Music as Thought

Music as Thought

LISTENING TO THE SYMPHONY IN THE AGE OF BEETHOVEN

Mark Evan Bonds

PRINCETON UNIVERSITY PRESS

PRINCETON AND OXFORD

Library of Congress Cataloging-in-Publication Data

Bonds, Mark Evan.

Music as thought : listening to the symphony in the age of Beethoven / Mark Evan Bonds.

   p.   cm.

Includes bibliographical reference and index.

ISBN-13: 978-0-691-12659-3 (hardcover : alk. paper)

ISBN-10: 0-691-12659-3

1. Symphony—19th century. 2. Music appreciation. 3. Music—Philosophy and aesthetics. I. Title.

ML1255.B68 2006

784.2′18409034—dc22   2005034091

British Library Cataloging-in-Publication Data is available

This book has been composed in Sabon

Princeton on acid-free paper. ∞

pup.princeton.edu

Printed in the United States of America

10 9 8 7 6 5 4 3 2 1

TO MY PARENTS

Marian Forbes Bonds and Joseph Elee Bonds

Der deutsche will seine Musik nicht nur fühlen, er will sie auch denken.

The German wants not only to feel his music, he wants to think it as well.
      —Richard Wagner, *Über deutsches Musikwesen* (1840)

Contents

Acknowledgments

I BEGAN WORK on this book during a year-long fellowship at the National Humanities Center in the Research Triangle Park, North Carolina, in 1995–96. My original project there, funded by the National Endowment for the Humanities, involved gathering and translating a wide range of critical commentaries on the symphony between 1720 and 1900. Although the finished product has turned out quite differently, the opportunity to assemble and work through such a wide range of documents opened my eyes and ears to new—or rather, very old—ways of listening to the symphony. I am grateful to the staff of the National Humanities Center for their support, particularly to Bob Connor and Kent Mullikin, and the library staff of Alan Tuttle, Eliza Robertson, and Jean Houston, who were able to track down some unusually obscure items on my behalf.

I am also grateful to the American Academy in Berlin, where as the DaimlerChrysler Fellow during the fall of 2002 I worked on something more nearly resembling the present book. Gary Smith, Paul Stoop, Marie Unger, and the entire staff there created a setting that provided the ideal mix of sociability and solitude needed for turning an idea into a book. Thanks, too, to Elmar Weingarten and Claudia von Grothe, my "godparents" in Berlin who helped me to experience first-hand, through the Berlin Philharmonic, the immediacy of the continuing artistic, social, and political traditions that link an orchestra and its listeners. A semester-long fellowship from the W. N. Reynolds Foundation through the University of North Carolina at Chapel Hill allowed me to remain in Berlin and continue my work there from January through June 2003. Through this fellowship, a good portion of this book happened to be written across the street from the cemetery in which Fichte and Hegel lie buried. While in Berlin, I also learned much from the students in the *Blockseminar* I directed at the Musikwissenschaftliches Institut of the Humboldt-Universität on the German music festival in the nineteenth century. My thanks to Hermann Danuser for inviting me to lead this seminar and to the dozen participants, who are no doubt still among the very few of their compatriots who have read Wilhelm Griepenkerl's extraordinary novel about "The Beethovenians" in its entirety (see chapter 5).

At the University of North Carolina at Chapel Hill, I am fortunate to work with exceptional colleagues, foremost among them Tim Carter, Annegret Fauser, and Jon Finson, all of whom gave useful advice in various ways and at various stages of this project. I have also benefited from the outstanding library resources and staff here, most notably Phil Vandermeer, Diane Steinhaus, Eva Boyce, John Rutledge, and Tommy Nixon. Bryan Proksch provided the graphics for the musical example.

Colleagues at other institutions have also been most generous in sharing their time and expertise with me over the years. These include Lydia Goehr (Columbia University), for stimulating conversations on Hanslick and Adorno; David Levy (Wake Forest University), for his help in securing a copy of Griepenkerl's *Das Musikfest* and for conversations on this novella and other aspects of Beethoven reception; James Parsons (Southwest Missouri State University), for his insights on Schiller and the Ninth Symphony and for helping me to navigate the otherwise impenetrable Deutsche Staatsbibliothek; J. Samuel Hammond (Duke University), for a variety of favors great and small but mostly great; and Michael Broyles (Pennsylvania State University) and William Weber (California State University, Long Beach), for their very helpful comments on an earlier version of the manuscript.

My greatest thanks go to my family. Dorothea, Peter, and Andrew have seen this book through since its inception, and it has taken us many places. I can only hope that through it all I have listened half as well as they have.

Portions of chapters 1 and 2 appeared in an earlier form in an essay entitled "Idealism and the Aesthetics of Instrumental Music at the Turn of the Nineteenth Century," in the *Journal of the American Musicological Society* 50 (1997): 387–420. All translations, unless otherwise indicated, are my own.

Introduction

WHILE BROWSING in the philosophy section of a bookstore a few years ago, I noticed a large image of Beethoven on the cover of a book. My first thought was that the item had been misshelved. On closer inspection, I saw that this was indeed a book about philosophy: volume seven of Frederick Copleston's classic *History of Philosophy*, covering the period "from the Post-Kantian Idealists to Marx, Kirekegaard, and Nietzsche." But none of those figures was on the cover—it was only Beethoven. What made this all the more puzzling is that Beethoven is never mentioned in the text, not even in passing. He was on the outside of the book, but not on the inside.

Why a composer on the cover of a book about philosophy in which he does not appear? And why Beethoven? Without wishing to put too much weight on the imagination of a book-jacket designer working in the late twentieth century, I believe this image does in fact capture a whole range of connections we routinely make about Beethoven's music and its capacity to say something about ideas, thought, and the pursuit of truth, even without the aid of words. These connections are more easily recognized than articulated, but generations of listeners since the composer's own time have been relating Beethoven's instrumental music—particularly his symphonies, the one genre on which his legacy rests more than any other—with ideas that go beyond the realm of sound.

This perception of instrumental music as a vehicle of ideas did not originate in responses to Beethoven or his symphonies, however. It predates the Ninth Symphony (1824), with its vocal finale about joy and universal brotherhood, and even the *Eroica* Symphony (1803), with its descriptive title and canceled evocation of Napoleon. The perception of the symphony as a means of thought was already in place by the late 1790s, before Beethoven had even begun to write symphonies at all. By the same token, the change cannot be ascribed to the works of any other composer, including Haydn and Mozart. This change, instead, was driven by a radically new conception of all the arts—including music—that emerged in German-speaking lands toward the end of the eighteenth century. People began to listen to music differently in the closing decades of the eighteenth century, and this change in listening opened up new perceptions toward music itself, particularly instrumental music.

The goal of this book is to trace the process by which purely instrumental music—music without a text and without any suggestion of an external program—came to be perceived as a vehicle of ideas in the decades around 1800, of just how and why the act of listening came to be equated with the act of thinking. Chapter 1 ("Listening with Imagination") outlines the emergence of a philosophical and conceptual framework in which instrumental music could be heard as an expression of thought. Chapter 2 ("Listening as Thinking") explores the process by which listening to untexted music came to perceived as a mode of thought, opening up avenues of insight not available through the medium of language by narrowing the gulf between subject and object, the particular and the universal, the phenomenal and the noumenal. Chapter 3 ("Listening to Truth") examines in detail the philosophical premises behind what is arguably the single most important and influential work of musical criticism ever written, E.T.A. Hoffmann's 1810 review of Beethoven's Fifth Symphony. The final two chapters ("Listening to the Aesthetic State" and "Listening to the German State") examine just how and why Beethoven's contemporaries began to hear symphonies—and not just his symphonies—as sonic paradigms of an ideal society. Some listeners heard in the symphony the projection of a cosmopolitan state transcending all political and linguistic boundaries, while others heard in it the aspirations of a nation-state that did not yet exist but that was becoming increasingly plausible during Beethoven's lifetime: Germany. In both instances, the symphony provided a model for the relationship of the individual to a larger whole, thus mirroring at a broader level the epistemological relationship of subject and object. And to Beethoven's generation—including Hegel, born in exactly the same year, 1770—the most immediate epistemological and social issues of the day were not really all that different from each other. The Absolute was perceived as the synthesis of the "I" and the "Not-I" in a point of nondifference, and this synthesis, by virtue of its all-encompassing nature, had to carried out at many levels, from the abstract to the concrete, from the individual to the social, from the noumenal to the phenomenal, from ideas to action.

The intersection of music, philosophy, politics, and social thought was scarcely a new phenomenon in Beethoven's lifetime. Socrates, in Plato's *Republic*, had warned that "the modes of music are never disturbed without unsettling of the most fundamental political and social conventions" (424c), and a long line of commentators from the Middle Ages onward had spoken to the ethical powers of music and its importance in the development of the individual and collective spirit. Another strand of thought linking music with the world of ideas lay in Pythagoreanism, the belief that all elements of the universe are ordered and guided by number and that music could offer special insights into the noncorporeal manifestations of number.

From the time of Plato through most of the eighteenth century, however, purely instrumental music was almost universally perceived as incapable of conveying ideas, for without the aid of a sung text, it could not articulate concepts with any appreciable degree of specificity. Music without words provided a "language of the heart" or a "language of emotions," but such a language was by its very nature inherently inferior to the language of reason. This age-old premise crumbled within the span of less than a decade at the end of the eighteenth century, opening the way for audiences—at least their more attentive members—to hear symphonies and instrumental music in general in a fundamentally new manner. They no longer approached these works solely as a source of entertainment, but increasingly as a source of truth. For E.T.A. Hoffmann (1776–1822) and others of his time, the symphony could function as a mode of philosophy, as a way of knowing. In the span of less than a generation, the act of listening had become associated with the quest for truth.

This transformation of perceptions took place with remarkable speed, for it was driven by two revolutions, both of which occurred during Beethoven's youth. The first of these was aesthetic. Immanuel Kant's self-proclaimed "Copernican revolution" in philosophy provided the basis for a fundamental reevaluation of aesthetics, including the long-standing premise that instrumental music, because it lacked words, could not convey ideas. The second revolution was social. The French Revolution of 1789 shook the political foundations of all Europe and raised fundamental questions about the nature of the state and its relationship to the individual. These issues took on special immediacy in German-speaking lands in the wake of Napoleon's conquests. Beethoven's generation was the first to think of "Germany" as a plausible political aspiration rather than as a mere abstraction. And the symphony had already established itself as the one genre of instrumental music capable of reflecting the sentiments of a large community. Unlike any other instrumental genre, it featured a synthesis of heterogeneous timbres, without a soloist; its voices were many but essentially equal. After the Revolution, Beethoven's contemporaries were all the more ready to hear the symphony as the sonorous manifestation of an ideal state, a society in which every voice could maintain its own distinct identity even while contributing to a harmonious whole. Such perceptions reinforced the growing idea that the performance of symphonies—regardless of their composer—represented a kind of ritualized enactment of community, be it civic, regional, national, or universal. Listeners in Beethoven's lifetime were inclined to hear the symphony as the expression of a communal voice, and many were inclined to hear it as a distinctively national genre at the very moment when German nationalism first began to emerge.

That these two revolutions should coincide with Beethoven's early professional career makes it all the more difficult today to separate what he wrote from the way in which his contemporaries heard it. But the distinction is important, for it can allow us to recover approaches to listening that have since been largely lost. When we listen to a symphony by Beethoven or anyone else today, we conceive of that work, quite naturally, as the product of a particular composer. The composer's name becomes, in effect, an element of the work's identity. This attitude has provided a basic framework for most histories of music, in which individual composers contribute in varying degrees to the development of the art. Yet this approach tends to divert attention from those qualities a given symphony shares with other works of its kind, qualities that emerge only when we consider the work within its generic context. (That the word "generic" more often than not has disparaging connotations is revealing in its own right.) Beethoven's contemporaries heard symphonies—symphonies in general—with a set of assumptions and expectations quite different from those most of us bring to the concert hall today. They were listening to Beethoven, to be sure; but they were also listening to a symphony. By reconstructing at least a portion of these assumptions and expectations from earlier times, we can begin to hear in these works qualities not otherwise so readily apparent today.

The question at hand, I should emphasize, is not whether or how Beethoven or any other composer of his era actually incorporated philosophical or socio-political ideas into their instrumental music. Such elements are unmistakable at times, as in the *Eroica* and *Pastoral* symphonies, or a host of other politically tinged works such as *Wellingtons Sieg* and the incidental music to *Egmont*. More subtle (and inherently more problematic) links between musical and nonmusical ideas can be present without such verbal indicators as well: the absence of overt programmatic clues does not in itself demonstrate the absence of some programmatic content in the mind of the composer. The Fifth Symphony offers a case in point. Listeners since Beethoven's time have sought to decipher its "meaning" through some sort of narrative program. When asked about the famous unison opening, the composer is reported to have replied: "Thus Fate pounds at the portal" ("So pocht das Schicksal an die Pforte"). The authenticity of the report is highly questionable: it comes from a single source, the notoriously unreliable Anton Schindler, Beethoven's on-again, off-again amanuensis, who first disclosed this alleged explanation thirteen years after the composer's death. In an attempt to exaggerate the closeness and extent of his relationship to Beethoven, Schindler is known to have added post-mortem entries in the composer's conversation books, and many of his anecdotes about Beethoven have proven demonstrably untrue. Yet the fact that this particular explanation of the Fifth Symphony should be taken up so readily in so many accounts of the work testifies to a deep-seated desire to connect purely instrumental music with the larger realm of ideas. This account, moreover, is entirely consistent with the verbal tag lines Beethoven himself explicitly associated with at least two of his subsequent compositions: the "Lebewohl" ("Farewell") motto in the Piano Sonata in E-flat Major, op. 81a; and the musical epigraph with the text "Muß es sein? Es muß sein!" ("Must it be? It must be!") appearing at the beginning of the finale of the String Quartet in F Major, op. 135.

The durability of Schindler's account also lies in the later course of instrumental music in the nineteenth century. Composers as diverse as Mendelssohn, Berlioz, Schumann, Liszt, and Wagner all agreed that music could and should be united with the broader world of ideas, objects, and events outside the concert hall. Mendelssohn's *Hebrides* Overture, Berlioz's *Symphonie fantastique*, Schumann's Symphony No. 1 ("Spring"), Liszt's symphonic poems, and Wagner's *Faust* Overture—to name only a few examples—openly connect musical and extramusical ideas. Allusions to other works of music offered yet another cryptic means by which composers could invest instrumental works with meaning of a kind.[1] And when composers proffered no such indicators or allusions, critics were quick to fill the void. The assumption was that composers did not always indicate the presence of extramusical elements in their works. Schumann and Brahms, for example, were notoriously reluctant to associate their later instrumental works with extramusical ideas, yet a surprising quantity of indirect evidence points to the presence of musical ciphers in at least some of their works.[2] By their very nature, these musical codes were a matter of secrecy, and the fact that they were not identified as such does not refute the hypothesis of their existence and meaning.

Many notable critics have looked beyond overt or covert programmatic elements to relate instrumental music to ideas. Theodor Adorno found in Beethoven's music a representation of social process through the relationship of individual movements to a larger whole. For Adorno, "Beethoven's music is Hegelian philosophy; but at the same time it is truer than that philosophy."[3] Scott Burnham, Berthold Hoeckner, and Michael P. Steinberg have pursued similar lines of thought more recently, seeking to identify specifically musical features in the music of Beethoven (and others) that have caused listeners to hear particular works as manifestations of broader forms of philosophical and cultural ideas.[4]

Still other strategies to locate meaning in instrumental music are grounded in biography. The best of these investigations have yielded rich rewards, helping us to understand why a composer might have written a particular work in a particular manner at a particular moment. Reinhold Brinkmann's analysis of changing concepts of time around 1800, for example, has much to tell us about the composer's psyche and its effect on his approach to composition at a critical juncture in his career, just as he was writing the *Eroica* Symphony. Lewis Lockwood's probing inquiry into the nature of heroism during this same period helps us to hear works such as the *Eroica* and *Fidelio* with heightened sensitivity to the composer's situation in Viennese society. Maynard Solomon's revelations about Beethoven's growing interest in Freemasonry and Eastern religions after 1812 illuminate with special intensity the often inward-looking nature of the late works, including the Ninth Symphony. And Stephen Rumph's examination of Beethoven's late compositions has shown the ways in which at least some of these works were shaped by the composer's political views.[5]

My own efforts to frame the question of music's relationship to ideas center on the act of listening. We have grown so accustomed to thinking of Beethoven's symphonies as a seminal force in the history of music (as indeed they were) that the role played by listeners in the transformation of attitudes toward instrumental music is easy to overlook. But the enormity of Beethoven's achievement has tended to obscure the slightly earlier yet no less momentous changes in the minds of the original audiences for this music. This was, after all, the first generation to approach listening as a way of thinking.

It is not my intention to minimize the originality or impact of Beethoven's music. Indeed, I have written elsewhere at length about the pervasive and enduring influence of his symphonies on composers of the nineteenth century.[6] My concern here lies in the broader premises that shaped the act of listening to symphonies during Beethoven's lifetime. Shifting attention from the works to their original audiences need not occur at the expense of the music. To the contrary: an enhanced appreciation of the modes of musical perception in the early nineteenth century can only deepen our understanding of this repertory.

My focus, then, is on the premises of perception rather than on the works themselves. For musical meaning, however one defines that deeply problematic concept, is a construct that arises out of the act of listening and is thus shaped as much by the listener as by the musical work being heard. Both are essential to the aesthetic experience. The double sense of "Thought" in this book's title acknowledges the fluidity of a process in which ideas can be perceived to reside both in the music ("thought" as a noun) and in the mind of the listener ("thought" as a participle). There can be no doubt that a work such as the *Eroica* changed expectations and assumptions about the nature of its genre and the capacity of instrumental music to serve as a vehicle of ideas. Yet these changes, as I argue in the first two chapters of this book, arose independently of any work or any particular repertory: they are the product of a far broader change in attitudes toward the very act of perception itself, the way in which a subject (the listener) apprehends an object (the musical work). By turning our attention to the act of listening, as opposed to the object of that perception, we can better appreciate the confluence of the aesthetic and social revolutions that so profoundly shaped the way audiences heard instrumental music in the closing decades of the eighteenth century and the early decades of the nineteenth.

Listening, unfortunately, is a notoriously subjective activity. Everyone listens differently, even to the same performance of the same work, and responses rarely get put into writing. And on those rare occasions when they do, writers are quick to apologize (and rightly so) for the inadequacy of words to capture the experience of listening. To complicate matters still further, the same individual can listen to the same work differently on different occasions, or even differently within the course of the same occasion, perceiving its beginning in one way, its middle in another, and its ending in yet another. Listening is a fundamentally inward activity that resists analysis.

One way out of this dilemma is to study the external indicators of listening. When, for example, did concert audiences become still and silent while listening? When did listeners begin to withhold applause until the very end of a symphony, as opposed to the older practice of responding at the end of each movement? It would be fascinating and instructive to know the answers to such questions for Beethoven's Vienna in as much detail as James H. Johnson has brought to light in his study of listening in Paris in the nineteenth century.[7] Yet even if such documentation were available, we would still face the question of just what was going on in the minds of those listeners even as their bodies remained silent and still.

Given the elusive nature of listening and the paucity of documentation, we must content ourselves with piecing together as best we can the broader premises that shaped listening within a particular place and time. Attitudes and expectations are critical here: we may or may not believe what we see, but we routinely see what we believe. The same holds for listening as well. We perceive in music what we are predisposed to perceive, and the predispositions of Beethoven's contemporaries differed from those of the Enlightenment as well as ours today in important respects.

I have chosen to focus on the act of listening to the symphony in German-speaking lands in the late eighteenth and early nineteenth centuries for a variety of reasons. Concentrating on a specific time, place, and repertory helps to ground what might otherwise be a hopelessly nebulous topic. Beethoven's contemporaries, fortunately, wrote great quantities of prose (and sometimes poetry) about the symphony, providing commentary on a repertory whose essence, with only rare exceptions, was purely musical. By reading between the lines of this criticism, we can begin to reconstruct those issues that were most important for the act of listening of a symphony. Why the symphony? It was a listener's repertory *par excellence*: more than any other form of instrumental music, it demanded an audience. Sonatas, trios, and quartets could be played in public as well, of course, but these and similar genres were just as often performed privately, without any listeners other than the musicians themselves. The old adage about the string quartet being a conversation among four rational individuals lasted for as long as it did in part because it captured the essence of the genre so well: one can listen in on a conversation, but the conversation is not conducted for the sake of the eavesdropper. With or without listeners, the string quartet and similarly intimate genres could sustain themselves quite nicely. The symphony, on the other hand, was never performed without an audience, and certainly not for the pleasure of the musicians (as any orchestral musician will be quick to attest). Even when performed within the confines of a court or aristocratic dwelling, even before it emerged into the public concert house in the nineteenth century, the symphony demanded a listening audience.

The geographical focus of my study on German-speaking lands derives from the intensity with which the symphony was cultivated there in the late eighteenth and early nineteenth centuries. Haydn, Mozart, and Beethoven are merely the best known of a large number of composers writing symphonies at the time. The Italian peninsula, France, England, and other regions and nations all had their own composers who cultivated the genre as well, but none even remotely rivaled the German-speaking regions of central Europe in the production of symphonies, nor does the corresponding critical discourse of these locales reflect the same degree of interest in relating purely instrumental ideas to the realms of philosophy and social thought. For these and other nationalities, vocal music, especially opera and song, remained central to the aesthetics of music.

In the end, this book seeks to recreate what might be called a historically informed listening practice, in an effort to heighten our sensitivity to the ways in which Beethoven's contemporaries heard instrumental music in general and symphonies in particular. As in the case of performance, modern reduplication of past practice is neither entirely feasible nor even wholly desirable. We deceive oursleves if we think we can undo our ears and eradicate altogether more recent notions of listening. And even if we could somehow reconstruct earlier modes of listening in all their fullness, we would certainly not want to restrict ourselves to them. We can, however, incorporate earlier modes of listening in such a way as to hear familiar music with new awareness and in so doing sharpen our own powers of perception.

Abbreviations

AfMw	*Archiv für Musikwissenschaft*
AmZ	*Allgemeine musikalische Zeitung* (Leipzig)
BAmZ	*Berliner Allgemeine musikalische Zeitung*
JAMS	*Journal of the American Musicological Society*
MQ	*Musical Quarterly*
NZfM	*Neue Zeitschrift für Musik*

Music as Thought

An Unlikely Genre: The Rise of the Symphony

THE EMERGENCE OF THE SYMPHONY as the most prestigious of all instrumental genres in the closing decades of the eighteenth century was in many respects an unlikely development. It was a relatively young genre at the time, having evolved only in the 1720s from the opera overture (often called a "symphony") into an independent, multimovement work. The symphony and overture continued to be so closely related that the two terms remained interchangeable into the 1790s. The number, character, and sequence of movements in a symphony, moreover, did not stabilize until the 1770s, when the familiar format of four movements (fast–slow–minuet–fast) begin to emerge as the norm. By this point, composers across Europe were writing symphonies for use at courts and in churches, theaters, and, increasingly, public concert halls. In terms of sheer numbers alone the eighteenth century stands out as the golden age of the symphony. The most comprehensive census of this repertory records some 16,558 different symphonies written and performed throughout Europe and the New World before 1800.[1]

For all its ubiquity, the symphony nevertheless remained a genre of only secondary importance within musical aesthetics prior to 1800. Opera continued to reign supreme in the mind (and pocketbook) of the public, and vocal music of all kinds captured far more attention in the press than any form of instrumental music. The surviving contemporary commentaries on Mozart's symphonies, for example, are nugatory; not until a decade after the composer's death did critics begin to write about any of these works in any kind of detail.[2] And while Haydn's two extended visits to England in the 1790s are on the whole fairly well documented, we often have no clear indication of which symphonies were played at which concerts. Reviews of these performances seldom venture beyond such bland characterizations as "bold," "original," "spirited," or "moving." This lack of critical engagement is typical of responses to instrumental music in general at the time, for music without words had long been viewed as a lesser art, capable of moving the passions but vague and imprecise. Even laudatory accounts of the symphony's power, such as those written by the composer Johann Abraham Peter Schulz (1774) and the composer and theorist Heinrich Christoph Koch (1787), appeared within larger contexts that give clear priority to vocal music or that view instrumental music essentially as vocal music without a text.[3]

All this began to change quite rapidly in the years around 1800, when the status of the symphony rose enormously. For most critics, it was the most prestigious of all instrumental genres, and for at least some critics, the most prestigious of all musical genres, vocal or instrumental. The reasons behind this sudden transformation in perception are traced in the first three chapters of the present study; for the moment, suffice it to say that by the last decade of Beethoven's life the symphony had become a "veritable touchstone for composers and listeners alike," as Adolf Bernhard Marx, Berlin's most influential critic of the time, noted in 1824.[4] It was held to be the most serious of all genres by virtue of the fact that it avoided virtuosity (in contrast to the concerto) and encouraged the cultivation of polyphonic textures through its multiple and diverse voices. And polyphony, by its very nature, placed greater demands on both composers and listeners than did the simpler homophonic texture of a melody and subordinate accomanipment. The symphony also demanded skill in orchestration across a wide spectrum of instruments, unlike the sonata or quartet. It was not a genre composers could take up lightly.

Accordingly, composers rarely stepped forward with a first symphony until they had proven their mettle in smaller, less demanding forms. Beethoven, for example, did not write his first symphony until he was thirty; up until that point his publications with opus numbers had consisted of short piano pieces, solo and duo sonatas, trios, string quartets, a septet, and two piano concertos. Beethoven's legacy would soon make the challenge of composing a symphony even more imposing. Schubert spoke of "finding the way toward the grand symphony" through quartets, while Brahms waited until he was forty-three to complete his own first essay in the genre, lamenting to the conductor Hermann Levi in the early 1870s that he would "never compose a symphony! You have no idea how it feels to our kind"—by this Brahms meant composers—"when one always hears such a giant marching along behind."[5]

The symphony's new aesthetic prestige in the first half of the nineteenth century was further enhanced, in an odd way, by its limited commercial appeal. No one writing such a work could be accused of pursuing monetary gain, for symphonies rarely turned a profit. They were time-consuming to write, expensive to publish, and cumbersome to perform.[6] Relatively few symphonies appeared in print before 1800, and these were almost invariably issued in parts rather than in score. One enterprising firm in London issued Beethoven's first three symphonies in score between 1804 and 1809, but this was an isolated enterprise of limited scope. The Fourth, Fifth, and Sixth Symphonies would not be available in this format commercially anywhere until the mid-1820s. Unlike piano music, songs, or other forms of chamber music, orchestral scores could not be marketed as a domestic genre; they appealed to a very small market of dedicated (and affluent) connoisseurs. When Robert Schumann offered his *Overture, Scherzo und Finale* to his publisher Friedrich Hofmeister in 1842, Hofmeister replied politely but firmly that he could not accept the work on financial grounds. "Orchestral works are in any case very dubious enterprises nowadays," he pointed out, and "almost all retailers with whom I have such business connections refuse to accept any orchestral works. There is no profit to be made from them; the cost of production simply goes unrecovered, even if the [composer's] honorarium is recouped after a few years, mainly through the publication of a four-hand arrangement. I do not hesitate, as a friendly well-wisher, to tell you this openly."[7]

Two- and four-hand piano arrangements compensated for commercial obstacles to some extent, as Hofmeister suggested, but even here the market was relatively limited.[8] One recent survey of symphonies published in German-speaking lands during the nineteenth century shows that even including piano arrangements, only 122 symphonies of any kind appeared between 1810 and 1860; this amounts to only about two or three works a year. The numbers increased somewhat in the later decades of the century, but no publisher could afford to stake his business on the genre.[9] The poor economic incentives of symphonic composition nevertheless contributed to the genre's cachet as the most prestigious form of instrumental music. In part because of its very unprofitability, the symphony enjoyed a certain aura of aesthetic superiority.

Changing patterns of patronage and performance venues also worked against the production of new symphonies in the late eighteenth and early nineteenth centuries. The contrasting careers of Haydn, Mozart, and Beethoven are illustrative in this regard. Haydn wrote the large majority of his 106 symphonies for the Esterházy family, whose court orchestra was by all accounts one of the finest in Europe. Performances, however, were closed affairs, open only to invited guests, and even then to a relatively small audience. What is believed to be the music room at Esterháza, the family's summer palace built by the music-loving Prince Nicolaus, could seat no more than about two hundred listeners. Public concerts opened up new venues for Haydn later in his career: he received commissions from both Paris (Symphonies nos. 82–87 and 90–92) and London (nos. 93–104), all of which were performed in larger spaces accessible to a paying public. But after returning from London in 1795, Haydn composed no more symphonies for the simple reason that he had no further commissions. In the meantime, Prince Nicolaus's successor had disbanded the Esterházy court orchestra in 1790. Mozart, in turn, wrote relatively few symphonies in the 1780s, for he lacked the kind of consistent patronage enjoyed at the time by Haydn. He composed at least some of his later symphonies, we know, for "academies," those occasional concerts produced and directed by the composer himself, leading an ensemble of musicians hired especially for the occasion. These works appeared on mixed programs that also included chamber music, improvisations, concertos, and vocal music of all kinds. Unfortunately, the surviving documentation on these events is thin, for concert life beyond the opera house was simply not an object of extended discourse in the Vienna of Haydn and Mozart.

Beethoven's early decades in Vienna coincide with the gradual shift from largely private to largely public performances. The *Eroica* Symphony was first performed in 1804 before an audience of invited guests in the palace of its dedicatee, Prince Lobkowitz. It then received its first genuinely public performance the following year. From the Fourth onward (1807), all of Beethoven's symphonies premiered in venues open to a paying public. The number of such concerts in Vienna remained relatively limited during the composer's lifetime, however. During the course of a typical year, Viennese orchestras performed his symphonies or movements from his symphonies six to ten times.[10] *Ad hoc* ensembles accounted for the vast majority of these performances; not until 1814 did the privately funded Gesellschaft der Musikfreunde initiate an ongoing series of concerts, and it would be almost thirty years before the establishment of the Vienna Philharmonic, in 1842.

In this respect, Vienna was typical of most major European cities. Standing civic orchestras such as Leipzig's Gewandhaus remained the exception, not the rule, during Beethoven's lifetime. Salomon's concert series in London ceased after Haydn's visits to England, and no comparable ensemble provided regular performance until the establishment of the Philharmonic Society in 1813. In Paris, the concerts of the Conservatory in the 1820s offered the first standing series of public orchestral performances since revolutionary times.

In light of external factors alone—poor economic incentives for composers and publishers, declining patronage, and limited public venues of performance—it is all the more remarkable that the symphony should rise to such prominence during Beethoven's lifetime. The standard explanation for this is of course the music itself, particularly the output of Haydn, Mozart, and Beethoven. Yet even this remarkable repertory cannot by itself explain the sea-change in attitudes toward the genre. There can be no doubt that these symphonies helped to promulgate the new-found aesthetic prestige of instrumental music, but they played a relatively minor role in its emergence. The principal impetus for this new outlook lies instead in changing attitudes toward the nature of art, the relationship of music and philosophy, and a new approach to the very act of listening itself.

CHAPTER ONE

Listening with Imagination:
The Revolution in Aesthetics

HISTORICALLY INFORMED PERFORMANCE PRACTICE has become a commonplace in the concert world in recent decades. Orchestras routinely perform Beethoven's symphonies on period instruments, and even nonperiod orchestras play in a manner that reflects a heightened sensitivity to performance traditions of the composer's time. Historically informed listening, on the other hand, has been much slower to develop. It rests, after all, on the consumer rather than the producer and is in any case far more difficult to reconstruct, for the evidence of how people actually listened to specific works of music in any given time and place is scant and by its very nature notoriously subjective. In a celebrated passage in *Howards End* (1910), the novelist E. M. Forster neatly captures an entire spectrum of modes of listening among six characters in a concert hall, all listening to the same work of music with six decidedly different reactions:

> It will be generally admitted that Beethoven's Fifth Symphony is the most sublime noise that has ever penetrated into the ear of man. All sorts and conditions are satisfied by it. Whether you are like Mrs. Munt, and tap surreptitiously when the tunes come—of course, not so as to disturb the others—; or like Helen, who can see heroes and shipwrecks in the music's flood; or like Margaret, who can only see the music; or like Tibby, who is profoundly versed in counterpoint, and holds the full score open on his knee; or like their cousin, Fräulein Mosebach, who remembers all the time that Beethoven is "echt Deutsch"; or like Fräulein Mosebach's young man, who can remember nothing but Fräulein Mosebach: in any case, the passion of your life becomes more vivid, and you are bound to admit that such a noise is cheap at two shillings.[1]

The responses range from the visceral (Mrs. Munt) to the technical (Tibby), programmatic (Helen), formalist (Margaret), nationalistic (Fräulein Mosebach), and purely social (Fräulein Mosebach's young man). Listeners, as Forster reminds us, have their own methods and motivations, and there is no reason to think that the audiences of Beethoven's era were any different in this regard. Indeed, the available documentation strongly suggests that the typical concert audience of the early nineteenth century covered just as wide a spectrum as that described by Forster a hundred years later, ranging from those who listened with rapt attention to those who used the occasion primarily to socialize, giving only passing attention (if any at all) to the music being played.[2] Any attempt to reconstruct listening practices of the past must therefore confront the challenge of reconciling an inevitable variety of responses toward a common object. The challenge is further compounded by the reluctance of these listeners to commit to writing just what those responses might have been on any particular occasion.

Still, there is much to be gained from trying to understand how the more attentive listeners of a particular place and time might have approached the music they heard, at least in the most general terms. Fortunately, the documented discourse on the aesthetics of the symphony in German-speaking lands during Beethoven's lifetime is extensive enough to allow us to reconstruct these earlier modes of perception in its broad outlines, to recreate a horizon of expectations of what informed listeners thought that instrumental music could and could not do.

FROM KANT TO HOFFMANN

Attitudes toward instrumental music changed markedly during the last decade of the eighteenth century and the first decade of the nineteenth. Many of the more sophisticated listeners of this time began to perceive it as equal if not superior to vocal music. This was a radically new perspective: at no previous point in the history of music had any prominent composer or critic argued for such a view. The power of instrumental music to move the passions had long been acknowledged, but without words, music's perceived ability to convey ideas had always remained suspect. Yet within the span of less than a generation, this new attitude toward instrumental music won increasing legitimacy, and its adherents would grow steadily in numbers throughout the nineteenth century.

The scope and speed of this change can be illustrated through two very different yet widely read sources of the time: Immanuel Kant's *Kritik der Urteilskraft* (*Critique of Judgment*), first published in 1790, and E.T.A. Hoffmann's review of Beethoven's Fifth Symphony, first published in the *Allgemeine musikalische Zeitung* of Leipzig in 1810. Both stand as landmarks in the history of aesthetics. Kant's treatise set off an intense debate about the relationship between art and philosophy that would dominate aesthetic debate through Hegel and beyond. One could disagree with Kant (and many did), but no one could ignore him. And it is scarcely an exaggeration to call E.T.A. Hoffmann's review of Beethoven's Fifth the most influential piece of music criticism ever written. It established a new standard for written discourse about music by integrating emotional response and technical analysis in unprecedented detail. Critics of subsequent generations would turn to it repeatedly as a model, and Hoffmann's images and method have continued to resonate to the present day. Particularly in its abridged form (1813), Hoffmann's comments gained a readership well beyond that of the journal in which it had originally appeared.[3] Had Hoffmann had been a solitary critic—if, in other words, his account had not resonated among his contemporaries—his review would have been swallowed up among the countless other notices of the day, filed away and forgotten. But his ideas were soon taken up by others, and the premises of listening he articulates in this review would soon be assimilated into the most basic assumptions of how to listen to music.

In his *Critique of Judgment*, Kant declared instrumental music to be "more pleasure than culture" (*mehr Genuß als Kultur*), for without a text, music could appeal only to the senses and not to reason. Kant marveled at instrumental music's potential to move listeners, but because it contained no ideas and was a purely temporal art, it remained merely transitory in its effect: once the sound of the notes had died, there was nothing left for the listener to contemplate. In his hierarchy of the arts, Kant classified instrumental music among those that were "agreeable" or "pleasing" (*angenehm*) but incapable of transmitting concepts. Like wallpaper, instrumental music was an abstract art that gave pleasure through its form but lacked content and was therefore inferior to vocal music.[4]

Kant's view of instrumental music, published when Beethoven was just nineteen, was thoroughly typical of its time. French aestheticians had been wrestling with the issue of instrumental music's "meaning" for decades and had concluded, almost unanimously, that without a verbal text, music alone could convey little of any significance. No one denied music's power or even its close affinity to language: Jean-Jacques Rousseau, in his *Essay on the Origins of Languages*, maintained that music and language shared a common origin and that the language of music, although "inarticulate," was "vivid, ardent, passionate" and had "a hundred times more energy than speech itself."[5] But the inability of music to express ideas remained a stumbling block. "To understand what all the tumult of sonatas might mean," Rousseau wrote in his *Dictionary of Music* (1768), "we would have to follow the lead of the coarse artist who was obliged to write underneath that which he had drawn such statements as 'This is a tree,' or 'This is a man,' or 'This is a horse.' I shall never forget the exclamation of the celebrated Fontenelle, who, finding himself exhausted by these eternal symphonies, cried out in a fit of impatience: 'Sonata, what do you want of me?'" Fontenelle's *bon mot* would be retold with relish by countless writers over subsequent decades: it became a kind of shorthand dismissal of the art of instrumental music on the grounds of vagueness and imprecision.[6]

Kant's German compatriots were equally unwilling to hear instrumental music as a vehicle of ideas. Johann Georg Sulzer, in his widely read encyclopedia of the fine arts published in the early 1770s, called instrumental music *unterhaltend* ("entertaining"), the same word that provides the basis for the modern-day German term *Unterhaltungsmusik*—that is, music meant to be enjoyed rather than contemplated, or as we might say more colloquially nowadays, "easy listening." Sulzer characterized "concertos, symphonies, sonatas, and solos" as "a not disagreeable sound, even a pleasant and entertaining chatter, but nothing that would engage the heart."[7]

By the time Beethoven was thirty-nine, Kant's hierarchy of the arts had been turned on its head. In his 1810 review of Beethoven's Fifth, E.T.A. Hoffmann declared instrumental music to be the highest of all art forms, for it opened up to listeners the realm of the infinite, "a world that has nothing in common with the external world of the senses." Precisely *because* of its independence from words, music could express that which lay beyond the grasp of conventional language. And Hoffmann was merely the most articulate in a series of prominent writers who had been arguing along much the same lines for more than a decade.

How can we account for this remarkable transformation of attitudes within such a short span of time, between Kant in 1790 and Hoffmann in 1810? At the simplest level, there are three variables to consider: (1) the instrumental music composed during this time, (2) the way in which this music was performed, and (3) the way in which it was heard. All three are closely connected, yet it is the first of these—the music itself—that has always been regarded as the primary force behind this new aesthetic. And on the surface, at least, the priority of the music in driving this change seems not only plausible but inescapable. Can it be entirely coincidental, after all, that the status of instrumental music rose so markedly during precisely the period in which Mozart's late symphonies were being discovered by a wider public, Haydn was composing his twelve symphonies for London (1791–95), and Beethoven was writing and publishing his first six symphonies (1800–1806)? Hoffmann himself appealed to the centrality of this repertory in having elevated instrumental music "to its current height" by tracing a steady progression of growing intensity among these three composers: Haydn's symphonies, according to Hoffmann, "lead us into vast green meadows, into a merry, bright throng of happy people." Mozart, in turn, "leads us into the depths of the spirit realm." But it is left to Beethoven's instrumental music to "open up to us the realm of the monstrous and immeasurable." It "sets in motion the lever of horror, fear, revulsion, pain, and it awakens that infinite longing which is the essence of Romanticism."[8]

Hoffmann also gives credit, in passing, to the steady improvement of performances, ascribing this to technical advances in instruments and to the increasing competence of players. The available evidence confirms these trends: contemporary accounts of early performances of the *Eroica* make us wince, but orchestras clearly warmed to the task over time. Rehearsals, once a rarity, were becoming more common, and there can be no question that the standards of performance were rising steadily as a result.

But Hoffmann has nothing good to say about listeners, and by the time he revised portions of his commentary on the Fifth Symphony in 1813, he had moved from indifference to contempt. Those listeners "oppressed by Beethoven's powerful genius" suffer because their "weak perceptions" cannot grasp "the deep internal coherence of every composition by Beethoven." Such deprecatory comments reinforce the largely erroneous but seeming ineradicable notion that Beethoven's music was not appreciated during the composer's lifetime. (Judging from contemporary reviews, critics did in fact find the music challenging at times but rarely oppressive, and already by the second decade of the nineteenth century, Beethoven was consistently acknowledged as the greatest living composer of instrumental music.) In any event, Hoffmann was not prepared to grant listeners any kind of positive role in instrumental music's newly elevated status. This new music, he claimed, demanded a more strenuous kind of listening, and audiences would have to elevate themselves to new heights of comprehension if they were to assimilate these works.

In this respect, Hoffmann's review created a paradigm that would be applied by virtually all subsequent commentators: Beethoven's music created a new aesthetic, one in which listeners were compelled to rise to the level of the composer. This basic model has persisted from Hoffmann down to the present. Hans Heinrich Eggebrecht, in the most comprehensive of all studies dealing with the reception of the composer's oeuvre, argues that a "language of reception never heard before appears spontaneously soon after 1800 in connection with Beethoven's music," while Scott Burnham, in his compelling account of how listeners have interpreted many of the composer's most important works, speaks of a "change of critical perspective engendered by Beethoven's heroic style."[9]

Yet this new kind of listening had already been a matter of intense discussion for well over a decade before Hoffmann's review. The unprecedented prestige of instrumental music was driven not by any composer or any particular repertory, but rather by a profound shift in aesthetics extending to the very act of listening itself. Ironically, the debate had been unleashed by Kant's *Critique of Judgment*, the same work that had dismissed instrumental music as something less than a fine art. Even while downplaying the status of music without words, Kant had provided the philosophical basis for the creative role of the beholder in all the arts, including music. The aesthetic revolution that took place during Beethoven's lifetime, then, focused not so much on any particular artist, composer, or repertory, but rather on the act of perception itself. For Kant, this meant a striving toward the reconciliation of the perceiving subject and the perceiving object; Johann Gottlieb Fichte conceived of the problem as the search for a means by which to integrate the "I" and the "Not-I"; Hegel sought to synthesize what he called the "identity of nonidentity" in a point of "nondifference" (*Indifferenz*). None of these writers was particularly sympathetic toward music. But others more sensitive to the art—Friedrich Schiller, Friedrich Schelling, Wilhelm Heinrich Wackenroder, Ludwig Tieck, Novalis, Jean Paul, Friedrich Schlegel, and eventually E.T.A. Hoffmann—would take up the implications of this new way of thinking about the act of perception as it applied to music.

IDEALISM AND THE CHANGING PERCEPTION OF PERCEPTION

The story of instrumental music's sudden emergence as one of the highest, if not the highest, of all the arts at the end of the eighteenth century is most commonly told from the perspective of Romanticism, that slightly later and notoriously slippery phenomenon whose chief characteristic, at least according to the conventional telling of this tale, is its tendency to favor emotion over reason. Whereas Enlightenment rationalists had almost universally dismissed instrumental music for its inability to incorporate and convey ideas, their Romantic successors, particularly in Germany, were quick to embrace music without words precisely because of its ability to function outside the strictures of language. Writers such as Wilhelm Heinrich Wackenroder, Ludwig Tieck, Novalis, Jean Paul, Friedrich Schlegel, and E.T.A. Hoffmann all praised instrumental music for its ability to transcend that which could be expressed in words. Instrumental music's lack of precision, long regarded as a liability, was now perceived as an asset.

More often than not, this new perspective has been viewed by later generations with deep suspicion, as an irrational and thus unsatisfactory basis on which to build any systematic aesthetic. From about the middle of the nineteenth century onward, a growing chorus of critics would dismiss the rapturous language used by the Romantics to describe the powers of instrumental music on the grounds that such accounts defy rational scrutiny. Many later commentators have responded to early Romantic aesthetics with thinly veiled scorn, beginning with Eduard Hanslick in his influential *Vom Musikalisch-Schönen* (*On the Musically Beautiful*) in 1854.[10] The noted philosopher and historian of aesthetics Francis Sparshott, writing in 1980, blamed Wackenroder's "rhapsodizing style" for having "permanently lowered the acceptable tone for serious writing on music. For the first time, cultivated men . . . conceived an unfocussed rapture to be a proper aesthetic response, thinking of musical techniques not as rational means of construction and expression but as occult mysteries." By this account, "Wackenroder's hysterically mystical view of music eventually invaded the writings of musicians themselves." Even Carl Dahlhaus, the one recent scholar who has done more than any other to illuminate the growing aesthetic prestige of instrumental music at the turn of the nineteenth century, refers dismissively to the "metaphysical excesses" of Tieck, Wackenroder, and Hoffmann.[11]

Equally troubling for many later critics is the apparent discrepancy between the early Romantics' claims for the power of instrumental music and the actual repertory they described—or rather, did *not* describe. Wackenroder, Tieck, Novalis, and Jean Paul rarely named specific works or composers, and in those few writings in which they did, their choices are all the more puzzling. Tieck, for example, in his important essay of 1799 on the symphony, discussed only a single work, an overture by Johann Friedrich Reichardt. This failure to address specific musical works has led several generations of scholars to advance the remarkable position that the aesthetics of the late 1790s anticipated a body of music yet to be composed and that the repeated references to "infinity" and "endless longing" in the works of Wackenroder, Tieck, and others are more nearly congruous with the music of Beethoven's "late" style than with the works of Haydn, Mozart, or the early Beethoven.[12] Particularly adamant on this point, Dahlhaus argued that the Romantic aesthetic preceded Romantic music and that Tieck's view of instrumental music "did not find an adequate object until E.T.A. Hoffmann borrowed Tieck's language in order to do justice to Beethoven." This new aesthetic, Dahlhaus maintained, "predicated the existence of instrumental music to which one could attach a poetically inspired metaphysics without embarrassing oneself with inappropriate dithyrambs."[13]

In point of fact, the early Romantics were working through a series of philosophical issues that had been under intense discussion since the early 1790s, and their "rhapsodizing style" played a central role in their approach not only toward instrumental music but toward the arts and philosophy in general. Their general failure to discuss specific works of music in any degree of detail reflects the origins of their thought within the traditions of philosophy rather than criticism. (Kant's *Critique of Judgment*, the seminal aesthetic treatise of the age, mentions very few specific works of art and dwells on none of them.) When E.T.A. Hoffmann finally did apply the premises and vocabulary of early Romantic aesthetics to a specific work of music, Beethoven's Fifth Symphony, these concepts had been in play for some time already.

The principal source for this new aesthetic of instrumental music was idealism. A venerable tradition of thought that traces its origins to the philosophies of Pythagoras, Plato, and Plotinus, idealism enjoyed a vigorous renewal in German philosophy and aesthetics toward the end of the eighteenth century through such figures as Johann Joachim Winckelmann, Karl Philipp Moritz, Kant, Schiller, Christian Gottfried Körner, Johann Gottfried Herder, Fichte, and Schelling. At first glance, the "rhapsodizing style" of Wackenroder and Tieck might seem to have little in common with the sober discourse of Winckelmann, Moritz, and Kant, yet these earlier writings provided the essential framework for what are widely considered to be the first manifestations of a Romantic musical aesthetic.[14]

In the broadest terms, idealism gives priority to spirit over matter. Without necessarily rejecting the phenomenal world, it posits a higher form of reality in a spiritual realm: objects in the phenomenal world—including works of art—are understood as reflections of the noumenal. From an aesthetic standpoint, idealism holds that art and the external world are consonant with one another, not because art imitates that world, but because both reflect a common, higher ideal. The work of art thus functions as a central means by which to sense the realm of the spiritual, the infinite; it exists in a sphere that is tangible yet not entirely natural. The artwork is artificial in the most basic sense of the word.[15]

Within the aesthetics of idealism, the true essence of the artwork could be grasped only through the power of imagination—*Einbildungskraft*— a faculty capable of mediating between the senses and reason, between the phenomenal and the noumenal worlds. The term itself, as used by Gotthold Ephraim Lessing, Kant, and Fichte, among others, combines an inward-directed activity ("*Ein*-bildung") with a sense of constructive power ("-kraft").[16] Christian Gottfried Körner, writing in 1795, emphasized that we value an artistic work "not by what *appears* in it, but according to what must be *thought*," that is, according to the reflective process demanded by the particular work.[17] For Körner and other idealists, the enjoyment of art was a process not of "idle reception," but rather of "activity." The distinction is crucial: late eighteenth-century aesthetics moved from the premise of passive effect to active construction. The new scenario rendered the listener less important in some respects but more important in others: less important in that the musical work's essence—as opposed to its effect—had become the focus of attention, and more important in that the listener was obliged to take an active role in constructing that essence through the application of the powers of imagination.

Idealism thus stands in marked contrast to the Enlightenment predilection for explaining the emotional power of music in essentially naturalistic or mechanical terms, that is to say, in terms of its effect on the listener. As a philosophical mode of thought, naturalism rejects the notion that anything in the universe lies beyond the scope of empirical explanation, holding that the mind and spiritual values have their origins in (and can ultimately be reduced to) material things and processes. Naturalism provided the philosophical basis for mimesis, the aesthetic doctrine that had prevailed throughout all the arts prior to 1800. By imitating nature or the human passions, a work of art, critics argued, could induce a corresponding emotional reaction in the mind and spirit of the listener.

But instrumental music never fit very well into the mimetic system, which had evolved around the more overtly representational arts of poetry, painting, and sculpture. By the second half of the eighteenth century, most critics viewed direct musical imitations of the external world with skepticism and at times outright derision. Human passions provided a more appropriate object of imitation, for here, as Rousseau pointed out, the composer "does not directly represent" in his music such things as rain, fire, and tempests, but instead "arouses in the spirit" of the listener "the same impulses that one experiences when beholding such things."[18] Still other writers opted for theories of "expression," but these systems ultimately depended on the principle of mimesis as well.[19] Even those few eighteenth-century writers who rejected musical mimesis altogether and espoused a kind of protoformalistic sensualism hastened to point out that music without a text was a merely agreeable (*angenehme*) art that stood beneath reason and thus outside the higher realm of beauty, the realm of the fine arts. (In German, the term *schöne Künste* means literally "beautiful arts," as does its French equivalent, *beaux-arts*.) Because it involved the free interplay of forms rather than of concepts, instrumental music was widely perceived, in Kant's oft-quoted formulation, to be "more pleasure than culture."

Many eighteenth-century writers—including Johann Mattheson, Charles Batteux, Johann Joachim Quantz, Rousseau, Johann Nikolaus Forkel, Johann Georg Sulzer, and Heinrich Christoph Koch—sought to explain the emotional power of instrumental music by regarding it as "the language of the heart" or "the language of the emotions."[20] This designation elevated the status of music without words by treating it as a language in its own right: this in itself represented a major step forward in the growing prestige of instrumental music. In the end, however, this approach perpetuated instrumental music's secondary status by situating it within the conceptual framework of language. From this perspective, instrumental music was defined in terms of what it lacked: specificity. No matter how powerful it might be, a language of emotions was by its very nature imprecise and ultimately irrational. A lack of precision could scarcely qualify as a desirable linguistic quality, least of all in the Age of Reason.

Idealism offered an alternative approach by shifting the focus of attention from effect to essence and by placing special importance on the active nature of aesthetic perception. Within the idealist aesthetic, the power of any given artwork lies in its ability to reflect a higher ideal and in the beholder's ability to perceive that ideal. Idealism did not deny the sensuous power of music. To the contrary: the aesthetics of idealism fostered some of the most soaring descriptions of instrumental music ever written. The object of description, however, had shifted from music's effect to music's essence or, more specifically, to the perception of an ideal realm reflected in that music. Within the idealist aesthetic, then, instrumental music remained an imprecise art, with the essential difference that listeners no longer considered this imprecision in relation to nature, language, or human emotions, but rather in relation to a higher, ideal world—to that "wondrous realm of the infinite" (*das wundervolle Reich des Unendlichen*), to use Hoffmann's celebrated phrase. From this perspective, vagueness was no vice. Commentators no longer felt compelled to justify instrumental music by engaging in the futile and inevitably trivializing effort to specify its objective "content." Instead, they changed the venue of contemplation from the material to the spiritual, from the empirical to the ideal. Freed from the obligation to explain the causal mechanism of their responses to music, idealist critics could revel in those responses all the more freely. One can, after all, be more readily forgiven for resorting to metaphorical excess in trying to describe the infinite, as opposed to one's personal reaction to a specific work of art. The early Romantics were most assuredly not the first to respond deeply and passionately to instrumental music; they were, however, members of the first generation to have at its disposal a philosophical framework in which to express such powerful emotions without embarrassment.

This resurgence of idealism in the eighteenth century owes much to the work of the archaeologist and art historian Johann Joachim Winckelmann (1717–68), whose concept of ideal beauty drew heavily on Plato.[21] For Winckelmann, the work of art did not imitate any single model in nature, but instead derived its features from a variety of different exemplars. The resulting "ideal figures, like an ethereal spirit purified by fire," were no mere composites, however: the high purpose of ancient Greek artists had been "to bring forth creations bestowed with a divine and suprasensory sufficiency" that were "freed from every human weakness."[22] In this sense, Winckelmann saw ideal beauty as deriving at least in part from the mind alone, independent of direct reference to experience. And although he at one point explicitly denied that ideal beauty holds any metaphysical significance, he argued elsewhere that the ideally beautiful has its archetype in God.[23] Herder accurately summed up the reception of Winckelmann's epoch-making *Geschichte der Kunst des Altertums* (1764) in describing the work not so much as an actual history of art as a "historical metaphysics of beauty."[24]

Plato's theories of beauty are equally evident in the *Allgemeine Theorie der schönen Künste* (*General Theory of the Fine Arts*, 1771–74), by the Swiss aesthetician Johann Georg Sulzer (1720–79). Sulzer followed the Greek philosopher's distinction among various categories of artistic imitation and idealization. The first and lowest category of artists consists of those who copy nature precisely and without discrimination. Artists who imitate nature more selectively belong to the second, higher category. The third and highest category consists of those for whom nature is not sufficient and who pursue the images of ideal forms. "One can generally say about an artwork that has not been copied from an object in nature that it has been made according to an Ideal, if it has received its essence and form from the genius of the artist."[25] But it apparently never occurred to Sulzer or anyone else of his generation to align instrumental music (or for that matter any kind of music) with the concept of the ideal; to do so would have been to elevate what was considered a merely pleasant form of diversion to the highest ranks of the fine arts—which is exactly what many of the Romantics would later do.

Karl Philipp Moritz (1757–93) helped to lay the foundation for this development in his later writings. From 1789 until his death, he lectured in Berlin on antiquity, mythology, and the history of art, and his audiences included Wackenroder, Tieck, Alexander von Humboldt, and the composer Johann Friedrich Reichardt. Moritz openly rejected mimesis as a basis of art, insisting instead that the true artwork must be self-contained and internally coherent and that it must exist for its own sake. He placed special emphasis on the act of aesthetic contemplation. In his essay *On the Unification of All the Fine Arts and Sciences under the Concept of the Perfected Thing in Itself,* he proclaimed that "in contemplating the beautiful, . . . I contemplate the object not as something within me, but rather as something perfect in itself, something that constitutes *a whole in itself* and gives me pleasure *for the sake of itself,* in that I do not so much impart to the beautiful object a relationship to myself but rather impart to myself a relationship to it."[26] For Moritz, the contemplation of the beautiful carried the added benefit of drawing attention away from the ills of mortal existence, if only momentarily. "This forgetting of the self is the highest degree of the pure and unselfish pleasure that beauty grants us. At that moment we give up our individual, limited existence in favor of a higher kind of existence."[27]

The belief that arts in general, and music in particular, could provide refuge from the failed world of social and political life was a key element of romantic aesthetics. Franz von Schober's "An die Musik," set to music by Schubert in 1817, captures perfectly the essence of this outlook:

Du holde Kunst, in wieviel grauen Stunden,	Thou wonderous Art, in how many gray hours,
Wo mich des Lebens wilder Kreis umstrickt,	When life's wild circle closed me in,
Hast du mein Herz zu warmer Lieb entzünden,	Did you enflame my heart to a warm love
Hast mich in eine beßre Welt entrückt!	Did you transport me to a better world!
Oft hat ein Seufzer, deiner Harf' entflossen,	Often a sigh, drifting from thy heart,
Ein süßer, heiliger Akkord von dir	A sweet, holy chord from thee,
Den Himmel beßrer Zeiten mir erschlossen,	Has opened up to me the heaven of better times,
Du holde Kunst, ich danke dir dafür!	Thou wondrous art, I thank you for this!

In a diary entry from the previous year, Schubert himself had observed that Mozart's music "shows us in the darknesses of this life a light-filled, bright, beautiful distance, toward which we can aspire with confidence."[28] When listening to music, Wackenroder's fictional Joseph Berglinger forgets "all earthly trivialities that are truly dust on the radiance of the soul"; this trivial dust is "cleansed" by music.[29] Tieck declares the modern symphony to be capable of "redeeming us from the conflict of wayward thoughts" and leading us "to a quiet, happy, peaceful land," while Hoffmann perceives "a wondrous spirit-realm of the infinite" through the prism of Beethoven's Fifth Symphony.[30]

Within the aesthetics of idealism, the composer assumed a new role as a mediator between heaven and earth, a divinely inspired human who could help to connect the mundane and the divine. When Carl Friedrich Zelter wrote to Haydn in 1804, he likened the elderly composer to a latter-day Prometheus: "Your spirit has penetrated into the sanctity of divine wisdom; you have brought fire from heaven, and with it you warm and illuminate mortal hearts and lead them to the infinite. The best that we can do for others consists simply in this: to honor God with thanks and joy for having sent you in order that we might recognize the miracles He has revealed to us through you in art."[31] Beethoven himself on more than one occasion cast his art as bridge between the earthly and the divine. In 1810 he urged a young admirer "not only to cultivate your art, but penetrate to its innermost; it deserves this, for only art and science elevate mankind to the divine."[32] Two years later he wrote to the publisher Breitkopf & Härtel of "my heavenly art, the only true divine gift of Heaven," and in 1824, writing to another publisher, he spoke of "what the Eternal Spirit has infused into my soul and bids me complete."[33] Writing to the Archduke Rudolph, Bishop of Olmütz, in 1821, Beethoven declared that "there is nothing higher than to approach the divinity more closely than other humans and from there promulgate the rays of the divinity among mankind."[34] It is unclear from the context whether Beethoven is referring to himself or to the addressee. And this is precisely the point: Beethoven considered his own calling a priesthood of sorts. Nor was he alone in this perception: one reviewer of the 1824 concert that premiered the Ninth Symphony and three movements from the *Missa solemnis* noted, "These new artworks appear as the colossal products of a son of the gods, who has just brought the holy, life-giving flame directly from heaven."[35]

Such views rest on the idealist aesthetic, whose philosophical cornerstone was laid in 1790 with the publication of Kant's *Critique of Judgment*. Building on his earlier *Kritik der reinen Vernunft* (*Critique of Pure Reason*, 1781) and *Kritik der praktischen Vernunft* (*Critique of Practical Reason*, 1788), Kant emphasized the creativity of perception and the capacity of the imagination to mediate between reason and the senses. It is not too much of an exaggeration to say that after Kant, beauty would be defined no longer as a quality within a given object, but rather as a function of subjective, aesthetic perception.

For Kant, spirit (*Geist*) is the "ability to present aesthetic ideas." He defined an "aesthetic idea" as "that representation of the imagination which induces much thought, yet without the possibility of any definite thought whatever, i.e., concept, being adequate to it." This representation of the imagination, consequently, can never be completely realized or rendered intelligible through language. Thus "it is easily seen that an aesthetic idea is the counterpart (pendant) of a rational idea, which, conversely, is a concept to which no intuition (representation of the imagination) can be adequate."[36] But Kant explicitly rejected the notion that purely instrumental music might incorporate aesthetic ideas; this art could be judged only on the basis of its form. He therefore relegated instrumental music—along with wallpaper—to the category of "free beauty." Vocal music, by contrast, belonged to the higher category of "dependent beauty" on the grounds that its text allowed the listener to find correlatives in the concepts of the objects being represented.

Kant clearly considered "free beauty" an inferior category of art, for the contemplation of mere form, without concepts, would eventually "make the spirit [*Geist*] dull, the object in the course of time repulsive, and the mind dissatisfied with itself and ill-humored."[37] He dismissed any ideas one might experience while listening to instrumental music as mere mechanical byproducts of associative thought. Unlike poetry, music speaks "only through sentiments and without concepts, and thus . . . leaves nothing to be contemplated." It was on this basis that he deemed untexted music to be "more pleasure than culture," even while affirming its power to move the emotions.[38]

Kant's emphasis on aesthetic cognition nevertheless provided an important opening for later writers grappling with the dichotomy between form and content. One of the most influential of these post-Kantian critics was Friedrich Schiller (1759–1805), who developed the tenets of aesthetic idealism in a series of widely read essays dating from the mid-1790s, beginning with an extended review of a collection of poetry by Friedrich von Matthisson. In a remarkable passage, Schiller argued that "although the *content* of emotions cannot be represented" in any work of art, "the *form* certainly can be." Schiller went on to point out that there is in fact a "widely beloved and powerful art that has no other object than the form of these emotions. This art is *Music.*"[39]

> In short, we demand that in addition to its expressed content, every poetic composition at the same time be an imitation and expression of the form of this content and affect us as if it were music. . . .
>
> Now the entire effect of music, however (as a fine art, and not merely as a agreeable one), consists of accompanying and producing in sensuous form the inner movements of the emotions through analogous external motions. . . . If the composer and the landscape painter penetrate into the secret of those laws that govern the inner movements of the human heart, and if they study the analogy that exists between these movements of the emotions and certain external manifestations, then they will develop from merely ordinary painters into true portraitists of the soul. They will leave the realm of the arbitrary and enter the realm of the necessary. And they may justly take their places not beside the sculptor, who takes as his object the *external* human form, but rather beside the poet, who takes as his object the *inner* human form.[40]

While still essentially mimetic in its assumptions, Schiller's pronouncement helped to move the focus of debate away from content and toward form. Like Hanslick, Schiller denied that music itself embodies emotional content; rather, it works through a process of analogical structure, mediated by the listener's imagination. The poet retains the ability to direct the imagination of his audience in a more defined direction, but even this capacity is limited, for while the poet can "indicate those ideas and allude to those emotions, he cannot develop them himself." Above all, he must not preempt the imagination of his readers. An overly precise indication of ideas or emotions would constitute a "burdensome limitation," because the attractiveness of an aesthetic idea lies in our freedom to perceive its content in a "boundless profundity." "The actual and explicit content that the poet gives is always finite; the potential content, which he leaves for us to project into the work, is an infinite entity."[41]

The "art of the infinite" and "infinite longing" play an even greater role in Schiller's essay "On Naïve and Sentimental Poetry" (1795–96). The dichotomy between the naïve (the natural and sensuous) and the sentimental (the reflective and abstract) corresponds roughly to the phenomenal and noumenal. The task of the modern poet is to bridge the gulf between the two. But because this cannot be realized on earth, the poet's striving for such a synthesis must necessarily remain "infinite." The genius of sentiment, according to Schiller, "abandons [phenomenal] reality in order to ascend to ideas and to rule over his material with his own freedom of activity."[42] In so doing, however, the artist runs the risk of devolving into a realm of meaningless abstraction. On precisely these grounds, Schiller elsewhere rejected those works of music by "recent"—unnamed—composers that appealed merely to the senses.[43]

Although Schiller was disinclined to comment at any length on the integration of the sensuous and the abstract in instrumental music, he helped to establish a framework for the reevaluation of this art in the work of his close friend Christian Gottfried Körner (1756–1831), who happened to be an accomplished musician. Körner's essay "On the Representation of Character in Music" was first published in 1795 in Schiller's journal, *Die Horen*. Following Schiller's lead, Körner rejected Kant's notion that instrumental music constituted a merely agreeable art rather than a fine art. The purpose of an agreeable art, Körner argued, is to please its audience by moving the emotions, through the process of *pathos*. Works of fine art, by contrast, exist as self-contained entities; their purpose is the representation of character, or *ethos*. Early in his essay, Körner neatly summarized the historical stages of eighteenth-century thought regarding the questions of imitation and representation in music:

> For a long time, the notion of what was worthy of representation in music was governed by remarkable prejudices. Here, too, there was fundamental misunderstanding about the principle that the imitation of nature should determine the art. For some, the mimicking of everything audible was considered the essential business of the composer, from the rolling of thunder to the crowing of the rooster. A better kind of taste gradually begins to spread. The expression of human sentiment replaces noise lacking a soul. But is this the point at which the composer is to remain, or is there a higher goal for him?[44]

The answer, he believed, is that the artist must go beyond the expression of transitory sentiment and complement that which is missing in individual, phenomenal exemplars: "He must *idealize* his material." Only through art, Körner maintained, can the infinite be made perceptible, however dimly, for it can otherwise only be imagined. Thus the artist "must raise us up to himself and represent the infinite in perceptible form."[45] For Körner, the characteristic is the symbolic manifestation of the ideal. Character is the quality that unites the realms of morality and aesthetics, and by associating music with moral character, Körner was able to elevate the status of instrumental music to that of a fine art.[46] He rejected the notion that music unsupported by dance, drama, or poetry could not, on the grounds of its vagueness, depict character. Körner stopped short of explictly articulating an essential equality between instrumental and vocal music, yet his brief essay represents an important advance in the emerging prestige of instrumental music.

By the end of the 1790s, the concept of the artwork as a perceptible manifestation of the ideal was being articulated ever more systematically by such figures as Johann Gottlieb Fichte (1762–1814), Friedrich Wilhelm Joseph von Schelling (1775–1854), and August Wilhelm Schlegel (1767–1845). Schelling, in particular, insisted that art and philosophy were in the end concerned with the same basic issue: to reconcile the world of phenomena with the world of ideas.[47] Like Schiller, he saw profound meaning in the congruence of artistic and natural forms and considered the artwork to provide a window on their essential unity. In his *System of Transcendental Idealism* (1800), Schelling advocated art as the key to perceiving the nature of this unity. His *Philosophy of Art*, in turn, based on lectures first delivered at Jena in 1802–3, has justly been called "the first explicit art-philosophy in the history of the Western world."[48] Art is the means by which the real and the finite can be synthesized with the ideal and the infinite. "Through art, divine creation is presented objectively, for both rest on the same imagining of the infinite ideal into the tangible. The exquisite German word *Einbildungskraft* actually means the power of an inward formation of the whole, and in fact all creation is based on this power. It is the power through which an ideal is at the same time something tangible, the soul the body; it is the power of individuation, which of all powers is the one that is truly creative."[49]

Within this framework, Schelling saw the "forms of music"—by this he meant rhythm, harmony, and melody—as "the forms of eternal things insofar as they can be contemplated from the perspective of the real. . . . Thus music manifests, in rhythm and harmony, the pure form of the movements of the heavenly bodies, freed from any object or material. In this respect, music is that art which casts off the corporeal, in that it presents movement in itself, divorced from any object, borne on invisible, almost spiritual wings." Rhythm, harmony, and melody are the "first and purest forms of movement in the universe. . . . The heavenly bodies soar on the wings of harmony and rhythm. . . . Borne aloft by the same wings, music soars through space to weave an audible universe out of the transparent body of sound and tone." Schelling openly acknowledged his debt to Pythagoreanism at this point, but insisted that Pythagorean theories had been quite poorly understood in the past.[50]

On this basis, then, one might reasonably expect that Schelling would deem instrumental music to be the highest of all arts precisely on the basis of its incorporeality, which in turn would allow the greatest possible range of freedom for imaginative perception. For Schelling, however, the contemplation of the ideal was but a means to the end of achieving the Absolute, which he defined as the integration of the material and the spiritual, the phenomenal and the ideal. Although the artist and the philosopher pursue the same essential task, the former does so by using symbolic forms in a manner he himself does not fully understand. The material of the philosopher, by contrast, is rational thought, which can be more readily idealized and then reintegrated into the realm of the phenomenal. Schelling therefore preserved the traditional hierarchy that accorded the place of honor to the verbal arts.

Schelling's work nevertheless provided an important advance in the aesthetics of instrumental music. He broke decisively with earlier systems based on the principle of mimesis, and he insisted on the metaphysical significance of all aesthetic intuition, including the perception of instrumental music. In this respect, Schelling's philosophy of art (which is in fact a philosophy *through* art) represents an aesthetic system qualitatively different from the one in which Kant, only a little more than a decade before, had deprecated instrumental music because of its purported inability to accommodate ideas. The rising tide of art-philosophy had lifted the status of all artistic vessels, including that of instrumental music.

Schelling's philosophy reverberates throughout the subsequent history of idealist aesthetics. August Wilhelm Schlegel's lectures on art (Berlin, 1801–2) also pursue the idea that the beautiful is a symbolic representation of the infinite and that the infinite becomes at least partly perceptible through the beautiful. The human spirit contemplating beauty is directed in "infinite striving" toward beauty. Schlegel used this premise to expose the inadequacy of earlier psychological, empirical, and sensualist theories of music. Sound is the "innermost" of the five senses, dealing with transitory phenomena in a play of successions; and music, as exemplified by the sound of the chorale (quite apart from any underlying text), provides us with "an intimation of harmonic perfection, the unity of all being that Christians imagine through the image of heavenly bliss."[51] Because of its incorporeality, "one must accord music the advantage of being ideal in its essence. It purifies the passions, as it were, from the material filth with which they are associated, in that music presents these passions to our inner sense entirely according to their form, without any reference to objects; and after touching an earthly frame, it allows these passions to breathe in a purer ether." All that remains after the experience of listening is "a single, immutable, and thoroughly infinite striving, reverent contemplation [*Andacht*]."[52] Friedrich Schlegel, the brother of August Wilhelm, concurred. He called hearing "the most noble of the senses" and praised it for its ability to take us "beyond the tyranny of the physical object." Because of its incorporeal nature, music was the one art most closely corresponding to the ever-fluid nature of the incorporeal "I." For Schlegel, music was "less a representational art than a philosophical language, and really lies much higher than mere art."[53]

IDEALISM AND THE NEW AESTHETICS OF LISTENING

Idealist vocabulary and categories of thought figure prominently in the musical aesthetics of the early Romantics. The emphasis on specific points varies from writer to writer, but many of the most basic terms and concepts derive from idealist philosophy.

Wilhelm Heinrich Wackenroder (1773–98) was the single most important figure in the articulation of a new aesthetic of listening at the end of the eighteenth century. Unlike most of the other writers discussed up to this point (with the notable exception of Körner), Wackenroder had substantial training in music. He received early instruction in his native Berlin from Karl Fasch, founder of the Singakademie, and he appears to have tried his hand at composition as well.[54] At Göttingen, Wackenroder studied under the theorist, historian, and composer Johann Nikolaus Forkel, and his keyboard skills were good enough to have elicited an invitation from a musical society in Bamberg for a public performance of a concerto by Haydn.[55] In the last years of his brief life, he collaborated with his friend Ludwig Tieck (1773–1853), a poet and playwright who in turn was responsible for the posthumous (anonymous) publication of Wackenroder's *Phantasien über die Kunst* (*Fantasies on Art*, 1799), to which Tieck added several essays of his own.[56]

Wackenroder's first major publication, *Herzensergiessungen eines kunstliebenden Klosterbruders* (*Outpourings from the Heart of an Art-Loving Monk*, 1796), attracted immediate attention. Published anonymously, it was thought for a time to have been written by none other than Goethe himself, and there was sufficient demand for the work to be reissued (along with the *Fantasies on Art*) in 1814 and in further subsequent editions. The *Outpourings* and *Fantasies on Art* incorporate all the essential elements of the idealist aesthetic. Nature and art are "two wondrous languages" of "mysterious power" granted to us by God "in order that mortals might grasp (as fully as possible) heavenly things in their full power."[57] Joseph Berglinger, Wackenroder's fictitious musician, declares music to be "the most wondrous" of all the fine arts because "it represents human emotions in a super-human manner" and "shows us all the movements of our emotions in a manner that is incorporeal, clothed in golden clouds of ethereal harmonies, above our heads."[58] Insofar as music is a language at all, it is "the language of angels." It is the "only art that leads us back to the most beautiful harmonies of the manifold and contradictory movements of our emotions."[59]

Music is the darkest and most powerful of all the arts. Its "waves" stream forth with "pure and *formless* essence . . . and particularly the thousandfold transitions among the emotions. In its innocence, this idealistic, angelically pure art knows neither the origins nor the impetus for its motions, and it does not know the relationship of its feelings with the actual world."[60] Here, Wackenroder encapsulates the creed of idealist aesthetics with remarkable concision. Music occupies a separate world of ideals, independent of earthly objects and emotions, and it has the power to lift us out of the ills of life to a higher region. Beyond this, we find virtually no attempt to explain a cause-and-effect relationship between work and listener in Wackenroder's writings, for the fundamental nature of discourse on music has changed: the perspective is no longer even remotely naturalistic.

Tieck shared these views on the essence of instrumental music, strenuously disavowing any connection of this art with the phenomenal world. Instead, he emphasized that musical notes "constitute a separate world unto themselves."[61] In one of the very few extended discussions of a specific work of music by early Romantic writers, he praised Johann Friedrich Reichardt's overture to a German-language adaptation of Shakespeare's *Macbeth* (1787). Tieck's choice of works has been widely misunderstood: it has been suggested that he knew nothing of the music of Haydn and Mozart, but this seems implausible for an artist intensely interested in music and living in Berlin during the late 1790s.[62] Reichardt's music to *Macbeth* was quite well known at the time, and the fact that it served as a prelude to one of Shakespeare's most famous dramas allowed Tieck to emphasize the greater emotional power of instrumental music over the subsequent stage production.[63] Tieck argued that the overture was capable of projecting its own complete and self-contained "drama" of a kind that "no poet could ever give us," not even Shakespeare. The music was a "drama without characters" that referred to no story and "relied on no laws of probability."[64]

Wackenroder and Tieck were both still in their twenties when they presented their idealist aesthetic of instrumental music. Many older writers, understandably, clung to more traditional outlooks well into the nineteenth century. Goethe, for one, appears never to have embraced the enhanced aesthetic status of instrumental music. Like many writers before him, he compared the string quartet to a conversation among four intelligent individuals, but the implicit imagery of music as a language was already old-fashioned by this time. But other critics of his generation gradually embraced the new mode of listening. Writing to Goethe in 1809, the composer Carl Friedrich Zelter described the act of listening as a process in which a physical response led to a heightened mental striving for a world beyond:

> There are certain symphonies by Haydn that in their loose, liberal progression bring my blood into a comfortable motion and give the free parts of my body the inclination and tendency to work outwardly. At these times, my fingers become softer and longer, my eyes wish to see something that until now no eye has ever glimpsed, the lips open themselves, that which is within me wants to go out into the open.[65]

Zelter's account manifests a curious but by no means incompatible mixture between older (passive, physical) and newer (active, mental) modes of listening in the early nineteenth century. Both the body and mind are moved at one and the same time; the spirit transcends the realm of the phenomenal and catches a glimpse of that which would otherwise remain inaccessible.

Other writers of this same generation also shifted their allegiance to the aesthetics of idealism during the closing years of the eighteenth century and the first decade of the nineteenth. The writings of Johann Gottfried Herder (1744–1803) illustrate this change particularly well, for his views on the nature and aesthetic worth of instrumental music changed markedly over the course of his life. His fourth *Kritisches Wäldchen* (*Critical Thicket*, written in 1769 but not published until 1846) maintained the conventional image of music as a language of passions, and within this conceptual design, instrumental music inevitably suffers because of its semantic obscurity. By the mid-1780s, Herder's views had begun to change. In an essay of 1785 entitled "Which Produces the Greatest Effect, Painting or Music? A Dialogue of the Gods," Apollo presides over a dispute on Mount Olympus between the goddess of music and the goddess of painting. Painting charges that Music is dark and confusing. Music responds that what is

> dark and confused in your emotions is due to your organ of perception, not my tones, which are pure and clear, the highest model of harmonious order. They are (as was once pointed out by a wise mortal inspired by me [i.e., Pythagoras]) the relationship and numbers of the universe in the most pleasant, facile, and powerful of all symbols. In criticizing me, my sister, you have therefore praised me. You have praised the infinite quality of my art in its innermost workings.

The goddess of poetry is summoned to judge the debate and finds in favor of Music, but she reminds her "that without my words, without song, dance, or other action, you must concede that for humans, your emotions remain perpetually in the dark. You speak to the heart, but to the understanding of how very few!"[66] Poetry thus reiterates the then-standard view that only through word or gesture can music become intelligible, but in so doing she emphasizes the shortcomings of human perception rather than the shortcomings of music itself.

Herder's late *Kalligone* (1800), in turn, reads like a thoroughly idealist tract. In rebutting Kant's *Critique of Judgment*, Herder unambiguously declared instrumental music to be the highest of all the arts because it provides a means of perceiving the Absolute, the realm in which distinctions between subjectivity and objectivity disappear. Music surpasses all other arts in the way the spirit surpasses the body, for music is spirit— *Geist*—and "related to motion, great nature's innermost power. What cannot be made visible to man—the world of the invisible—becomes communicable to him in its [music's] manner, and in its manner alone."[67] Herder emphasizes *Andacht*—reverent contemplation—as the cognitive quality that moves the listener to a "high, free realm" when hearing music without words. A more spiritual version of Kant's *Einbildungskraft, Andacht* implies a sense of active reflection combined with reverence for the divine, the infinite.[68] Through reverent contemplation, the aesthetic experience was now seen to take place in a transcendent sphere, "pure and free above the earth."[69] Herder's insight is critical to understanding the Romantic aesthetic, for it was not a change in the contemporary repertory that was transporting listeners to a higher realm, but rather a change in the perceived nature of aesthetic cognition—which is to say, a change in attitudes toward listening.

Christian Friedrich Michaelis (1770–1834), although only slightly older than Wackenroder and Tieck, is another writer whose works reveal a similar change in outlook. Michaelis published two separate pamphlets entitled *Über den Geist der Tonkunst* (*On the Spirit of Music*, 1795 and 1800) both of which take as their point of departure Kant's *Critique of Judgment*. Although willing to grant instrumental music a higher aesthetic status than had Kant, Michaelis nevertheless adhered in these early essays to the view of instrumental music as "more pleasure than culture."[70] By 1804, however, in a commentary on Herder's hierarchy of the arts, Michaelis acknowledges that the individual and the ideal can be integrated most readily and thoroughly through music alone and that the infinite can be expressed through the finite in a more vivid manner than in any other art.[71] By 1808, in an essay entitled "On the Ideal in Music," Michaelis had abandoned the naturalist perspective altogether and openly embraced idealism. Music "presents entirely and purely the spirit of art in its freedom and individuality" and conjures up before our fantasy "such an entirely individual world that we would search in vain for an original in artless reality."[72] The ecstatic tone of Wackenroder and Tieck is missing, but the perspective is recognizably the same.

Michaelis's "conversion" to idealism is typical of his time. The notion of the artwork—and the work of music, in particular—as an earthly manifestation of the Absolute won widespread acceptance in the first decade of the nineteenth century. The vocabulary of idealism pervades much of the criticism written during this time: Music is widely described as "supernatural," "mystic," "holy," "divine," "heavenly." The mechanical associations with the passions were no longer the central concern they had been only a short time before; instead, the emphasis had shifted toward the premise that music is the reflection of a higher, more spiritual realm. The anonymous reviewer of Wackenroder and Tieck's *Fantasies on Art* in Leipzig's *Allgemeine musikalische Zeitung*, for one, seems to have taken the idealist aesthetic as a given: the essence of art, he observes almost in passing, is to "manifest the supra-sensuous, to unite the finite and the infinite." And it was a mistake, this reviewer argues, to draw a parallel between sounds and colors (in Wackenroder's essay "Die Töne") on the grounds that the corresponding play of sensations between sounds implicitly relegates music to the agreeable rather than to the fine arts.[73]

Idealist premises are also evident in the lengthy and perceptive "Observations on the Development of Music in Germany in the Eighteenth Century," by Johann Triest, a pastor in Stettin, published in the *Allgemeine musikalische Zeitung* in 1800–1801. Triest argued that instrumental music is no mere receptacle for vocal music, nor derived from it, but is instead fully capable of incorporating aesthetic ideas. Triest thus preserved Kantian terminology while extending the domain of instrumental music beyond the realm of the merely sensuous. Even more so than vocal music, instrumental music is able to incorporate "spirit and life" by intimating an ideal.[74] In the works of Shakespeare and Mozart, according to the playwright, novelist, and critic Franz Horn, writing in 1802, there is no longer "any conflict between the ideal and the real, the internal and the external"; instead, the "infinite is made manifest for the fantasy" of the beholder.[75] And it is altogether telling that Heinrich Christoph Koch should include "Ideal" as an entry in the abridged version of his musical dictionary of 1807, even though it is not to be found in the much larger original edition of 1802. Here, Koch emphasizes the freedom of the listener's imagination and speaks of a "poeticized world" (*erdichtete Welt*) within which the images of our fantasy can play.[76] And for the critic Amadeus Wendt, the goal of the composer is to create in sensuous form "an image of the infinite."[77]

E.T.A. Hoffmann (1776–1822) thus appeared on the scene of idealist aesthetics at a relatively late stage: the basic concepts and vocabulary of his music criticism were already well established by the time he began writing reviews for the *Allgemeine musikalische Zeitung* in 1809. Like earlier writers, Hoffmann perceived music as occupying an altogether separate sphere beyond the phenomenal, thereby endowing musical works with the power to provide a glimpse of the infinite. Instrumental music "discloses to man an unknown realm, a world that has nothing in common with the external sensuous world that surrounds him, a world in which he leaves behind him all feelings that can be expressed through concepts, in order to surrender himself to that which cannot be expressed" in words. In vocal music, it is only because the text is "clothed by music with the purple shimmer of Romanticism" that we can be led into "the realm of the infinite."[78] When united with a text, music is forced to descend to the realm of common, everyday life and "speak of specific passions and actions. . . . Can music proclaim anything else but the wonders of that region from which it descends to us to resound?" In an utter reversal of traditional aesthetic hierarchies, Hoffmann left open the possibility that vocal music could achieve the exalted realm of instrumental music if the poet could raise himself to the level of the composer and do justice to the music.[79]

As in earlier writings influenced by the idealist aesthetic, Hoffmann's music criticism abounds with sacred metaphors. He adopted Schelling's view of the artist as a high priest capable of providing mankind with a glimpse of a distant "spirit-realm," and he perceived musical harmony as "the image and expression of the communion of souls, of union with the eternal, with the ideal that rules over us and yet includes us."[80] Hoffmann saw the origins of music in the liturgy of the church and emphasized that music's divine nature had now extended into the secular sphere as well. Thus, while he acknowledged that "instrumental music had elevated itself in recent times to a level of which the old masters [before Haydn and Mozart] had no concept," it is important to recognize that his aesthetic applies to vocal as well as instrumental music, and not merely to the music of the present and recent past.[81] The sacred works of Palestrina and Leo are just as capable of providing a glimpse of the divine as are the symphonies of Haydn, Mozart, and Beethoven. The presence or absence of a text and the style of the music are ultimately less important than the essential nature of music itself. Beethoven's instrumental compositions gave Hoffmann the immediate impetus for some of his most inspired essays, but they did not provide him with the philosophical and aesthetic outlook that underlies these writings.

Hoffmann's particular contribution lies in his superior prose and his ability to integrate philosophical and aesthetic concepts with more technical issues of musical detail. I shall return to Hoffmann's account of Beethoven's Fifth Symphony in chapters 2 and 3; for the moment, suffice it to say that the idealist aesthetics of instrumental music had already developed largely outside the domain of music criticism and almost entirely outside discussions of (or even familiarity with) the music of Beethoven. Beethoven's music, in short, did not create a revolution in listening; he was, however, the direct and immediate beneficiary of this new outlook. Symphonies, until only recently consigned to the same category of the "agreeable" arts as wallpaper, were now beginning to be perceived as manifestations of the infinite and, as such, as vehicles of truth.

CHAPTER TWO

Listening as Thinking: From Rhetoric to Philosophy

THE AESTHETICS OF IDEALISM opened up new approaches to listening just at the time when Beethoven began to make his mark on the musical world. His early Romantic contemporaries were now describing the act of listening in radically new terms, as an active rather than a passive process. The act of listening to music had never been conceived in quite this way before. Two very different accounts of listening, one from 1739, the other from 1792, capture the contrast between these two modes of listening. Both resonate with passion, but they rest on two very different aesthetic premises. "When I hear a solemn symphony in church," Johann Mattheson declared in 1739, "a sense of reverential awe falls over me. If an instrumental chorus joins in, this brings about an elevated sense of wonder within me. If the organ begins to storm and thunder, a divine fear arises in me. And if everything concludes with a joyful Halleluia, my heart leaps within my body."[1] For Mattheson, listening was an intense yet ultimately passive process in which a certain type of music produced a certain type of response. His account falls into an "If x, then y" kind of pattern, one of cause and effect.

The "true way of listening" that Wackenroder described in a letter of 1792 to Tieck follows an altogether different process:

> It consists of the most attentive observations of the notes and their progression; in the complete surrender of the soul to this torrential stream of emotions; in the distancing and withdrawal from every disruptive thought and from all extraneous sensuous impressions. For me, this voracious quaffing of the notes is associated with a certain strain that cannot be tolerated for all that long. And for this reason, I believe I may assert that one is capable of perceiving music in a participatory manner for one hour at the most.[2]

Unlike Mattheson, Wackenroder describes listening as an activity independent of the music he hears: listening is something he *does* to the music. Instruments, voices, text, volume, genre—none of this matters. Wackenroder was certainly capable of giving a more technical account had he wished to do so. What concerns him most in this account of listening is the sense of exertion. Paradoxically, even the "complete surrender of the soul" can be accomplished only with effort, by consciously distancing himself from all external stimuli other than the music. This enables him to listen in a "participatory manner" that requires a strenuous engagement of the imagination. This is not to suggest that Mattheson and his contemporaries used no imagination while listening to instrumental music or that their emotional responses to this music were somehow less intense than those described by Wackenroder and other early Romantics. But the new premise of an engaged, "participatory" perception had changed the basic perception of the act of listening.[3]

The idealist aesthetic assumes that anyone contemplating a work of art must reconstruct that work in his or her own mind if that work is to exercise any significant effect. As an aesthetic based on the philosophical premise of a free and absolute self, idealism accommodates multiple and widely differing interpretations of a given work of music. The contrast with earlier modes of musical listening could not be more striking. Under the doctrine of mimesis, conflicting interpretations of the emotional content of an instrumental work had long been perceived as an inevitable consequence of the presumed deficiencies of instrumental music itself. The implicitly derisive question Rousseau had attributed to the *philosophe* Fontenelle—"Sonata, what do you want of me?"—resonated for as long as it did not only because the limited ability of instrumental music to represent nature was deemed unsatisfactory, but also because the very premise that one might have to "work" while listening was itself nothing short of preposterous.[4] When Rousseau himself described the desired construction of an aria's melody, his guiding principle for the composer was to choose those techniques that would "move," "sway," "agitate," and "transport" the listener.[5] Compositional technique, under the old aesthetic, was ultimately governed by the effect of the resulting music on the listener. Within the idealist aesthetic of the late eighteenth century, by contrast, listeners were routinely expected to "work," to bring their imagination to bear on the object at hand. The fact that an instrumental composition could generate widely differing accounts of its "content" was accepted as a consequence of the music's capacity to reflect a higher ideal. That this ideal might be only partially comprehensible was scarcely a fault of the medium itself.

LISTENING IN A RHETORICAL FRAMEWORK

The Enlightenment's conception of music as a language reflects the broader practice of hearing music within the framework of rhetoric. The goal of the composer and performer, working in tandem, was to move the listener. Charles Batteux's widely read *Les beaux arts réduits à un même principe* (*The Fine Arts Reduced to One Common Principle*, 1746) sums up the matter quite neatly:

The word instructs us, convinces us: it is the medium of reason. But tone and gesture are media of the heart; they move us, win us over, persuade us. The word expresses passions only by means of the ideas with which the sentiments are associated, as though a reflection of them. Tone and gesture reach the heart directly, without any detour.[6]

Over and over throughout the seventeenth and eighteenth centuries, composers were likened to orators, instrumental compositions to word-less orations. By elaborating and transforming a central musical idea, theorists of the time argued, composers of instrumental music were able to construct and convey a series of musical thoughts analogous in struc-ture to those found in a verbal oration. The parallels between music and language were expounded in countless treatises of the time, which borrowed terms from grammar (theme, phrase, sentence, period, para-graph, antecedent, consequent, etc.) to explain the technical elements of musical form.[7]

Nor were such accounts limited to technical writings on music. Even though it does not evoke rhetoric explicitly, one particularly rich passage from Karl Philipp Moritz's novel *Andreas Hartknopf* of 1786 illustrates vividly in a very short space the essence of late eighteenth-century atti-tudes about the conceptual model of music as a language:

Hartknopf took his flute out of his pocket and accompanied the magnificent recitative of his teachings with appropriate chords. He translated, while fanta-sizing, the language of reason into the language of sentiments, and in this he was served by

Music.

Often, when he had spoken the antecedent phrase of a sentence, he then blew the consequent phrase on his flute.

He breathed thoughts from reason into the heart, just as he breathed thoughts into the tones of the flute. . . .

How is it that solemnity and dignity can be expressed through equal rhythms? Lively sentiments through unequal rhythms? Happiness through three or four short tones between two longer ones? Turbulence and wildness through one or two short notes before a long one? Ponderousness through ♪♪♩? Wherein lies the similarity between the symbols and the thing indicated?

Whoever finds this out will be capable of creating an alphabet for the lan-guage of emotions, out of which a thousand magnificent works can be con-structed.—Is the music of mortals not a child's rattle the moment it ceases to follow Great Nature, the moment it stops imitating her?[8]

This kind of passage could not possibly have been written in the nine-teenth century. It is nearly contemporaneous with the publication of Rousseau's *Essay on the Origins of Languages*, which maintained that music and language share a common origin but that the language of music was could "speak" in its own right. Within this outlook, Moritz posits a system of signs and equivalencies that moves fluidly between the language of reason and an imaginary language of emotions.

Moritz and his contemporaries probably recognized (at least from time to time) that this kind of language was a useful fiction and that no one would ever write its "alphabet." The image of music as a language nevertheless remained deeply engrained in Enlightenment thought. And the corollary to this image was that the composer was responsible for creating a work whose expression was intelligible to listeners. Technical issues of musical form, in fact, were often justified or rejected on the grounds of their comprehensibility. Johann Friedrich Agricola, for example, criticized another composer's concerto movement because its internal ritornellos had introduced new musical ideas. The problem with this unconventional practice, Agricola pointed out, was that it would bring the listener's attention into "disorder" and thereby dissipate the effect of the work. Along more general lines, Forkel recommended that composers adhere to "the highest possible distinctness and clarity" in constructing musical periods (itself a term borrowed from grammar, tantamount to a "sentence"), not merely for the sake of following convention, but because listeners would otherwise "become either tired or distracted" and consequently be "in no condition to follow the course of the whole and receive the pleasure expected from the piece." Other pedagogical manuals of the time make similar recommendations on similar grounds.[9]

This was not, however, a prescription for mindless simplicity. The ability to make the unfamiliar seem familiar was regarded with special admiration. Haydn, in particular, was praised for his ability to present the most demanding technical artifices in a readily comprehensible manner—for of what use is an incomprehensible language? Ernst Ludwig Gerber, in a biographical sketch first published in 1790, singled out Haydn's gift of writing music that "often seems familiar" in spite of its contrapuntal sophistication. Johann Ferdinand Ritter von Schönfeld, in his *Yearbook of the Music of Vienna and Prague for 1796*, lauded Haydn's ability to develop ideas in a manner that was at once both simple and artistic.[10] And whereas Johann Karl Friedrich Triest had likened the music of C.P.E. Bach to the poetry of the mystically inclined Friedrich Gottlieb Klopstock, he declared that "if one had to distill the essence of Haydn's art into two words, they would be *kunstvolle Popularität* ["artful popularity"] or *populäre Kunstfülle* ["popular richness of art"]."[11] The image of the eighteenth-century Haydn as an orator capable of reaching and moving the masses persisted well into the nineteenth century. In a biography first published in 1810, just after the composer's death, Ignaz Theodor Ferdinand

Arnold called Haydn a "clever orator," and Giuseppe Carpani lauded Haydn's ability to present the most unusual and even bizarre ideas in a manner that was "learned" without being "arid," "clear" yet "erudite."[12] Stendhal, who in his *Vie de Haydn, de Mozart, et de Métastase* drew liberally on Carpani's account of the composer, elaborated still further on the image of Haydn as an orator, adding a lengthy account of the difficulties involved in giving eloquent expression to any idea. Even as late as 1828, the Würzburg Kapellmeister and Professor of Music Joseph Fröhlich was pointing to Haydn's rhetorical abilities to present complex ideas in an intelligible fashion.[13]

All these accounts rest on the unspoken assumption that it is the responsibility of the composer to make his music readily comprehensible. The framework for this kind of listening is rhetorical: the burden of intelligibility lies with the composer. Listeners are not expected to exert themselves in following the trajectory of a musical discourse. A certain degree of attentiveness was of course required on the part of the listener, and critics began emphasizing this quality of attentiveness more and more over the course of the eighteenth century.[14] But in the end, it remained the composer's obligation to reach the listener, not vice versa.

Listening in a Philosophical Framework

The new paradigm of listening that emerged out of the aesthetics of idealism around 1800 abandoned the premise that music was a language. The musical work was perceived no longer as an oration, but rather as an object of contemplation, a potential catalyst of revelation accessible to those who actively engaged the work by listening with creative imagination, with *Einbildungskraft*. By the first decade of the eighteenth century, the onus of intelligibility was rapidly shifting from composer to listener. This new framework of listening was in effect philosophical, based on the premise that the listener must strive to understand and internalize the thought of the composer, follow the argument of the music, and comprehend it as a whole.

In an aphorism often quoted even in its own time, Friedrich Schlegel asserted at the turn of the nineteenth century that music has "more affinity to philosophy than to poetry," that is, as a way of knowing rather than as an expression of emotion or ideas per se. Schlegel pronounced the need for "all pure music" to be "philosophical and instrumental," and he urged others to go beyond considering instrumental music from "the flat perspective of so-called naturalness"—that is, from the mechanistic perspective of cause and effect—and to recognize it instead as a vehicle of philosophy.[15]

E.T.A. Hoffmann's review of Beethoven's Fifth Symphony represents the first attempt to apply this philosophical framework to a specific composition. It articulates the shift from the Enlightenment's perception of music as a language, operating under the principles of rhetoric, to Romanticism's perception of music as a source of truth, operating under the principles of philosophy. This review also happens to be *the* central document in the reception of Beethoven's music during the composer's lifetime. Beethoven's music and the idea of listening in a philosophical framework have thus become inextricably linked. But the close—almost complete—identification of this new mode of listening with the works of Beethoven has tended to obscure the origins and significance of this new mode of listening outside his music, and for that matter outside the music of any other composer that came before him.

It is worth reminding ourselves that Hoffmann's review was one of the earliest published commentaries to link Haydn, Mozart, and Beethoven in a single breath, and it was the first to proclaim Beethoven the greatest of the three.[16] In reviewing Beethoven's new symphony, then, Hoffmann was faced with the immediate task of connecting the young composer to his more celebrated predecessors even while setting him apart. This was no small challenge. Hoffmann's solution was to present the music of Haydn and Mozart within the earlier, rhetorical framework of listening and to present Beethoven within the newer, philosophical mode of listening. A closer examination of the relevant passages from the review will reveal this basic distinction.

Hoffmann credits Haydn and Mozart as having been the first to show us the art of instrumental music "in its full glory," but he accords Beethoven the honor of having "penetrated to its innermost essence." The instrumental compositions of all three "breathe a similar Romantic spirit, which rests upon a similar inner grasp of the distinctive essence of this art," yet the "character of their compositions differs markedly":

> The expression of a child-like, jovial personality prevails in Haydn's compositions. His symphonies lead us into vast green meadows, into a merry, bright throng of happy people. Youths and maidens float past in circling dances. . . . A life full of love, full of bliss, as before the Fall, in eternal youth; no sorrow, no pain, only a sweet, melancholy yearning for the beloved object that floats in the distance out of the glow of dusk. . . .[17]

> Mozart leads us into the depths of the spirit realm. Fear surrounds us, but because it does not torture us, it is more an intimation of the infinite. Love and melancholy resound in lovely voices; the night of the spirit-world descends in a bright purple shimmer, and with inexpressible longing we follow those figures who gesture to us familiarly to join them in their ranks, and who soar through

the clouds in an eternal dance of the spheres. (For example: Mozart's Symphony in E-flat Major, known as his "Swansong.")[18]

Thus Beethoven's instrumental music also opens up to us the realm of the monstrous and immeasurable. Burning rays of light shoot through the deep night of this realm, and we become aware of giant shadows that surge back and forth, closing in on us in ever narrower confines until they destroy us, but not the pain of endless longing. . . .[19]

There are multiple tropes at work here, most significantly a move from the beautiful (Haydn's music, characterized by a pastoral scene) to the sublime (Beethoven's music, characterized by thunderbolts, deep night, and the supernatural), with Mozart's music occupying a space somewhere in between. Hoffmann also traces a trajectory from childlike innocence (Haydn) to the superhuman (Mozart) to the divine (Beethoven). This kind of teleological progression has been a source of constant irritation to Haydn scholars, for it reinforces the image of the composer as a harmless, slightly doddering old man whose music is innocent and charming but ultimately trivial. Mozart fares better in this regard, but for Hoffmann, it is Beethoven who crowns the triumvirate.

I shall return to Hoffmann's imagery in chapter 3; for the moment, let us consider more closely the pattern of his verbs. "Haydn's symphonies *lead us* into vast green woodlands. . . ." This is exactly the same verb as that associated with Mozart, who also "*leads us*," but into a different place, "the heart of the spirit realm." The nouns associated with Mozart are more mysterious—love and melancholy, spirit voices, an approaching night with a bright purple shimmer—but what Mozart does is the same as what Haydn does: he leads us. In both instances, the composer bears the burden of intelligibility. Beethoven, on the other hand, does not lead us at all. Instead, his music "*opens up* to us" the "realm of the monstrous and the immeasurable." And what is opened up to us is truly extraordinary. Flashes of light shoot through the "deep night of this realm," allowing us to perceive "giant shadows that surge back and forth." The allusion to Plato's cave here is unmistakable. Listening to Beethoven's music, we become aware—dimly—of a higher form of reality not otherwise perceptible to us.

A similar pattern emerges in Hoffmann's second series of comparisons, which follows hard on the heels of the first.

Haydn grasps Romantically the human element of human life; he is more commensurable for the majority [of listeners].

Mozart takes up more the superhuman, the wondrous element that abides in inner spirit.

Beethoven's music sets in motion the lever of horror, fear, revulsion, pain, and it awakens that infinite longing which is the essence of Romanticism.[20]

Here, the contrast is on agency. Haydn and Mozart act as individuals, leading us, but Beethoven is invisible. It is his *music* that sets in motion the lever of the sublime. The distinction is significant, for it underscores the fundamentally different nature of the listening experience within the new aesthetics of idealism. In his 1813 reworking of his review, Hoffmann reverts at this point to the image of music as a language when he takes up the question of intelligibility, of how listeners might make sense of this music.

Yet how does the matter stand if it is *your* feeble observation alone that the deep inner continuity of Beethoven's every composition eludes? If it is *your* fault alone that you do not understand the master's language as the initiated understand it, that the portals of the innermost sanctuary remain closed to you?

[A]nd at the center of the spirit realm thus disclosed the intoxicated soul gives ear to the unfamiliar language and understands the most mysterious premonitions that have stirred it.

It is as though the master [Beethoven] thought that, in speaking of deep mysterious things . . . one may not use ordinary words, only sublime and glorious ones.[21]

Hoffmann gives the traditional image of music as a language a new twist: in Beethoven's hands, instrumental music has become a kind of secret code, understood only by an elite group of initiates. It is a language unconcerned with rhetoric, at least in the traditional sense of that term: the artwork exists as an autonomous entity, within a world of its own. If we as listeners lack sufficient imagination, Hoffmann tells us, we will not be able to enter that world, for it is not part of Beethoven's purpose to *lead us.*

This is not to say that Beethoven's music—or the music of any other composer, for that matter—can ever operate wholly outside the framework of rhetoric. The Fifth Symphony is full of rhetorical devices and strategies that draw us into its web, and Beethoven uses essentially the same stock of techniques that composers had been using for centuries: repetition, variation, contrast, interruption, silence, and so on. What has changed, however, is the listener's basic orientation toward these techniques. The individual who assumes it will be his or her responsibility to make sense of the work at hand attends to it in a manner far different from the listener who relies on the composer to act as a guide, as an orator.

Hoffmann's account thus traces a path by which the listener moves from the passive framework of rhetoric (Haydn and Mozart) to the active framework of philosophy (Beethoven): it is precisely this emphasis on the responsibility of the listener that distinguishes the new mode of listening from the old. That Hoffmann should ascribe the essential difference of the aesthetic experience to Beethoven's music—as opposed to a new way of listening to music in general, already in place before Beethoven had begun to write symphonies—has only blurred the issues. Hoffmann could not, in good conscience, claim that Beethoven had appeared on the scene without precedent of any kind, and it is to his credit that he aligned the younger composer with Haydn and Mozart. Hoffmann was entirely justified, moreover, to make distinctions among the musical styles of the three composers. Yet many of the most important features Hoffmann identifies as uniquely Beethovenian in fact derive more directly from attitudes toward listening than from elements within the music.

Beethoven's greatness, for Hoffmann, comes at the expense of the listener, a shadowy figure who is "led" by Haydn and Mozart to ever-higher realms, only to fall flat when confronted by the music of Beethoven. The incomprehensible artist of genius and the hopelessly dim public—the juxtaposition has become so commonplace since Hoffmann's time that this, too, is a novelty we scarcely notice at first. But what other reviewer had ever heaped such open scorn on his readers? This in itself is no small milestone in the history of musical aesthetics. Yet in an odd way, Hoffmann's contempt testifies to the newly established responsibility of listeners to take an active role in attending to the music, to make sense of the work at hand. Even while reducing the listener to a position of befuddled ignorance, Hoffman places that individual squarely in the center of things.

ART AS PHILOSOPHY

When read against earlier accounts of instrumental music, Hoffmann's review stands out for its urgency of tone. Beethoven's Fifth and works like it are perceived no longer as vehicles of entertainment but as vehicles of truth. Listening becomes a way of knowing.

Once again, Kant is the key figure in the emergence of this new perspective. He considered every work of beauty to be the product of genius, which he defined as "the talent (a gift of nature) that gives art its rules. Because this talent—an innate productive capacity of the artist—is itself an element of nature, one might also put it in this manner: Genius is the inborn disposition (*ingenium*) through which nature gives the rule to art."[22] But while genius gives rules to art, a work that merely imitates an existing product of genius lacks the originality characteristic of a work of beauty, for it lacks precisely that unpredictable quality of nature and the unconscious—genius—that provides the artwork of beauty with its essential character. To avoid creating the appearance of chaos, works of art would always be obliged to follow certain rules; true art, however, incorporates the unpredictable, indescribable, and ultimately unknowable element of originality. The quality of genius is such that no one, including even the artist, can adequately describe how the ideas within the artwork came to be there. Nor can anyone fully explicate the nature of the artist's accomplishments. For Kant, this is what distinguishes art from science. He illustrates the difference by contrasting Newton with the poets Homer and Wieland. Newton, Kant maintains, could demonstrate his conclusions through a series of step-by-step deductions, whereas neither the ancient nor the modern poet could adequately explain or teach to others the process by which he had created his poetry. The difference was not one of profundity or significance—Kant held Newton in the highest esteem—but rather one of process. Artistic creation, unlike scientific thought, could not be deduced by the powers of reason alone, for the quality of genius inherent in art precluded such deduction.[23]

It was on this basis that Kant differentiated between aesthetic and rational ideas. He defined an "aesthetic idea," it will be recalled, as "that representation of the imagination which induces much thought, yet without the possibility of any definite thought whatever, i.e., concept, being adequate to it, and which language, consequently, can never get quite on level terms with or render completely intelligible."[24] This is an extraordinary assertion, for it opens up the possibility that language, in the end, is something less than the ultimate vehicle for the expression of ideas. Language had long been considered the sole and sufficient means by which to express concepts. But an aesthetic idea is one that cannot be adequately expressed through a concept, which is to say, through words. By calling the aesthetic idea a "counterpart" to a rational idea, Kant conspicuously avoids placing it at a lower level of value. In still broader terms, Kant's definition of the aesthetic idea reflects a growing conviction during the last quarter of the eighteenth century that ideas could not be separated from the language in which they were expressed, that truth could not be captured solely or even primarily through a series of declarative statements, and that language was not even necessarily the best means of expressing ideas in the first place. Descartes had asserted that ideas could be contemplated by a detached mind, but Kant and his contemporaries—Hamann and Herder, and then later Schelling, Schleiermacher, and Wilhelm von Humboldt—were gradually coming to the realization that language constitutes an element of the world it seeks to describe and thus cannot step outside itself to represent that world objectively. Language could no longer provide an immutable basis for the articulation of truth.[25]

Kant nevertheless upheld the place of poetry as first in the hierarchy of the arts, not because of its ability to express specific ideas and emotions, but rather because of its ability to transcend them. In this sense, Kant was arguing for the priority of language *in spite of* its specificity. More than any other art, poetry could trace its origins "almost entirely to genius" and resist being shaped "according to rules or examples." Poetry "expands the mind" by giving the greatest degree of "freedom to the imagination," which in turn induces a "wealth of thought to which no verbal expression is completely adequate."[26] Although a particular poetic image might be specific in its own right, the thought to which this image, this metaphor, might give rise could be inexhaustible. And in the end, it was the inexhaustibility of interpretation that distinguished the fine arts from the merely agreeable. For later writers such as Novalis, Friedrich Schlegel, and E.T.A. Hoffmann, as we shall see, this inexhaustibility of interpretation would be associated with infinite longing (*unendliche Sehnsucht*) and extend beyond the verbal and plastic arts to include music.

But Kant refused to take this step, relegating instrumental music to the realm of the agreeable arts on the grounds that it did not incorporate concepts that could provide a basis for contemplation. If instrumental music were to be admitted to the realm of the fine arts at all, Kant argued, it would have to be considered the lowest of the lot, for he deemed the "play of thoughts" aroused during the process of listening to be mere by-products of a quasi-mechanical association. Kant ascribed the appeal of instrumental music to an apparent association of musical and verbal expressions: like so many commentators of his generation, he fell back on the conventional image of music as a "language of emotions," a kind of inarticulate speech without specificity. Instrumental music, for Kant, lacked the material substance to stand up as an object of aesthetic contemplation. It moved from sentiments (*Empfindungen*) to indistinct ideas, whereas the verbal and plastic arts moved from distinct ideas to sentiment.[27]

In the end, however, Kant's hierarchy of the arts proved far less important than his theory of aesthetic perception. Over the following decade a series of influential writers would use the *Critique of Judgment* as a starting point from which to reevaluate the relationship of art and philosophy. Friedrich Schlegel, Friedrich Hölderlin, Novalis, Schelling, and Friedrich Schleiermacher, among others, openly endorsed the eradication of any basic distinction between philosophy and art. In the closing years of the eighteenth century and the early decades of the nineteenth, they advocated nothing less than a merger of art and philosophy, on the grounds that both were engaged in the same enterprise: the pursuit of truth. They considered poetry, drama, and prose as venues by which the rationality of philosophy could be synthesized with the sensuousness of art to foster a higher form of consciousness than was available through deductive reasoning alone. Novalis, Hölderlin, Friedrich Schlegel, and Clemens Brentano all wrote novels centered on the philosophical problem of subjectivity, the relationship of the perceiving subject to the external world.[28] Even the ponderously systematic Schelling wrote a novel (*Clara; or, On Nature's Connection to the Spirit World*), and the novelist Jean Paul wrote a treatise on aesthetics. What all these diverse writers shared was a resistance to being labeled as "philosopher" or "poet." In their minds, the two callings were indistinguishable. As Jean Paul put it in the preface to his novel *Das Kampaner Tal* (1797), "critical philosophy proves . . . that we are immortal; but not everyone stands close enough to its cathedra to hear its quiet proofs. I hope it [philosophy] will not accuse me of anything more serious than a change of clothing. But the verbal arts [*Dichtkunst*] are the electrical condenser of philosophy," which consolidate the "electrical spider's web" of philosophy into "lighting bolts that convulse and heal."[29]

For the early Romantics, then, epistemology and aesthetics merged into a single enterprise that could be served equally well by both philosophy and poetry. The act of aesthetic perception became a philosophical activity because it went to the heart of what they considered to be the central questions of epistemology. The document known as "The Oldest Systematic Program of German Idealism" (ascribed variously to Hegel, Schelling, and Hölderlin), written in 1797, proclaimed that

> I am now convinced that the highest act of reason is an aesthetic act since it comprises all ideas, and that *truth* and *goodness* are fraternally united only in beauty. The philosopher must possess as much aesthetic power as the poet. People without an aesthetic sense are only philosophers of the letter. The philosophy of the spirit is an aesthetic philosophy.[30]

Friedrich Schlegel proclaimed that *Poesie*—literature, or in a broader sense, the arts in general—"must begin where philosophy ends." His idea of a "progressive universal poetry" (*Universalpoesie*) would combine philosophy with poetry and rhetoric, criticism with creation, science with art, all in a form of writing that made no distinction between art and philsophy.[31] Schlegel expanded on these thoughts in his lectures in Cologne in 1804–5:

> Philosophy thought of in a completely pure way does not have its own form and language; pure thought and pure knowledge of the *Highest*, of the *Infinite*, can never be adequately represented. But if philosophy is to communicate it must take on form and language, it must employ every means to make the representation and explanation of the Infinite as distinct, clear, and comprehensible as is at all possible; it will in this respect wander through the realm of every science and every art, in order to choose any aid which can serve its purpose. To the extent to which philosophy encompasses all kinds of human knowledge in art, it can appropriate the form of every other science and of art.[32]

The theory of art as a vehicle of truth was most fully developed by Schelling, who in his *System of Transcendental Idealism* (1800) famously asserted that art was in fact "the only true and eternal organon and document of philosophy, which always and continuously documents what philosophy cannot represent externally."[33] Building on the tradition of Kant, Schelling viewed the process of artistic creation as one in which the unconscious manifests itself through the conscious, thereby synthesizing the two. He emphasized art's unique capacity among human endeavors to unite necessity (nature) and freedom (genius). The human mind cannot see itself in its unconscious form, Schelling argued, for to perceive the unconscious would in itself be an act of consciousness. But because it incorporates the unconscious (through the gift of genius, a product of nature), "the artwork alone" is capable of providing us with a reflection of "that which cannot be reflected through anything else, namely, that which has already divided itself within the I. Thus what the philosopher allows to be separated in the basic act of consciousness, and what is otherwise inaccessible to any other form of intuition, is reflected through the products of the miracle of art."[34]

Echoing Kant's thoughts on the nature of the aesthetic idea, Schelling argued that the artist of genius incorporates into the artwork, in an almost instinctual manner, "an infinity which no finite reason is capable of fully developing." And "so it is with every true work of art, in that every one of them is capable of being expounded *ad infinitum*, even though one can never say whether this infinity was present within the artist himself, or is present only in the work of art."[35] For Schelling, anything that does not evoke the infinite, either immediately or on reflection, cannot be considered a work of art.[36] It is only through aesthetic perception that we can recognize the primordial but otherwise inaccessible identity of the conscious and unconscious. No sequence of deductive thought can achieve this, for every law-bound explanation, by its very nature, rests on an earlier explanation, which itself rests on a prior explanation, and so on. Only through the contemplation of the infinite through the finite (the work of art), Schelling maintains, can we hope to break out of this endlessly regressive sequence and experience the Absolute directly.[37]

Novalis similarly emphasized the role of art in presenting the infinite in finite form. He considered the uninterpretable sensuous fullness of the artwork—its infinite nature—to be a manifestation of that which cannot be deduced through logical reasoning. The artwork, for Novalis, was the only means by which to represent that which could not otherwise be represented.[38]

By the reckoning of Schelling, Novalis, and others, art alone reflects the underlying identity of the conscious and the unconscious. Art is "thus precisely for this reason paramount to the philosopher, for it opens to him, as it were, the holiest of all holies, that place in which burns in One Flame, so to speak, an eternal and primordial unification of that which nature and history have rent asunder."[39] Artists alone can objectify this other world, for they work under the influence of a power that separates them from all other humans, even if the artists themselves can never fully understand this power. And like all the other early Romantics, Schelling saw this condition as an opening to a different world. Through art, we become aware—albeit through a "half-opaque cloud"—of "the land of fantasy for which we long" or, as E.T.A. Hoffmann would put it a decade later, writing about his response to Beethoven's Fifth Symphony, the "realm of the infinite."[40]

This view of art as a vehicle of truth—as *the* vehicle of truth—changed the very ground of both philosophy and art, giving rise to a poetic style of discourse very different from the systematic, deductive method so carefully cultivated by Kant and his immediate followers. Later generations would be quick to dismiss the Romantics for their supposed abandonment of rigorous thought and their tendencies toward the mystical. In recent decades, however, the philosophical accomplishments of the Romantics have been reevaluated in a new light. This is due in part to the recovery of sources that had long remained unpublished, but in even greater measure to the postmodernist recognition that all knowledge is contingent, that the search for a single fixed point of philosophical certainty will remain forever elusive. Far from having their heads in the clouds, the early Romantics recognized just how far their heads actually were from those clouds, and they carefully thought through the consequences of this recognition. Rather than try to eliminate the unknowable, the Romantics embraced it as a fundamental basis of knowledge. The paradox is not as profound as it may seem at first. Novalis, Friedrich Schlegel, Hölderlin, the early Schelling, and others were simply applying their recognition of the inaccessibility of the Absolute in a consistent, nondogmatic fashion. They used the essential inaccessibility of the Absolute as the basis for a new system of knowledge that suspended reality between the material and ideal.[41]

Recognizing the interminable nature of regressive thought, the early Romantics for the most part preferred to articulate their insights through those fleeting moments of totalizing synthesis experienced in the perception of the beautiful. This aesthetic experience, more than any other, was both an opening and an inducement to unify all the faculties of the mind in a way that traditional systems of philosophy, with their endless chains of definitions and conditions, could not. For the early Romantics, the act of aesthetic perception could reveal more about the nature of the Absolute than any series of linguistically based philosophical assertions or empirical observations. Holistic rather than deductive, the new poetic philoso-

phy cultivated the genres of the fragment and aphorism with special intensity, in the conviction that a moment of insight could provide a window
on the Absolute through its all-encompassing synthesis of opposites. The
new approach rested on the belief that truth—the Absolute—could best
be comprehended (insofar as it could be comprehended at all) through
example rather than through explanation. The new vehicle of philosophy
was no longer the discursive treatise based on reductive logic, but the
work of art.

CHAPTER THREE

Listening to Truth: Beethoven's Fifth Symphony

THE NINETEENTH CENTURY'S NEW PARADIGM of listening created the need for a new kind of didactic discourse about music, aimed at those members of the public eager to elevate their knowledge and tastes. The very notion of explicating a work of instrumental music in depth—E.T.A. Hoffmann's most immediate goal in his review of Beethoven's Fifth Symphony—was a fundamentally new kind of enterprise. There were antecedents, to be sure: Johann Nikolaus Forkel had given a series of lectures in what amounts to music appreciation in the 1770s, but this kind of undertaking was the exception rather than the norm.[1] The proliferation of music journals, composer biographies, and concert guides in the decades after 1800 (and particularly after 1820) would feed into the ideology of connoisseurship so eloquently described by Leon Botstein.[2] These new aspirations, as Botstein argues, grew in part out of the wider striving for *Bildung* (education, self-improvement), in part through changes in the production and consumption of music—that is, in the shift from aristocratic salons to the public concert hall. But the association of *Bildung* with the act of listening was also driven by basic changes in the underlying premise of listening itself. Journals such as the *Allgemeine Literatur Zeitung* and its musical counterpart, the *Allgemeine musikalische Zeitung*, regularly featured essays that to one degree or another addressed the central issues of contemporary philosophy.[3] By 1800, music critics were beginning to use the verb *verstehen* ("to understand") when speaking about specific works of music.[4] More than any other art, instrumental music nevertheless continued to resist verbal elucidation and "understanding," at least in the conventional sense. Even though the idea of art as a mode of philosophy was widely acknowledged by 1800, it would be another decade before anyone would attempt to apply this new outlook to music in any appreciable degree of detail and specificity.

E.T.A. Hoffmann may seem at first an unlikely figure to fulfill this role, for he is best remembered today as a fantasist, a teller of fairy tales about nutcrackers who slay seven-headed mice, cats who write memoirs, and evil magicians who craft enchanted eyeglasses. Yet Hoffmann lived in an age when philosophy and art, including fantastical prose, were widely perceived to be in pursuit of a common goal. His fiction consistently engages with the central philosophical problem of the day: how to bridge the gap between the phenomenal and the noumenal, the physical and the spiritual.[5] Hoffmann's music criticism is no different in this regard, for in his 1810 review of Beethoven's Fifth Symphony, he touches on virtually all the central themes of the philosophical debate about the relationship of art and philosophy that had been under way in the preceding decade. The philosophical elements of this review are not immediately obvious to us today, for Hoffmann makes no direct reference or appeal to the philosophical discourse of his time. And the review certainly does not read like a philosophical tract; much of it is written in the poetic, aphoristic tradition of Hölderlin, Novalis, and Friedrich Schlegel. But this in itself reflects Hoffmann's debt to these and other writers of his time, as does his mixture of aesthetic and technical approaches toward a single object. The most prominent features of his review—his emphasis on the sublime, the infinite, organic form, and Beethoven's place within the history of music—all relate to a broader agenda that seeks to align music with the pursuit of truth. His review can be read, in effect, as an explication of Schelling's assertion that art is "the only true and eternal organon and document of philosophy, which always and continuously documents what philosophy cannot represent externally."[6]

THE INFINITE SUBLIME

The central importance of the sublime in Hoffmann's review of Beethoven's Fifth has long been recognized, even though Hoffmann uses the term itself only once. The essential qualities of the sublime were vastness of scope, unpredictability, and a capacity to overwhelm the senses. Unlike the beautiful (with which it was invariably contrasted), the sublime was perceived to elicit reactions of fear and pain rather than pleasure. For Edmund Burke, the sources of the sublime could be found in "whatever is fitted in any sort to excite the ideas of pain, and danger, that is to say, whatever is in any sort terrible, or is conversant about terrible objects, or operates in a manner analogous to terror." Burke, whose writings circulated widely in German-speaking lands in the second half of the eighteenth century, considered the sublime to be "productive of the strongest emotion which the mind is capable of feeling."[7] Hoffmann's references to "the monstrous and immeasurable" and the "lever of fear, horror, revulsion, [and] pain" set in motion by Beethoven's music stand very much within this tradition.

Hoffmann was also surely aware of the long-standing association of the sublime with the symphony as a genre.[8] Johann Abraham Peter Schulz's account of the symphony in Sulzer's *Allgemeine Theorie der schönen Künste* (1771–74) had emphasized this point with singular clarity. For

Schulz, the symphony was "especially suited to the expression of the grand, the solemn, and the sublime" not only because of the massed forces of its sound, but also because of its "apparent irregularity of melody and harmony," its "sudden transitions and shifts from one key to another, which are the more striking the weaker the [harmonic] connection is" between the two principal keys of a movement. Schulz went on to liken the symphony to a Pindaric ode, the quintessentially sublime poetic genre of antiquity.[9] Heinrich Christoph Koch, in the most extended German-language compositional treatise of the late eighteenth century, repeatedly associates the symphony with the sublime. And Franz Xaver Niemetschek, an early biographer of Mozart, writing in 1798, described Mozart's late symphonies, particulary the "Prague" (K. 504), as works "full of surprising transitions and a fleet, fiery course, so that they immediately predispose the soul to the expectation of something sublime."[10]

But the sublime was more than a matrix of aesthetic qualities: it was perceived by many as an epistemological means toward the integration of the finite and the infinite. Like the sublime, the infinite was a concept whose vastness was simply too great for the mind to comprehend, and from the 1740s onward, a long series of influential writers had argued that contemplation of the infinite (through the sublime) could elevate the human spirit in a manner that contemplation of the finite (through the beautiful) could not. As John Baillie noted in his *Essay on the Sublime* (1747), "Vast Objects occasion vast Sensations, and vast Sensations give the Mind a higher Idea of her own Powers."[11] Burke similarly argued that the infinite could create feelings of awe and fear in the beholder through its sheer size and endlessness. This sense of terror, moreover, had the ability to overwhelm the powers of reason, thereby transporting the mind to a higher state.

Kant preferred to focus on the transcendent qualities of the sublime. Precisely because contemplation of a sublime object could overwhelm the senses, either through sheer size and scale (what Kant called the "mathematical sublime") or through power (the "dynamic sublime"), he considered the sublime capable of inciting the mind "to abandon sensibility and occupy itself instead with ideas involving a higher finality," that is, to integrate reason and the senses, the objective and the subjective, in a point of identity.[12] Kant offered two specific examples of the sublime that are especially revealing in this regard. The first was the Biblical commandment against making any graven image of God; he considered this prohibition "perhaps the most sublime passage in Jewish law," for it recognized humankind's inability to represent the divine, the absolute, in sensuous form. And within his account of "The Faculties of the Mind Which Constitute Genius," Kant singled out for special praise "the well-known inscription upon the Temple of Isis (Mother Nature): 'I am all that is, and that was, and that shall be, and no mortal hath raised the veil from before my face.' " Kant averred that there had "perhaps never been a more sublime utterance, or a thought more sublimely expressed" than this.[13] Beethoven held this passage in equally high esteem: he kept a copy of it under glass on his working desk, in a spot where he might see it every time he sat down to work, as if to keep before himself, both literally and figuratively, the relationship of the sublime to the absolute.[14]

This potential of the sublime to elevate the human spirit to a higher level of synthesis appealed deeply to Schiller, who considered "the ability to perceive the sublime" as "one of the most glorious capacities of human nature," one that could transport the individual beyond all limitations of the senses and allow us to "judge according to the statutes of the spirits."[15] "The sublime creates for us a way out of the sensuous world," Schiller maintained, a world to which beauty would otherwise keep us bound. And the sublime does this in a manner that is "not gradual (for there is no transition between dependence and freedom), but instead sudden," and in a way that would provide a "revelation of our true calling." Schiller contrasts the ensnaring beauty of Calypso with the liberating sublimity of Mentor, who with a single stroke had freed Odysseus from his captivity.[16]

Hoffmann's repeated emphasis on "longing for the infinite" (*Sehnsucht des Unendlichen*) thus emerges as something more than an emotional response to Beethoven's Fifth Symphony. It is part of a broader strategy to reveal the epistemological dimension of the infinite. His more astute readers would have recognized this goal at once, for "longing for the infinite" was an activity squarely associated with philosophy, and specifically with the attempt to reconcile subject and object in the Absolute. For Friedrich Schleiermacher, knowledge of God and knowledge of the Absolute were one in the same and could be achieved only through a "longing for the infinite, for the One in All."[17] Friedrich Schlegel held that "consciousness of the infinite" is a sensation "from which all philosophy derives" and that there is "nothing higher in humanity" than the "longing for the infinite." The very "essence of philosophy lies in longing for the infinite, and in the development of understanding."[18] This longing for the infinite, moreover, "must always be longing. It does not appear in the form of intuition. The ideal never permits itself to be perceived. The ideal is cultivated through speculation."[19] We can perceive the infinite only negatively and only insofar as we sense the presence of that which cannot in fact be represented in any form.

But how could abstractions such as infinity and the absolute be related to a specific work of music? This was Hoffmann's principal challenge when he sat down to write his review of Beethoven's Fifth Symphony. It was one thing to theorize about music's potential in the abstract, as Herder, Wackenroder, Tieck, and Friedrich Schlegel had done a decade before; it was quite another to relate these ideas to specific works of music, for surely not every composition was equally capable of creating the same degree of longing in listeners.

This challenge was compounded by the necessity of distinguishing *this* new symphony from all others before it, particularly those by Beethoven's most illustrious predecessors in the genre, Haydn and Mozart. As shown in chapter 2, Hoffmann addressed this problem in part by shaping his accounts of these composers around two contrasting modes of listening: the traditional framework of rhetoric for Haydn and Mozart and the new framework of philosophy for Beethoven. But this alone could not justify his extraordinary claims on behalf of the Fifth Symphony, for the music of all three composers, by Hoffmann's own account, "breathes the same Romantic spirit, which lies in their profound grasp of the innermost essence of the art," its ability to evoke the infinite.

The infinite, however, cannot be divided or evoked to varying degrees, for infinity is an absolute, indeed, *the* absolute. How could Beethoven's music be more infinite than that of his predecessors? Hoffmann found the solution to this dilemma in the writings of his favorite author, Jean Paul. In his *Vorschule der Aesthetik* (*A Preliminary Study of Aesthetics*, 1804), Jean Paul had pointed out that while "there are no degrees of infinity, there are degrees of the sublime." A "stormy sky and a stormy sea," he observed, are more sublime than "a starry night over a sleeping sea," and "God is more sublime than a mountain." All evoke the infinite, but through different degrees of sublimity. And the sublime, according to Jean Paul, was "applied infinity" (*das angewandte Unendliche*).[20]

Hoffmann's nouns set Haydn, Mozart, and Beethoven apart from one another, even while keeping them together as a group by emphasizing degrees of "applied infinity." He describes their music through a series of carefully calibrated images meant to evoke ever-greater degrees of sublimity.

DISTANCE AND SCALE. Haydn's music conjures up a green meadow extending beyond what the eye can see [*unabsehbar*]. But this endlessness reflects the limitations of the senses: it only *seems* infinite.[21] The figures beckoning us through Mozart's music reside in a higher sphere, in the clouds. The image of the sky is qualitatively different, for it is not earth-bound and stretches beyond any known limitation. The realm evoked in Beethoven's music lies beyond measurement (*unermeßlich*) and occupies, in effect, all space and no space. Hoffmann is deliberately obscure on this point, in keeping with the obscure nature of the sublime: he aligns Beethoven's music with no physical location at all.

FEAR AND PAIN. Haydn's music transports us to a world with "no suffering, no pain." The bucolic scene Hoffmann describes is prelapsarian, "full of bliss, as before the Fall, in eternal youth." Pain and suffering are unknown qualities in a world of innocence. Mozart's music, by contrast, creates a sensation of fear that "grips" or "surrounds" us (the verb *umfangen* carries both connotations). But this is a fear without pain (*Marter*), and the figures that beckon are still "friendly."[22] The effect is to create an intimation (*Ahnung*) of the infinite. Beethoven's music completes the progression by "destroy[ing] us, but not the pain of infinite longing." Hoffmann draws here on Burke's notion of the sublime as a kind of imagined death, a presentiment of an after-life in which pain and suffering are intensified even though the body itself is no longer alive.

NIGHT AND OBSCURITY. Commentators on the sublime agreed that the night is by its very nature more sublime than the day, and Hoffmann applies varying shades of darkness to achieve his ends. Haydn's music conjures up a scene of permanent twilight: the mountains and meadows glow in the fading sun, yet the scene never darkens beyond this. Mozart's music ushers in the "bright purple shimmer" of night: the sun has set, but the night still retains a degree of color. Beethoven's music transports us to the "realm of deep night" illuminated only by sudden flashes of light coming from an unknown source. This is a universe of total blackness alternating with brief moments of intense light. Jean Paul, in his *Vorschule der Ästhetik*, had asserted that the "empire of the Romantic is divided into the eastern-dawn realm of the eye and the western-evening realm of the ear and thus resembles in this respect its relative, the dream."[23] For Hoffmann, the deepest night was the realm of the most intense dream.

FLASHES OF LIGHT. Only in response to Beethoven's music does Hoffmann summon up the image of the thunderbolt, the quintessential emblem of the sublime in nature. This imagery also captures the Romantic conviction that the Absolute could not be deduced or grasped but only glimpsed in brief yet intense flashes of insight. Jean Paul's image of the verbal arts as the "electrical condenser" of philosophy has already been noted; its lightning bolts can "convulse and heal" the spirit in an instant.[24] Friedrich Schlegel also used the metaphor of the lightning bolt to suggest that the synthesis of the finite and infinite could be presented and grasped only fleetingly. And for Hegel, it is lightning that will "reveal, in an instant, the image of a new world."[25] The illumination we experience in Beethoven's Fifth Symphony, Hoffmann suggests, is far brighter than what we experience in the symphonies of Haydn and Mozart, but it is transitory and fleeting: a moment later we are plunged back into complete darkness.

TIME AND TIMELESSNESS. The world evoked by Haydn's music is static, a moment of perpetual twilight, an unchanging moment in time. Mozart's music ushers in the onset of night, a process of gradual change. But Beethoven's music "opens"—suddenly—the "realm of the monstrous and immeasurable." Time stops altogether, for once this realm has been revealed to us, we find ourselves in a literally timeless universe.

THE MOVE TO INCORPOREALITY. Haydn's music conjures up the image of "youths and maidens who float past in round-dances." The dance is not earth-bound, for the dancers float (*schweben*: the term also suggests the idea of "hov-ering"). The dancers evoked by Mozart's music are even more ethereal, mere figures (*Gestalten*). We are not told whether they are male or female, old or young. Theirs is the "eternal dance of the spheres" that "flies through the clouds." The dance becomes increasingly abstract, mirroring the motions of the planets according to the Pythagorean doctrine by which the motions of the heavenly bodies create a music inaudible to mortal ears.[26] Beethoven's music completes the progression to incorporeality by eliciting no reference to dance at all. The body has disappeared: we perceive neither dancers nor figures but only "giant shadows." The figures that cast these shadows are beyond our perception; the allusion to Plato's cave and the world of ideals, as noted be-fore, could not be more striking.[27] Beethoven's music in fact "destroys us," even while leaving us with the "the pain of infinite longing." The body is eradi-cated, but not the psyche: one is reminded of the phenomenon of "phantom limb pain" sometimes experienced by amputees.

These images of the sublime all point toward the Absolute as an eradica-tion of difference between the (bodily) subject and the (ethereal) object. And the Absolute, Hoffmann implies, can be glimpsed through the agency of the Fifth Symphony.

HISTORY AS KNOWING

Hoffmann's successive gradations of the sublime reflect a progression to-ward the Absolute that is both chronological and teleological. This kind of trajectory would provide a template—sometimes subtle, sometimes not—for virtually all subsequent histories of music dealing with the late eighteenth and early nineteenth centuries: the innocent Haydn subsumed by the ethereal Mozart, who in turn is subsumed by the transcendent Beethoven.[28] Whether or not this last step represented a culmination—the end of music, to paraphrase Hegel—would remain a matter of intense debate throughout the nineteenth century, particularly in the realm of the symphony.[29]

The framework of the debate, however, was clearly Hegelian, one that saw history not merely as a record of the human past but rather as an unfolding of the human spirit (*Geist*) through a series of steps leading toward ever higher states of consciousness. In his *Phänomenologie des Geistes* (*Phenomenology of Spirit*, 1807), Hegel had argued that human consciousness could be recognized only through history and that the essence of *Geist* (often also translated as "mind") was revealed through its transformation and growth over time. History was now viewed as a means of epistemology, as a way—in fact, the *only* real way—of arriving at truth.

Hoffmann's review of Beethoven's Fifth embraces this approach, for his account opens with an encapsulated (if tendentious) history of evolving attitudes toward instrumental music. In so doing, he outlines a series of ever-higher states of human consciousness.[30] He begins his narrative with myth, reminding us of the fabled powers of wordless music in the ancient world: It was Orpheus's lyre-playing, not his singing, that had opened the portals of the underworld.[31] The next stage in this progression is the more immediate human past. Here, Hoffmann portrays the history of instrumental music as having consisted largely of composers who did not recognize its true nature and who therefore composed music intended to imitate specific emotions or—worse still—actual objects or events. In his original review (1810) he actually cites Carl Dittersdorf by name (presumably, the symphonies he wrote based on Ovid's *Metamorphoses*, composed in the early to mid-1780s) and derided as well "all the recent *Battles of Three Emperors*," a generic reference to a variety of compositions produced soon after the Battle of Austerlitz in 1805—which is to say, quite recently. But Hoffmann is careful to couch all these dismissals in the past tense. Because they did not recognize the true nature of instrumental music, Dittersdorf and other composers like him had created "laughable errors" that are "to be punished with complete oblivion."[32] Hoffmann also conveniently ignores Beethoven's own *Pastoral* Symphony, with its celebrated thunderstorm, a work that had received its premiere alongside the Fifth in 1808 and had been published in May 1809, only a month after the Fifth, by the same firm, Breitkopf & Härtel.

To maintain this tendentious trajectory of historical progress, then, Hoffmann treats programmatic works as products of the past, as if they did not belong also to the present. He discusses vocal music in the present tense on the grounds that it represents a more advanced stage of the art, for by clothing "every passion . . . and even that found in life" in "the purple shimmer of Romanticism," it leads us "out of life into the realm of the infinite." The words enhance the music, in other words, not vice versa. But the "magic of music" is so powerful and "growing ever more powerful" in its effect that music had to break the chains connecting it to every other art—which is to say, every art bound by the quality of representation to the earthly world.

As history, Hoffmann's account is transparently selective and misleading. But this is precisely the point. By calling attention to works that illustrate the supposed inadequacies of the past (e.g., Dittersdorf's programmatic symphonies) and by ignoring those that manifest their continuing presence (e.g., Beethoven's *Pastoral* Symphony), Hoffmann creates a narrative that outlines a steady progression toward the fulfillment of self-consciousness. The path he traces is strikingly similar to Hegel's account in the *Phenomenology of Spirit*, in which humankind moves from an epistemology that Hegel contemptuously describes as naïve and immediate (*unmittelbar*) to one of Absolute Knowledge.

It is at this point that Hoffmann begins his account of Haydn, Mozart, and Beethoven. As in Hegel's *Phenomenology*, historical progression correlates to phases of the day, which in turn reflect ever-higher forms of consciousness. The day ends with the night, and Hoffmann gives no reason to suggest that time will run cyclically, that we will ever again return to a state of ignorance or innocence in a future dawn. In much the same way that Hegel had posited an eventual end of history, Hoffmann offers no speculation as to the future of music, only ruminations on its path from ignoble past to glorious present. The unstated but inescapable message here is that in the symphonies of Beethoven, music has reached its culmination, its own moment of historical timelessness.

The question of future historical progress would become a flashpoint of critical debate in the middle of the nineteenth century. Could music progress in any substantive way beyond Beethoven? The question may seem naïve in retrospect, but it was very real at the time. Whatever their differences of opinion, parties on both sides of the issue agreed on the basic trope of progress and the challenges it posed. A. B. Marx's 1824 essay on Beethoven's symphonies rests on a premise of Hegelian unfolding, though it leaves open the question of future progress. Robert Schumann, in his 1835 review of Berlioz's *Symphonie fantastique*, openly raised the question of whether the symphony had any future at all but concluded that Berlioz's new work pointed a way forward.[33] Wagner was more pessimistic, repeatedly asserting that no composer of instrumental music after Beethoven could advance the art in any significant way. For Wagner, the symphony was a genre of the past; only a fusion with with the "fertilizing seed" of the word could ensure the future progress of music. Even as late as 1889, in the first edition of *Grove's Dictionary of Music and Musicians*, the composer C. Hubert H. Parry would feel compelled to apologize for tracing the history of the symphony beyond Beethoven.[34] By this time, the question of historical progress (or the lack of it) had established itself as a central issue in virtually all narratives of recent music. The fundamental premise of this debate is already present in Hoffmann's essentially Hegelian approach to the history of symphony.

The Synthesis of Conscious and Unconscious

Hoffmann's emphasis on Beethoven's reflective powers (*Besonnenheit*) is yet another element of a strategy to demonstrate the ways in which a work of music can function as a vehicle of philosophy. On the surface, at least, this portion of Hoffmann's review rebuts the composer's critics, including some in earlier volumes of the same *Allgemeine musikalische Zeitung* who had accused him of an excess of musical ideas in his works. One reviewer commenting on the Piano Sonatas, op. 10, in 1799, for example, had complained that Beethoven was too often inclined "to pile thoughts wildly upon one another" and to "group them in a somewhat bizarre manner and in a way that produces, not infrequently, an obscure artificiality [*dunkle Künstlichkeit*] or an artificial obscurity [*künstliche Dunkelheit*]."[35] Even favorable reviews from this time occasionally take note of the overwhelming variety of contrasting ideas in Beethoven's works and the attendant difficulty of absorbing new works in a single hearing.[36] It was partly for this reason, then, that Hoffmann chose to emphasize Beethoven's *Besonnenheit*, a quality that German writers of the time typically described as the objective counterpart to subjective emotion. The word's root verb, *besinnen*, means "to contemplate," and *Besonnenheit* stands for all that is conscious and deliberate in the act of artistic creation, the refinement applied to moments of unconscious inspiration.

But Hoffmann's comments go well beyond the rebuttal of earlier criticism, for the synthesis of fantasy and reflection lies at the heart of an epistemological argument. As the synthesis of all opposites, the Absolute necessarily integrates art and nature, the conscious and the unconscious; any artwork that might provide us with a glimpse of the Absolute must necessarily do the same. Inspiration alone, as Schelling had emphasized, is insufficient in the creation of art, for in the form of genius it is a "wholly blind power whose effect lies in its capacity to reject all judgment and even intuition itself." Because such inspiration resists contemplation, it must be tempered if the artwork is to be intelligible—not in the sense of making the difficult seem familiar, but in the sense of transforming the raw power of inspiration into a form that will allow itself to be contemplated in any form whatsoever.[37] *Besonnenheit* is required not so much for intelligibility as for completeness. It is a requisite element for wholeness. Only through a synthesis of rational technique and the irrational genius could an artwork integrate the finite and infinite.

Jean Paul, for one, had incorporated this very concept into his *Vorschule der Ästhetik* at many points in addressing the fundamental paradox of the artist both to maintain and to overcome the division between subjectivity and objectivity.[38] As described by Jean Paul, *Besonnenheit* entails a self-distancing that allows the artist of genius to detach himself from his work. He identifies "a higher form of *Besonnenheit*" that "distances and divides the inner world into an I and its realm, into a creator and his world," and he goes on to point out that *Besonnenheit* is a quality necessary for philosophers and poets alike: both must be capable of self-reflection, and this common activity reinforces the relationship of poetry and philosophy.[39]

Hoffmann uses many of the same words to describe the process by which Beethoven gains perspective on the raw products of his innate genius. As far as *Besonnenheit* is concerned, Beethoven is every bit the equal of Haydn and Mozart, for Beethoven "separates himself from the inner realm of tones and rules over this realm as unfettered lord."[40] Hoffmann couches his point here in explicitly philosophical terms. *Er trennt sein Ich von dem innern Reich der Töne*—his more astute readers would have instantly recognized in this passage the language of Fichte, whose subjective idealism rested on a separation and higher integration of the "I" and the "Not-I."

What remains beyond the integration of subject and object—and something always lies beyond it, for the quest is infinite—serves to remind us that knowledge is by its very nature open-ended. Given the lofty position of the Fifth Symphony, Hoffmann suggests, incomprehensibility is not in itself a bad thing. Surely Hoffmann had in mind here Friedrich Schlegel's widely read essay *On Incomprehensibility* (1800), which had argued that great works of art are never completely understandable, that we perceive them differently each time we approach them, and that only through a residual incomprehensibility can we, as beholders, truly extend our capacity to understand, even if our understanding ultimately remains imperfect.[41] The striving, as Hoffmann insists, is necessarily infinite.

Hoffmann's emphasis on *Besonnenheit* also reinforces his larger-scale objective of differentiating Beethoven from his predecessors. His claim that Haydn, Mozart, and Beethoven are all "Romantic composers" whose instrumental works "breathe the same Romantic spirit" emphasizes their commonality. Yet while he praises Haydn and Mozart as "the creators of the new instrumental music," he singles out Beethoven as the "first to show us the art in its full glory," and the reason for this, he maintains, is that Beethoven was the first to "contemplate" this art "with full love and penetrate to its innermost essence." The idea that love should be the distinguishing element in Beethoven's compositional approach to instrumental music seems hardly worth taking seriously until we recognize that for Jean Paul, love was the most extreme manifestation of *Unbesonnenheit*, a forgetting of one's self, the most subjective of all subjective modes of perception.⁴² When assimilated into Beethoven's objectivity—his *Besonnenheit*—the synthesis becomes all the more profound.

ORGANIC COHERENCE

Closely related to the striving for ever-higher stages of self-consciousness is the process of organic growth in which an underlying coherence is revealed over time through a process of unfolding. Plato and Aristotle had provided a basis for the idea of organic form in ancient philosophy, and in his *Critique of Judgment*, Kant had pointed to the artwork as an analogue of organic nature, in which means and end were one in the same. The organism soon became the preferred metaphor for explaining the relationship between the parts and the whole, not only in the work of art but in the very process of thought itself. Herder, Goethe, Schiller, Fichte, Schelling, August Wilhelm and Friedrich Schlegel, Novalis, and Schleiermacher all drew on this imagery to elucidate the structure of human consciousness and its relationship to art.⁴³

"The True is the Whole," Hegel famously declared in the Preface to his *Phenomenology of Spirit*, but only through the process of unfolding (*entfalten*) can the essence of that truth be grasped. For the Whole, the Absolute, is the result of a long process of becoming; it is only at the conclusion of this process that we can recognize the end for what it is.⁴⁴ Hegel compares the development of human consciousness to the stages of growth in a living organism: the bud gives way to the flower, the flower to the fruit. An acorn contains the essence of the oak tree but not its actuality, which unfolds and can be recognized only through its stages of development over time. Hegel emphasizes the corresponding simplicity of existence itself in the human *Geist*, which also reveals itself through a process of unfolding in which consciousness becomes increasingly aware of itself.⁴⁵

Hoffmann uses precisely the same imagery of the plant and the same verb (*entfalten*, to unfold) to describe the organic coherence of Beethoven's Fifth, emphasizing both the simplicity and the rich potential of the work's opening idea:

> Aesthetic surveyors have often complained about the complete lack of inner unity and inner coherence in the works of Shakespeare, for only deeper inspection reveals that a beautiful tree with its leaves, flowers, and fruits grows and unfolds from a single seed. In the same manner, only a very deep study in Beethoven's instrumental music reveals the high degree of reflection [*Besonnenheit*] that is inseparable from true genius and which is nourished by study of the art.⁴⁶

At this point in the 1813 revision of his original review, Hoffmann expands on the organic potentiality of the symphony's opening theme:

> Nothing could be simpler than the two-measure main idea of the opening Allegro. It is presented in unison at first, and the listener cannot be certain of even its key. . . . How simple—it must be said again—is the theme on which the master establishes the basis of the whole, yet how wonderfully do the secondary and transitional ideas follow in their rhythmic relationship to it, unfolding more and more and in such a way as to reveal the character of the Allegro, which was only hinted at by the main theme. All the ideas are brief; almost all of them consist of only two or three measures, and yet the winds and strings constantly exchange them. One might believe that from such elements only something fragmented and incomprehensible could result. But instead, it is precisely the ordering of the whole and the constant and rapid repetition of ideas and individual chords that raise the feeling of an ineffable longing to the highest degree.[47]

From a technical point of view, Hoffmann stresses throughout his review the close interrelationship of seemingly contrasting ideas. The rhythm of the celebrated opening motif (short-short-short-LONG) metamorphoses over time to generate almost every subsequent theme of significance throughout the symphony as a whole. Even the triumphant theme of the finale can be heard to derive from this opening idea. This relationship represents something more than the commonly expressed desire for "variety in unity" or "unity in variety." For Hoffmann, the relationship of parts within a whole is a matter not merely of artistic economy, or even of artistic coherence, but of a striving toward the Absolute, for only through an all-embracing whole in which every element plays an essential function can the nondifference of opposites be realized.

In this respect, too, the category of organic coherence allows Hoffmann to emphasize the distance between Beethoven and his predecessors. The image of the musical work as an organic whole manifests itself in a variety of ways at the end of the eighteenth century. Repeat signs for both halves of sonata-form movements (exposition and development-plus-recapitulation) begin to drop precipitously in the 1790s and even more drastically in the first decade of the nineteenth century.[48] It is also around this time that composers began to explore more fully the possibilities of thematic metamorphosis across individual movements. Haydn and Mozart had explored such possibilities on occasion, but rarely as overtly as in Beethoven's Fifth Symphony. When Haydn brings back a literal return of the third movement in the middle of the finale of his Symphony no. 46 (1772), for example, the effect seems more local, in spite of the underlying thematic connections between the two movements.[49] And when Mozart introduces a thematic idea from the third movement of his String Quartet in A Major, K. 464, within the course of the work's finale, the connections are once again more subtle than the comparable links within Beethoven's Fifth.[50] And thereby hangs the tale: the process of thematic unfolding is so basic to the Fifth as a whole that the unexpected return of a previous movement in the finale serves only to draw attention to what was already audible at the very surface of the music in every movement.

BEYOND THE SUBLIME

The musical qualities Hoffmann emphasizes in his review of the Fifth Symphony—the unfolding of a central musical idea, the close integration of contrasting gestures, a trajectory leading from struggle to triumph, all within a general framework of the sublime—are the same qualities that later generations would come to associate with the composer's "heroic" style. One of the reasons why works such as the Third and Fifth symphonies and the *Egmont* Overture have resonated so consistently over time, as Scott Burnham has argued, is that they are perceived to model human consciousness and, specifically, the fundamental processes of becoming and self-overcoming. In the unfolding of a central musical idea, in the close integration of contrasting gestures, and in a trajectory that traces a path from struggle to triumph, we hear what amounts to an idealized progression of life itself.[51] Yet as even Burnham is quick to acknowledge, not all of Beethoven's music is "heroic," not even all the symphonies from the composer's so-called heroic period. How, then, are we to hear such works as the Fourth Symphony, the Violin Concerto, or the String Quartet op. 59, no. 3? Are these somehow less capable of revealing the Absolute?

Hoffmann's emphasis on the sublime (and, by extension, the "heroic") obscures the capacity of its implied opposite—the beautiful—to transcend the Kantian divide between subject and object. Many writers of Beethoven's era perceived the beautiful as equally capable of inducing a sensation of psychic wholeness, and they equated the beautiful as well as the sublime with the infinite. Kant himself maintained that the beautiful was by its very nature inexhaustible, for it lies beyond concepts that can be articulated adequately through words. If it could be expressed through concepts (such as Newton's laws of mechanics), an object could not be considered beautiful. Schelling argued that the beautiful is the infinite represented in finite form and disputed the significance of any sharp distinction between the sublime and the beautiful. August Wilhelm Schlegel similarly defined the beautiful as a symbolic representation of the infinite, as something toward which the spirit directed itself in "infinite striving." For Schlegel, a work of art could easily incorporate elements of both the sublime and the beautiful in such a way that neither predominates.[52] Even

Jean Paul connected the infinite with the beautiful, declaring that "the Romantic is beauty without limitations, or the *beautiful* infinite, just as there is a *sublime* infinite."[53]

This more widely embracing view of beauty offers an alternative to Hoffmann's use of the sublime alone as the measure of infinity and, by extension, of art's capacity to provide insights into the Absolute. Relatively few of Beethoven's works, after all, can measure up to such an immense yardstick. In his subsequent (1813) review of Beethoven's Piano Trios, op. 70, also published in the *Allgemeine musikalische Zeitung*, Hoffmann says nothing about infinite longing, giant shadows, or deep night.[54] Instead, these trios evoke the imagery of a garden and (later on) a painting. Contrasting emotions—joy and pain, sorrow and ecstasy—coexist but are not synthesized in the totalizing manner Hoffmann describes in connection with the Fifth Symphony. The tropes of sublimity are now absent, in part because the need to compare Beethoven with earlier composers (Haydn and Mozart) is no longer so pressing, in part because the more intimate genre of the piano trio does not lend itself as well to ideas of sublimity. While still ascribing superior powers to instrumental music, Hoffmann uses imagery here that operates on a far smaller scale than what he had used in his review of the Fifth. Whereas the listener had been all but destroyed in hearing the Fifth, the soul who takes in the piano trios is "delighted" (*entzückt*), and it "understands" the "most secret longings." *Verstehen* (to understand) does not carry with it the same imagery of identification between the self and the object, of a complete synthesis of emotions within the process of assimilating (or trying to assimilate) the sublime. One does not understand the Absolute; the best one can hope for is a glimpse of it, for in the end it is a matter that passes all understanding.

Hoffmann's emphasis on the sublime in his review of the Fifth Symphony also runs counter to the core belief among all the Romantics that there was no single path leading to the Absolute, to the synthesis of subject and object. Novalis and Friedrich Schlegel, in particular, emphasized that only through a variety of inherently contradictory approaches could mankind even begin to hope for a glimpse of the Absolute, a fleeting recognition of its all-embracing essence.

This fundamental longing for a synthesis of opposites helps to explain the Romantic predilection for irony, a perspective that allowed for (and, indeed, demanded) the recognition that two wholly contrasting points of view could be equally valid and mutually reinforcing. Irony undermines the presumptions of a privileged vantage point and a fixed philosophical perspective. Many of the most memorable aphorisms from the pen of Novalis and Friedrich Schlegel rest on inherent contradictions that on the surface seem nonsensical but that at a deeper level capture the essence of an all-synthesizing Whole. Schlegel claimed that "it is equally fatal for the spirit [*Geist*] to have a system and to have none. One must therefore decide to combine both."⁵⁵ The inherent incompatibility of such extremes—having a system and not having one—defies rational reconciliation. This kind of paradox manifests the ultimate inaccessibility of the Absolute on any enduring basis. In the end, however, this inaccessibility was something to be embraced, not avoided or explained away. Novalis maintained that philosophy, in searching for a fixed principle, was by its very nature an "endless activity" because no such first cause could ever be found. But the fact that this process was endless did not negate its value. The only Absolute accessible to us, Novalis maintained, is one that would "allow itself to be recognized only negatively, in that through our actions we discover that no actions allow us to find that which we seek."⁵⁶

This idea of multiple, shifting, contradictory, yet ultimately equivalent perspectives permeates early Romantic thought, in fiction as well as in philosophy. For in the hands of Novalis, Friedrich Schlegel, Jean Paul, and Hoffmann, irony does more than merely expose the inadequacy of discursive logic: it affirms even as it negates. By undermining the premise of referential meaning, by opening up the possibilities of multiple (and even contradictory) meanings, irony establishes a distance between one's perspective and one's self, a necessary first step toward the ultimate goal of bridging the gulf between subject and object. It is for this reason that Jean Paul speaks of the "annihilating or infinite idea" of humor, or as we would call it today, irony. What is annihilated is a fixity of perspective, and what fills the void is infinity.

This same approach could extend to listening as well, particularly in works that demand a reconciliation, in the listener's mind, of seemingly disparate elements. And in no other repertory of the time is the demand for a transcendent perspective more pressing than in the music of Beethoven, particularly in his late works, written from about 1820 onward. Here, juxtapositions of the profound and trivial, the great and small, the sincere and humorous, are more prominent than ever before. The String Quartet in B-flat Major, op. 130, offers unusually striking instances of irony on multiple levels. The cycle as a whole is full of apparent contradictions. The opening movement begins with a series of starts and stops, a series of seemingly unconnected ideas that cannot agree even on a basic tempo. The second movement is as breathtakingly brief as it is fast. The pointillism heard at the end of the fourth movement gives way to the celebrated Cavatina, in which the first violinist imitates a *prima donna* so overcome by emotion that she can barely get the words out of her mouth, "singing" in manner that Beethoven marks *beklemmt* ("constricted," or more literally, "caught in a vise"). But is the emotion genuine or feigned? Only an ironic perspective can accommodate these alternatives with equal weight. Contradictory possibilities continue into the work's finale. To follow this heartfelt aria, Beethoven originally wrote a lengthy fugue as a finale, a tour-de-force of contrapuntal artifice with its own "overture" and an array of learned fugal devices. At least partly at the urging of his publisher, Beethoven detached the finale, published it as a separate work—the *Grosse Fuge* ("Great Fugue"), op. 133—and composed in its place a new finale that could scarcely have been more different in character, a lighter and much shorter movement. The "severe, apocalyptic, utterly radical fugue," as Joseph Kerman describes the original finale, was "supplanted by a quiet, sunny, Haydnesque Allegro."[57]

The motivations behind this substitute finale have been dealt with at length on many occasions, and each of the two endings has had its advocates over the years.[58] But the possibility that these two finales might represent equally valid yet utterly opposite perspectives on a similar "object"— the quartet as a whole—seems to have gone unconsidered. Beethoven had incorporated ironic elements into his music (including this particular quartet) throughout his life, and now, at the end of his career, he seems to have raised the technique of irony to new heights, providing, in this instance, two very different endings to one and the same work. Financial considerations and his publisher's urgings certainly played at least some role in his decision to write a second finale, but these factors in themselves seem inadequate, given what we know of Beethoven's reluctance to conform to public tastes, particularly in the last decade of his life. Nor do these factors shed any light on why the substitute finale should be so utterly different in kind from the original. In its double state, one ending with the Great Fugue, the other ending with the more modest Allegro, this quartet would seem to exemplify in music Friedrich Schlegel's definition of an idea as a "concept perfected to the point of irony, an absolute synthesis of absolute antitheses, the constant and continuously self-generating exchange between two conflicting thoughts."[59]

The idea of two contrasting yet equally valid finales takes on special significance in light of credible reports that Beethoven had second thoughts about the last movement of the Ninth Symphony as well. His pupil Carl Czerny reported that Beethoven had at one point described the choral finale as a mistake (*Missgriff*) and given serious consideration to replacing it with an entirely instrumental movement.[60] It cannot be entirely coincidental that the two most monumental finales of the late period—the *Grosse Fuge* and the setting of Schiller's *An die Freude*—should have occasioned second thoughts, acted on in one instance, merely contemplated in the other. We do not know what shape the reputed alternative finale to the Ninth might have taken, but the very fact that it would not incorporate voices is enough to establish its conception as one radically different from the finale we know.

Irony of this kind, moreover, need not be restricted to individual works: it can be applied to Beethoven's output as a whole. As Lewis Lockwood has recently argued, we can better understand the corpus of his music in its entirety by viewing Beethoven "not as a 'primarily heroic' composer who sometimes lapsed into the use of other aesthetic models, but rather as a composer seeking all his life to be a universal artist, who could control tragedy, comedy, and an infinite number of expressive modes that fall somewhere between."[61] By this reckoning, Beethoven's music achieves its own kind of intra-opus synthesis in which the parts constitute far more than the sum of the whole.

In the end, we must recognize that more than one path can lead to musical truth, and indeed that there are multiple ways to conceive the very notion of musical truth. Theodor Adorno's idea of the "truth content" in an artwork resides in that work's ability to resist reconciliation, even while striving, paradoxically, to achieve reconciliation. All art is an illusion, Adorno argues, but a work's truth content lies in its ability to transcend that illusion.[62] Jerrold Levinson's distinction between "correspondent truth" and "propositional truth" in music offers yet another, very different perspective. For Levinson, "correspondent truth" relates to the structural parallels between a musical work and the emotion it arouses in the listener, while "propositional truth" relates to the emotional plausibility of a work's various parts in their temporal succession.[63] The details of these and other concepts of musical truth need not detain us here, the important point is that, as the Romantics themselves would argue, no one approach alone leads to truth, and no truth stands alone.

Toward the end of his *Aesthetics*, published posthumously and based on lectures he had given in Berlin in the 1820s, Hegel identified the fundamental essence and purpose of art as "the liberation of the spirit [*Geist*] from the content and forms of finitude, with the presence and reconciliation of the Absolute in what is apparent and visible, with an unfolding of truth which is not exhausted in natural history but revealed in world-history."[64] A generation before, no one would have thought to endow the art of instrumental music with such weighty responsibility, and Hegel himself, like Kant a generation before, seems to have had little sympathy for music without words. But, like Kant, Hegel contributed to a framework within which writers more sympathetic to the art—A. B. Marx, Robert Schumann, and Ferdinand Hand, among others—would promulgate the conviction that instrumental music can and does convey ideas and that it offers a means of understanding the world outside the more traditional framework of discursive reasoning. The "discovery" of Arthur Schopenhauer's *The World as Will and Representation* in the 1840s and 1850s, a work that had languished in obscurity since its original publication in 1819, reinforced the conviction that instrumental music and philosophy were inseparable. All the arts except music, according to Schopenhauer, were reflections of the Will, the instinctual, nonrational impetus behind all existence. Music, however, was an objectification of the Will itself. Nietzsche and Wagner would both embrace this perspective, further solidifying the connection between music and truth. Listening had become a way of knowing.

CHAPTER FOUR

Listening to the Aesthetic State: Cosmopolitanism

NOT ALL LISTENING turned inward. The most basic philosophical problem of the age—the reconciliation of subject and object, of the "I" and
the "Not-I"—was playing itself out on a larger scale as well, in an extended and often heated debate about the relationship of the individual
to society as a whole. The all-encompassing breadth of the symphony
proved particularly conducive to turning the minds of engaged listeners
toward the broader challenge of reconciling personal autonomy with social order. The monumental yet timbrally diverse nature of the genre led
many of Beethoven's contemporaries to hear the symphony as a projection of an ideal state in which personal liberties could flourish within an
structured framework, and in which the needs of the community could
function in harmony with the needs of the individual. Opinions on exactly
what form this ideal state order might take varied from individual to individual and across time. In the broadest terms, however, the principal social ideals in early nineteenth-century German-speaking lands centered
on cosmopolitanism and nationalism. These responses should not be distinguished from one another too rigidly, for none excludes the others. The
images of the symphony as a sonorous analogue of humanity (cosmopolitanism) or of a particular state (nationalism) both derive from a creative
tension between the many and the whole, between the individual and
universal. During Beethoven's lifetime, moreover, cosmopolitanism and
nationalism were not yet perceived as the polar opposites they would later
become. The fissures that would eventually crack their shared foundation
would not emerge until the early nineteenth century and even then were
slow to develop.

THE COMMUNAL VOICE OF THE SYMPHONY

In a conversation with his wife shortly before his death in 1883, Richard
Wagner mused on the essential difference between Beethoven's symphonies and all his other instrumental works. "In the sonatas and quartets,"
Cosima recorded her husband as having said, "Beethoven makes music;
in the symphonies, the entire world makes music through him."[1]

Whether he realized it or not, Wagner was articulating a long-standing perception of the genre of the symphony—and not merely those by Beethoven—as the expression of a communal voice. This outlook owed much to the large scale of these works: their length, the size of the performance forces, the physical size of the performance venue, and above all the synthesis of diverse timbres within an essentially polyphonic texture. From the second half of the eighteenth century onward, commentators on the symphony consistently pointed to this last quality as the genre's most distinctive feature. What critics emphasized over and over again was not merely the equality of voices, but also their sonorous variety. Polyphony, after all, could be found in virtually any genre, but the symphony was perceived as different from all other forms of instrumental music in its synthesis of such a wide range of contrasting timbres: woodwinds, brass, percussion, strings, and all in great numbers. This was a projection not of similar instruments but of diverse voices.

This characteristically polyphonic texture was won at the expense of a certain degree of melodic beauty. "The German symphonists," François Jean de Chastellux had pointed out as early as 1765, "are less concerned with finding simple musical motives than with producing beautiful effects through the harmonies they draw out of the large number of different instruments they use. . . . Their symphonies are a type of *Concerto* in which the instruments each shine in turn, in which they provoke and respond to one another, dispute and reconcile."[2] The composer Johann Abraham Peter Schulz, writing in Sulzer's *Allgemeine Theorie der schönen Künste* in the early 1770s, emphasized the symphony's capacity to "weave all the voices in and out of one another in such a way that all parts, when played together, create a single melody that is incapable of accompaniment," in which "every voice makes its own particular contribution to the whole." Schulz went on to criticize three of the leading composers of his day for writing symphonies that sounded too much like arias performed on instruments. He deemed certain movements by Johann Gottlieb Graun, Carl Heinrich Graun, and Johann Adolph Hasse to be "feeble" in spite of their melodic beauty. Only occasionally, according to Schulz, did these composers succeed in achieving the "true spirit of the symphony" by blurring a clear division between primary and secondary voices.[3] Schulz's critique would be turned on other composers in later centuries as well. Schubert's symphonies, in particular, suffered from a perceived overabundance of lyricism considered incompatible with a postulated symphonic ideal.

No other genre of instrumental music was heard against this standard. Chamber music claimed an equally polyphonic texture but could not offer much in the way of timbral diversity. Nor were chamber works heard to embody the sentiments of a large or terribly diverse group. The string quartet, for example, was routinely compared to a conversation among a small group of individuals. This imagery underscores at once both the intimacy and timbral homogeneity of the genre. And while the concerto for orchestra and soloist provided both size and timbral contrast, it was necessarily dominated by the soloist, who stood apart from (and implicitly above) the main body of the orchestra. The concerto also suffered from a perceived tendency toward empty virtuosity. The symphony alone was heard as the one instrumental genre in which all the participants could lay claim to an essentially equal stake in a very large whole. The issue did not turn on profundity: expressive depth could be achieved in many ways by many different kinds of music, including even the most miniature of songs. The real issue was one of tone, and only the symphony was perceived as expressing the voice of community.

This perception is reflected in the repeated image of the symphony as a chorus for instruments. Lessing, writing in the 1760s, compared the orchestral overture—the symphony—and interludes of the spoken theater to the chorus in ancient Greek drama, whose function had been to give voice to the collective whole.[4] La Cépède echoed this idea in 1785, noting that "just as there is a need to introduce the chorus into the drama," so too can "all of the orchestra play in manner that is quite brilliant and distinct, representing a multitude that adds its clamors to the cries of passion that have emanated from the most interesting characters." Such imagery would become even more common in the early nineteenth century. Heinrich Christoph Koch noted in 1802 that the symphony "has as its goal, like the chorus, the expression of a sentiment of an entire multitude." The French theorist Jérôme-Joseph de Momigny argued in 1805 that because it was "destined for a large gathering of persons," the symphony "must have at once both grandeur and popularity. The composer should choose his subject from scenes of nature, or from scenes of society that are most capable of moving and engaging the multitude, without however descending at any time to that which is base and trivial."[5] The imagery that E.T.A. Hoffmann used to describe the symphonies of Haydn, Mozart, and Beethoven consistently evokes the idea of vast space and numbers. One anonymous German critic, writing in 1820, asserted that in the symphony, as in a work for large chorus, there appears "the universality of humanity, in which everything that is individual finds itself melted as discrete entities within the whole."[6]

The various programmatic interpretations imposed on otherwise nonprogrammatic works further manifest the perception of symphonies as expressions of a collective voice, these programs invariably involve large crowds. Momigny's 1803 analysis of the first movement of Haydn's Symphony 103 in E-flat Major ("Drumroll") is typical in this regard. A large assembly has gathered to pray for relief against the terrors of a storm and its thunder (represented by the symphony's opening drumroll); the group rejoices at the arrival of sunny weather and cowers collectively at the resumption of the thunder when the slow introduction makes an unexpected return (at m. 202). In his programmatic interpretation of a chamber work, by contrast—Mozart's String Quartet in D Minor, K. 421—Momigny is reminded of Dido's anguish at Aeneas's departure from Carthage. The grief expressed here is personal, not collective.[7] The many programmatic interpretations of Beethoven's Seventh Symphony, in turn, evoke images of some kind of communal gathering, be it a peasant dance or wedding (first movement), a priestly ceremony (second movement), or a bacchanal (finale).[8]

Composers were well aware of the symphony's communal tone. In a letter to a Parisian publisher of 28 August 1789, shortly after the beginning of the French Revolution, Haydn announced his intention to call one of four symphonies he proposed to write a "National" Symphony.[9] The work was never composed, but the idea is revealing in its own right. Such a designation would have been unthinkable for a new quartet or concerto: only the symphony could convey the requisite quality of massed expression. Muzio Clementi's Third Symphony (1832), entitled "Great National Symphony," incorporates "God Save the King," the national anthem of his adopted homeland. And it is scarcely coincidental that the most celebrated of all musical expressions of communal ideals in any genre is to be found in a symphony. Beethoven's Ninth, with its choral finale on Schiller's *An die Freude*, revolves around a text whose social and political implications were widely recognized long before 1824. Indeed, one of the composer's early sketches for the opening words of Schiller's text indicates it as part of a "Sinfonie allemand."[10]

This kind of communal tone had in fact already been perceived in at least some of Beethoven's earlier symphonies. An anonymous reviewer in Leipzig's *Allgemeine musikalische Zeitung* described the ending of the *Pastoral* Symphony as a "choral song" (*Chorgesang*) in praise of nature.[11] And Adolf Bernhard Marx, surveying Beethoven's symphonies in 1824, before he had heard the Ninth Symphony or seen a copy of it (and likely before he had even heard *of* it), compared the genre of the symphony to the hymn, on the grounds that both expressed the emotions of a large body, a veritable chorus.[12] In this sense, Beethoven's incorporation of a chorus into the Ninth extended the genre in its performance forces but not in its fundamental tone.

In the wake of the Ninth, critics embraced the idea of the symphony as a genre of collective expression all the more readily. Gottfried Wilhelm Fink maintained in 1835 that a symphony is "a story, developed within a psychological context, of some particular emotional state of a large body of people," a "representation of the *Volk* [*Volksrepräsentation*] through every instrument, drawn into the whole."[13] Ernst Gottschald, reviewing Schumann's Second Symphony in 1850, insisted that a composer of symphonies could realize the fullest potential of the genre only by sublimating himself to the highest order of universality, transcending even nature itself.[14] A. B. Marx, comparing Beethoven's sonatas and symphonies in 1855, was careful to point out that while both genres were capable of great depth of expression, the tone and nature of that expression necessarily differed. He praised the profundity of such works as the Piano Sonatas, opp. 110 and 111, but distinguished the expression of the "individual-subjective piano" from that of the chorus and the symphony, which address general conditions "in the grand sense of ancient tragedy."[15] August Reissman pointed out in 1878 that a true symphony does not present the subjective spirit of the individual, but rather "that objective spirit fulfilled by the manifest command of the world-spirit."[16] The most extended exposition on the idea of the symphony as a genre of communal expression would come from the pen of the distinguished German music critic Paul Bekker in the early twentieth century.[17]

Such responses stand in marked contrast to the more common perception of these works as emanating from the creative psyche of an individual composer. In a literal sense, of course, they do: no one would suggest that the symphonies of Haydn, Mozart, or Beethoven are somehow products of collective authorship. But the real question, once again, is one of tone. Who is "speaking" in these works? Whose voice, whose persona, do we hear in these symphonies? To the extent that this question is raised at all, the answer, almost invariably, is that we are hearing the composer's voice. This is particularly true in the case of Beethoven, whose persona is perceived most forcefully in his "heroic" works, most notably the Third, Fifth, and Ninth Symphonies, which follow a trajectory leading from struggle to triumph. The confluence of the composer's life and the aesthetics of the heroic are perceived to intersect with special clarity in the *Eroica* Symphony, whose very title aligns itself with the idea of heroism, and whose canceled reference to Napoleon connects it to the single most powerful individual of the composer's era. But the hero, by definition, is an individual who stands apart from the crowd, apart from society, and even the *Eroica*'s most literal interpreters have understood this work to be about more than any one individual, be it Napoleon or the more abstract idea of an unnamed, prototypical hero. Through this music, the individual self—the hero—is heard to be projected in such a way as to transcend the state of limiting selfhood. Scott Burnham has eloquently described this perception of self-overcoming as one in which the passionately individual is made to sound as a larger organic universality. This is because the passionately individual self, which is heard to be projected by the music, *is all there is*: one does not hear a world order against which a hero defines himself—one hears only the hero, the self, fighting against its own element. Thus the "superclosure" effect of the "organically unified musical masterpiece": there is no world beyond the piece, no fading horizon, no vanishing point of perspective. All is in the piece, and the piece is all; all is now. The feeling provoked by this music is one of transcendent individuality, or merger with a higher world order in the name of Self. This effect is identical to that enunciated in the Idealist trajectory of Hegel's phenomenology, with one overwhelmingly important exception: Beethoven's music is heard and experienced; it is a concretion with a degree of compression and concentration that Hegel's philosophy could never hope to reach.[18]

The quintessential individual, the hero, is *aufgehoben*, to use that multivalent word employed by Hegel to indicate at once subsumption, cancellation, and elevation. By being absorbed into a higher form of expression, the individual is integrated into the universal. The persona of the individual—Beethoven, Napoleon, or anyone else, for that matter—is heard within a transcendent context.

The transcendentally heroic, however, is only one of many means by which to express the universal, for the symphony was a genre that by its very nature was associated with the universal. When Wagner claimed that the "entire world" made music through Beethoven's symphonies, he was not speaking of any particular symphony but about Beethoven's symphonies in general. And from a broader perspective, he need not have limited his comments to Beethoven at all, for the perception of the symphony as the expression of a communal voice was already established even before Beethoven had begun to make his mark on the genre.

THE IMPERATIVES OF INDIVIDUAL AND SOCIAL SYNTHESIS

At the end of the eighteenth century, Friedrich Schlegel famously summed up the spirit of his age by identifying its three most characteristic "tendencies": the French Revolution, Fichte's *Wissenschaftslehre*, and Goethe's *Wilhelm Meisters Lehrjahre*. The juxtaposition of the political, philosophical, and literary was intended to provoke. "Whoever takes exception to this grouping," Schlegel noted, "whoever thinks that no revolution can seem important unless it is loud and material—that individual has not yet elevated himself to the high and broad perspective of the history of humankind."[19]

For Schlegel, all three "tendencies" were revolutionary, for each manifested a turning point in the history of the human spirit. Fichte's *Wis-*

senschaftslehre (1794–95)—or to cite its full title, *Die Grundlage der gesammten Wissenschaftslehre* (*Foundation of the Entire Theory of Knowledge*)—was hailed for having surmounted the Kantian dualism between subject and object. For writers of Schlegel's generation, the *Wissenschaftslehre* seemed to offer, if only for a brief time, a solution to the limits of knowledge identified but not overcome by Kant. The shortcomings of the treatise became apparent soon enough: one recent commentator has noted that for all its brilliance, the *Wissenschaftslehre* had only "a brief life. Like a rocket, it quickly rose to the heights . . . only to explode in mid air."[20] It nevertheless inspired a new generation of thinkers to continue wrestling with the most basic issues of epistemology and to develop their own approaches to the relationship of subject and object, between the individual and the external world, the world of mind and the world of matter. The most prominent of these figures included Hölderlin (b. 1770), Hegel (b. 1770), Novalis (b. 1772), Schelling (b. 1775), and Schlegel himself (b. 1772). Every one of these writers was an exact or near contemporary of Beethoven (b. 1770).

Goethe's novel *Wilhelm Meisters Lehrjahre* (*Wilhelm Meister's Years of Apprenticeship*, 1795–96) was received with equal and ultimately more enduring enthusiasm. It, too, was perceived as revolutionary, for it provided a model of personal self-realization for those who did not enjoy the privilege of aristocratic birth. Through the medium of the novel, Goethe offered a paradigm of *Bildung*, a concept that encompasses education, experience, and the formation of an individual personality all at once.[21] As the novel's title character explains in a letter to his brother: "I have an irresistible desire to attain the harmonious development of my personality such as was denied me by my birth. . . . Add to that my fondness for poetry and everything connected with it, the need to develop my mind and my taste, so that, in the pleasures I cannot do without, I may gradually come to see good only in what is good, and beauty only in what is truly beautiful."[22] Friedrich Schlegel, in his lengthy review-essay on the *Lehrjahre,* pointed to this novel as having addressed at its core "the art of all arts, the art of living."[23]

One particularly appealing element of this novel for readers of the time was its dual emphasis on the development not only of the individual but of the individual's larger place in society. The plot, such as it is, revolves around Wilhelm's search for a suitable profession. He rejects the materialism of his merchant father and pursues instead a career in the theater, only to become disillusioned with its world of perpetual semblance. He eventually finds his true calling as a physician, which offers him the opportunity to engage in "purposeful activity" (*zweckmäßige Tätigkeit*) useful to society as a whole. The formation of the self, in short, is inseparable from the productive integration of the self into the larger world.

Schlegel recognized that this idea of integration was revolutionary, hence his juxtaposition of Goethe's novel with Fichte's treatise and the recent events in France.[24] What all three phenomena share is a striving to overcome fragmentation, to make whole that which had been separated: subject and object, in the case of Fichte's philosophy; individual and society, in the case of Goethe's novel; levels of society, in the case of the French Revolution. All three manifest the fundamental drive of humanity to achieve a fuller degree of self-realization in ways ranging from the abstract (Fichte's epistemology) to the concrete (the French Revolution). These extremes are mediated by the individual (the title character of *Wilhelm Meisters Lehrjahre*), who must use both thought and action to acquire the kind of *Bildung* needed to integrate himself into the larger whole of society. What Schlegel considered characteristic of his era, then, was not merely these three phenomena in and of themselves—important as each might be in its own right—but their collective breadth and interconnectedness.

These "tendencies" all resonate with the writings of Schiller, Fichte, and other contemporary philosophers. A broad span of the educated German-speaking public found in these works a mechanism by which to better themselves, to develop their own views of the world, and ultimately to assume control of their own personal lives in a society otherwise dominated by rigid hierarchies of social, political, and economic power. These individuals saw self-cultivation (*Bildung*) as the means by which to determine their own destinies.[25] Beethoven himself was quite typical in this regard. He received a fairly minimal formal education but continued to pursue higher intellectual goals throughout his life. "From my childhood onward I have striven to grasp the meaning of the better and wiser people of every age," he wrote to the publishers Breitkopf & Härtel in 1809. The journal-diary that Beethoven kept between 1812 and 1818 documents the breadth and voraciousness of his intellectual interests. It includes two passages copied directly from an edition of Kant's *Universal Natural History and Theory of Heaven* that Beethoven owned, and it reflects an ongoing project to assimilate the central philosophical and social thought of his era.[26]

Following Schlegel's line of thought, then, we can see that the symphony is likewise very much a "tendency" of its age and equally revolutionary, for listeners were beginning to hear in this music a kind of totalizing synthesis with implications that reach far beyond the walls of the concert hall. It is not my claim that Haydn, Mozart, Beethoven, or any other composer of the time wrote their symphonies with such effects in mind (though as we shall see there is at least some circumstantial evidence to suggest that this may well have been the case). But there can be no doubt that Beethoven's more astute contemporaries heard these symphonies in relation to the most pressing epistemological, social, and political issues of their day.[27]

THE STATE AS ORGANISM

The predominant image of the state throughout the Enlightenment was that of a mechanism. Philosophers and political theorists of the time conceived of the state as a machine by which to establish social order and protect the rights of the individual. John Locke's *Second Treatise of Civil Government* (1690), the American Constitution (1787), and the French National Assembly's *Déclaration des droits de l'homme et du citoyen* (*Declaration of the Rights of Man and the Citizen*, 1789) all embody this basic outlook. Enlightened absolutism could accommodate this conception of the state just as readily as democracy: A. L. Schlözer's widely read *Allgemeines Staats-Recht* (*General Law of the State,* 1789) identified the goal of the state as the well-being and protection of its citizens and their property, with the monarch bearing responsibility for the efficient operation of the state. Schlözer even went so far as to compare the monarch to a "Director of Machinery" (*Maschinendirektor*).[28] Throughout this and other writings shaped by Enlightenment thought, the state hovers in the background as a kind of necessary evil, something to be tolerated because of its usefulness but not embraced with any degree of enthusiasm in its own right.

The Revolution and subsequent Terror accelerated the pace of this transformation. Inspired by the ideals of personal liberty that had driven the storming of the Bastille but horrified by the social chaos that had ensued, most of the early Romantics embraced an ideal of government based on the metaphor of the state as an organism rather than a machine, its constituent parts functioning in a system of mutual interdependence.[29] Within this organic conceptualization of the state, the individual's first obligation to society was to achieve the highest possible degree of self-realization so that he or she might in turn contribute in the fullest manner to society as a whole. *Bildung* became a central goal not only of the individual but of society as well. The process of self-realization could not take place in isolation. Goethe's *Wilhelm Meisters Lehrjahre*, as Friedrich Schlegel had quickly recognized, was a harbinger of this new outlook. For Novalis, "flight from the communal spirit is death." A state was necessary in order for the individual to "become and remain a person. A person without a state is a savage. All culture emanates from the relationship between person and state."[30]

This organic relationship between state and individual provided a model of society that could avoid both tyranny from above (absolutism) and chaos from below (liberalism, based on the supreme autonomy of the individual). It offered a paradigm of social thought in which the individual could retain a sense of autonomy without being isolated. In a series of commentaries from the 1790s and early 1800s, Fichte put forward a model of the ideal community devoted to the self-realization of the individual and the corresponding self-realization of the community as a whole. "The duty of the state," Fichte argued, "does not consist only in protecting the mass of goods accumulated by somebody." Its true aim, rather, "is to procure for its subjects that which is their due as members of mankind."[31] Fichte declared the state to be an "indivisible organic whole" that enabled its individual members to develop to their highest potential.[32] Along similar lines, Schelling maintained that the individual could attain maturity only within the context of the state, an organism of interdependent individuals.[33] Schelling also used the aesthetic concept of "unity in variety" (*Einheit in der Vielheit*) to describe the integration of the individual into the community. "Every state is perfect to the extent that each individual member, as a means to the end, is in itself a goal."[34] Hölderlin, Novalis, Schiller, and Friedrich Schlegel advanced similar arguments. The central message of all these texts, as the scholar Frederick Beiser notes, "was as inspiring as it was explosive: that the common people have the right to change society according to the demands of reason, and that the highest good is not a heaven beyond the earth but a just society on it."[35]

The image of the state as an organism necessarily entailed some form of democracy, for the ultimate integrity of the state was seen to reside in mutually beneficial exchanges among its citizens. And if the blood-letting of post-revolutionary France was to be avoided, the citizenry as a whole had to constitute something more than a mob. Here the early Romantics took as their model not France but Periclean Athens—or more accurately, an idealization of a Periclean Athens that cultivated beauty as a means of developing the spirit of the individual and the community alike. Plato's image of the *polis* as an artwork in its own right became the basis for a new conception of ruler and ruled. Winkelmann, pointing to the example of classical antiquity, went so far as to claim that political democracy was a necessary precondition for the realization of artistic beauty, and vice versa.[36] In attempting to explain the political and artistic achievements of ancient Greece over and against those of all other civilizations both before and after, Winkelmann and others in his wake posited an unbreakable connection between beauty and democracy. In his essay *Glaube und Liebe* (*Faith and Love*, 1797) Novalis urged the new king of Prussia, Friedrich Wilhelm III, to abandon the long tradition of running the state like a factory and to treat it instead as a work of art in which the monarch's role would be to act as "the artist of artists," with each citizen an artist in his own right. "The ruler creates an infinitely diverse theater, where the stage and parterre, the actors and spectators, are one, and where he is at once poet, director, and hero of the piece."[37] Such imagery is remarkably similar to that used to describe the symphony at the time, emphasizing the simultaneous autonomy of the individual voices and the harmony of the whole and, as we shall see, the spiritual communion of performers and listeners.

SCHILLER'S IDEA OF THE AESTHETIC STATE

The most important and widely discussed treatise of the time advocating the development of the aesthetic to social ends was Friedrich Schiller's *Über die ästhetische Erziehung des Menschen* (*On the Aesthetic Education of Man*, 1795), an essay in the form of a series of letters to a fictitious recipient. Schiller argued that no truly effective government could be based on such abstract principles as the rights of the individual or on the categorical imperative that Kant had put forward in his *Critique of Practical Reason* ("Act only according to that maxim by which you can at the same time will that it should become a universal law"). While Schiller did not disagree with either of these postulates as principles of action, he considered them inadequate as foundations of the state, for neither took into account the powerful appeal of the senses. As abstractions, they failed to reconcile the rational and the sensuous, and every attempt at political reform would be "untimely, and every hope based upon it . . . chimerical, as long as the split within man is not healed [*aufgehoben*], and his nature so restored to wholeness that it can itself become the artificer of the State, and guarantee the reality of this political creation of Reason."[38] Schiller viewed the "construction of genuine political freedom" as "the most perfect of all artworks," and only through beauty could mankind make its way to freedom. Only through the contemplation of beauty could the individual—and, by extension, society as a whole—overcome the divisions of life between duty and inclination, mind and body, form and content, finite and infinite.[39]

Schiller thereby reversed Plato's banishment of arts from the state. The arts, according to Plato, presented mere semblances of the truth and thus appealed more to the senses than to reason. Schiller considered this approach to governance unsound, for it demanded a repression of the sensuous in favor of the rational. He dismissed as vapid the constant reminder that a feeling for beauty refined morals and argued instead (in the tradition of Kant) that aesthetic contemplation was essential for a sense of psychic wholeness. Only through the mechanism of what Schiller called the *Spieltrieb* ("play drive") could the divisions between subject and object be reconciled.[40] He viewed the rational and the sensuous not as irreconcilable opposites but as complementary forces whose fusion, through the activity of aesthetic contemplation, could restore wholeness to the individual and ultimately to society in general. Through *Spieltrieb*, ethical duty and sensuous inclination could be reconciled in a genuinely harmonious fashion, without one being sacrificed in favor of the other. And only through aesthetic contemplation, stimulated through the work of art, could this synthesis be achieved.

For Schiller, then, aesthetic education would play as vital a role in the welfare of the state as in the welfare of the individual, for every person "carries within him . . . a purely ideal human being" whose life's goal is to "reconcile the ever-changing manifestations of the self with its ever-constant unity." This archetypal being, which can be perceived more or less in every individual, is "represented by the state, the objective and, as it were, canonical form in which individual subjects in all their variety seek to reconcile themselves." But this reconciliation can derive only from the inner reconciliation of the individual between reason (which demands unity) and nature (which demands diversity). "Once man is inwardly at one with himself," Schiller maintained, "he will be able to preserve his individuality however much he may universalize his conduct, and the state will be merely the interpreter of his own finest instinct, a clearer formulation of his own sense of what is right."[41]

In the *Aesthetic Letters*, Schiller outlines three principal types of states. The "dynamic state" imposes laws from above, while the "ethical state" subjects the individual to the will of the whole. Only the "aesthetic state" could consummate the will of the whole without compulsion through the wholeness of its individual constituents. "Though it may be his needs which drive man into society, and reason which implants within him the principles of social behavior, beauty alone can confer upon him a social character. Taste alone brings harmony into society, because it fosters harmony in the individual."[42]

For Schiller, the art form most capable of promoting a synthesis of individual and communal development was the theater. Already in 1784 he had argued that the stage was a "moral institution" whose "jurisdiction begins where the domain of secular law leaves off." Like Lessing before him, Schiller advocated the establishment of a German national theater as a means of developing a national culture:

> If we were to experience our own national theater, then we too would be a nation. What bound Greece so firmly together? What drew the *Volk* so irresistibly to its stage? Nothing other than the patriotic content [*der vaterländische Inhalt*] of the plays, the Greek spirit, the great overriding interest of the state, of the better humanity that breathed within these works.[43]

But Schiller cannot be construed on these grounds as a German nationalist, at least not in the modern sense of that term. He deemed "patriotic interest" of importance only for "immature nations, for the youth of the world." "It is a poor and mean ideal to write for *one* nation," he wrote to his friend Christian Gottfried Körner; "to a philosophic mind, this limitation is thoroughly unbearable."[44]

Could such a state in fact be achieved in reality? Schiller remained deliberately vague on this point, emphasizing instead that the prerequisite for the aesthetic state lay in the individual rather than in any body of laws. "As a need, [the state] exists in every finely attuned soul; as a realized fact, we are likely to find it, like the pure Church and the pure Republic, only in some few chosen circles, where conduct is governed, not by some soulless imitation of the manners and morals of others, but by the aesthetic nature we have made our own. . . ."[45] Schiller realized he was advocating a delicate balance that would be difficult to achieve and even more difficult to sustain, yet useful nonetheless as a regulative idea. His idea of the aesthetic state is in any event not to be confused with those many states before, during, and since his time that have used aesthetic means to achieve political ends. He would have seen this as simply another ploy by the dynamic state (based on power from above) to extend its reach, to persuade through art. Schiller's aesthetic state emanates from the individual.

GOETHE'S PEDAGOGICAL PROVINCE

Goethe was equally cosmopolitan in his outlook, and in the deeply allegorical novel of his old age, *Wilhelm Meisters Wanderjahre* (*Wilhelm Meister's Journeyman Years*, 1821, revised 1829), he used the symphony to illustrate the ideal art form that embraced the cultivation of both the individual and society as a whole. The novel's central theme, as in the earlier *Wilhelm Meisters Lehrjahre*, is the self-realization of the individual and the consequent harmonious self-realization of society. *Bildung* is a continuum that links the individual and the collective.

Nowhere is this continuum more evident than in the "Pedagogical Province" in Book Two of the *Wanderjahre*. Here, Wilhelm and his son, Felix, enter that portion of an unnamed utopian realm in which the young learn various languages, arts, and crafts—learn, in short, how to become productive members of society. Music is fundamental to this process: harmony is evoked repeatedly as a metaphor in the development of both the individual and the ideal society. The preceptor who acts as their guide explains that the simplest pleasures and lessons are enlivened and impressed on the memories of students through song. Musical education is the basis for such diverse skills as orthography, penmanship, and arithmetic. When Wilhelm expresses surprise that there are no instruments to be heard or seen, he is told that instrumental music is cultivated in a separate region of the Pedagogical Province. Indeed, different instruments are cultivated within different districts there. The discords of beginning instrumentalists are restricted to designated points isolated from the rest of society. As Wilhelm's guide explains it, "there is no more sorrowful affliction to be endured in a well-ordered civil society" than "the proximity of someone who is just starting to learn how to play the flute or violin." In the Pedagogical Province, beginners go into the wilderness of their own free will and work in isolation to earn the privilege of approaching the inhabited portion of the world.[46]

As it turns out, the Region of Instrumental Music contains still further layers of ability. Wilhelm's visit happens to coincide with a festival celebration peculiar to this region, and he and his guide travel a considerable distance through valleys and forests and across streams to reach an area in which every house is situated far enough from the one next to it so that neither pleasing nor displeasing notes can be heard between them. At last Wilhelm reaches "a broad area surrounded by buildings and shadows where great masses of people were waiting, taut with the greatest attention and expectation." As he enters this space, he hears a "mighty symphony" being performed by all the instruments. He marvels at its simultaneous strength and gentleness. On closer inspection, Wilhelm realizes that there are actually *two* orchestras before him and that of these, only one of them is actually playing. The second orchestra, seated at the side of the first, consists of "younger and older students, each holding his instrument at the ready, but without playing it; these were the ones who were not yet able or not yet daring enough to join in with the Whole." Seldom a performance goes by, Wilhelm is told, in which one or more of these aspiring talents actually does join in with the orchestra as a fully-participating member.[47]

In this transparently allegorical account, the individual players must go through a long process of education before they are capable of contributing to the whole. Specialization is the prerequisite to harmonious society; a general education provides only the milieu in which a specialization can have its effect. "Practice and become an accomplished violinist," one character observes early on in the novel, "and the conductor will gladly direct you to your place within the orchestra."[48] The harmonious society, in turn, is represented by a symphony, not a concerto. No soloist dominates, and every instrument contributes its own distinctive and indispensable sound to the larger whole.

Goethe's Pedagogical Province owes much to the teachings of three contemporaries: his friend Carl Friedrich Zelter (1758–1832), conductor of the Berlin Singakademie; Hans Georg Nägeli (1773–1836), the founder of the Zurich Singinstitut; and the Swiss pedagogue Heinrich Pestalozzi (1746–1827), a disciple of Rousseau. All three advocated music, particularly singing, as a means of inculcating young children with a sense of social belonging. Zelter and Nägeli helped to establish choral societies throughout German-speaking lands, sometimes as mixed choruses (following the model of the Berlin Singakademie), but more often as men's choruses.[49] Zelter and Pestalozzi both played an important role in persuading the Prussian Minister of State, Wilhelm von Humboldt, to incorporate music into that nation's pioneering system of compulsory public education. In 1809, Humboldt would declare music to be "a natural bond between the lower and higher classes of the nation," on the grounds that it appealed in unmediated fashion at a level so basic to the human spirit that "even the lowest, uneducated classes" could respond to it. Through education (*Bildung*) and improved musical performance, this kind of response could be enhanced still further. "All the elements of the nation," Humboldt argued, could thus "be united, irrespective of their difference of circumstance."[50] Education was an essential element of nation building, and by the second decade of the nineteenth century, at least in Prussia, music had become an officially recognized component of education.[51]

In associating the symphony with an ideal social order, Goethe's account also resonates with long-standing perceptions of the genre as a model of society. Pre-revolutionary images of the orchestra as a polity had tended to emphasize the authority of the leader, the machine-like precision of the players, or both. Charles Dufresny, for example, had noted in 1699 that "everything hinges on the sovereign of the orchestra, a prince whose power is so absolute that by raising and lowering his scepter in the form of a roll of paper he holds in his hand, he regulates every movement of the fickle populace."[52] But post-revolutionary accounts would take a decidedly different approach. Heinrich Christoph Koch observed in 1795 that "an orchestral part represents a member of a society, which, stirred by a common sentiment, expresses that sentiment." In the case of multiple instruments playing the same part (such as any of the strings), the performers must play together strictly if they are, as a unit, to represent a particular element of society.[53] Robert Schumann, in turn, writing in 1835, looked with alarm on the growing importance of the conductor as a threat to the social equality of the orchestra, which "must stand as a republic, acknowledging no higher authority."[54] Gottfried Wilhelm Fink's account of the symphony from 1838 uses much the same vocabulary. A symphony is more difficult to compose than a work of chamber music, just as it is more difficult to rule a state than a household:

[E]ach orchestral instrument must be treated as a particular individual according to its own individual nature. Each must be accorded its own particular sounding and singing, as if there reigned the greatest freedom within a republican state of high priests, in which each individual gladly submits himself to the divine idea. In this last point lies the basis for the closest possible association of the greatest mastery and highest degree of lawfulness with individual freedom. Moreover, whenever such masses characteristically deport themselves as individually as possible, the characteristics of the individual must emerge not in some hazy freedoms, but rather within the fully robust bounds of nature. The musical idea—in which and with which every individual instrument proclaims itself according to its properties—must therefore be all the more broad, multivalent, and widely applicable if it is to move within the whole in unencumbered fullness and extend itself.[55]

This is all very much in keeping with the agenda of the aesthetic state. Social harmony could rest only on a foundation of individuals who had themselves achieved a requisite level of personal self-realization. Goethe's allegory of the two orchestras, all the members of one playing a symphony, individual members of the other waiting for just the right moment to join in, captures perfectly Schiller's ideal of the aesthetic state. Indeed, the conception of personal wholeness as a necessary condition for the individual's integration into society helps to explain the apparently exclusionary aspect of one passage in Schiller's *An die Freude* that Beethoven incorporated into the finale of his Ninth Symphony. More than one commentator has puzzled over how the "circle of joy" is not accessible to all:

Wem der große Wurf gelungen,	Whoever has had the great fortune
Eines Freundes Freund zu sein;	To be a friend to a friend;
Wer ein holdes Weib errungen,	Whoever has won for himself a dear wife,
Mische seinen Jubel ein!	Let him mix his jubilation into the whole!
Ja—wer auch nur eine Seele	Indeed, even he who can call only a single soul
Sein nennt auf dem Erdenrund!	His own in the entire world!
Und wer's nie gekonnt, der stehle	And whoever has not been able to do this must creep,
Weinend sich aus diesem Bund!	Tearfully, out of this circle!

This act of exclusion from the circle of joy is not because of any character defect, but rather because the individual in question has not yet attained a sufficient degree of personal self-realization. The one who has been cast out is in fact not cast out at all, for he is not rejected by society. Rather, he lacks the capacity to join it. Joy is achieved through synthesis, and this cannot be accomplished through solitary self-contemplation.[56]

CHAPTER FIVE

Listening to the German State: Nationalism

THE IDEAL of a cosmopolitan, aesthetic state outlined by Schiller and Goethe held powerful sway over the European imagination throughout the first half of the nineteenth century. But even the most optimistically inclined were prepared to concede that such a state was destined to remain an ideal, far removed from the *Realpolitik* of the post-Napoleonic era. Some, like Hegel, envisioned an aesthetic state emerging out of existing polities, such as Württemberg, Bavaria, or Prussia. Most, however, conceived of this aesthetic state as "Germany," an imagined entity coinciding more or less with the aggregate of all German-speaking lands. Like the cosmopolitan state, this national state was also an abstraction, but it was one whose realization became increasingly plausible over the course of the early decades of the nineteenth century. Concepts of the symphony, long perceived as a distinctively "German" genre, changed accordingly, with cosmopolitanism eventually giving way to nationalism.

GERMAN NATIONALISM

Concepts of Germany changed enormously during Beethoven's lifetime. For the Viennese audience listening to the premiere of his First Symphony in 1800, Germany was a long-standing yet essentially fictive entity loosely united by a common written language but otherwise diverse in its manners of speech, customs, and political governance. Vienna itself was the de facto capital of the Holy Roman Empire, a weak confederation of more than three hundred Central European polities that as a whole lacked any clearly defined identity. "Germany" was a shorthand expression used to describe that wide swath of Central Europe in which German, in all its dialects, was the primary language.

For the Viennese audience that heard the premiere of the Ninth Symphony in 1824, Germany remained an abstraction, but within the span of less than three decades it had now become a plausible aspiration. Its territorial outlines, structure, and cultural identity would remain a matter of ongoing debate—with the proclamation of the Second Reich in 1871, it would in fact exclude Austria—but at the time of the Ninth's premiere, the notion of a pan-German state was very much alive in the public mind.

The idea of a united Germany, moreover, was inextricably linked to a belief in the principles of representative democracy. Hopes for unification rested on political reform, and the advocates of national unity were invariably advocates of democracy.

By 1824, these hopes had been tempered through a series of raised and dashed expectations. The French Revolution gave inspiration to the forces of freedom and democracy east of the Rhine, but the Terror demonstrated the pitfalls of eradicating the monarchy with a single blow. Napoleon's conquests, welcomed at first by the forces of reform in German-speaking lands, devolved into what would be perceived increasingly as a foreign occupation. The ensuing Wars of Liberation catalyzed German nationalist sentiment, and the decisive victory against the French at the Battle of Leipzig in 1813 gave new hope to those seeking some form of a unified Germany based on democratic principles. In the end, however, these aspirations would be crushed by the Congress of Vienna (1814–15), which restored the essentials of the status ante quo across the European continent.

The German Confederation, created toward the end of the Congress of Vienna as an association of thirty-nine sovereign states and four free cities, provided little in the way of either unity or democracy. Prussian authorities soon began shutting down some of the more liberal publications that had sprung up toward the end of the Napoleonic era: Joseph Görres's *Rheinischer Merkur*, the *Tagesblatt der Geschichte*, the *Deutsche Blätter*, and Ernst Moritz Arndt's *Der Wächter* were all abolished in quick order.[1] The joint causes of political reform and national unity suffered their most serious setback in 1819 after the assassination of the playwright August von Kotzebue, a political agent for the Russian legation at Mannheim. The crime itself was of limited significance, but it raised the specter of chaos. Memories of post-revolutionary France were still vivid, and the event provided local governments and the Confederation with the pretext for a series of repressive measures aimed at individuals and groups advocating political unity and basic liberties of speech, press, and association. The most sweeping of these new laws, the Karlsbad Decrees, outlawed student fraternities (*Burschenschaften*), allowed governments to appoint special agents to oversee the ideologies of university faculty and students, and tightened censorship laws still further. The driving force behind these new laws was Prince Klemens von Metternich, nominally the Austrian minister of state but in fact the single most powerful individual within the Confederation.

By the early 1820s, then, the institutions of communal expression in German-speaking lands, never large to begin with, had grown even smaller in scope and number. Parliamentary debate in various assemblies was strictly controlled, and proceedings rarely appeared in print.[2] Public

gatherings of any kind could not be taken lightly, and government infor-
mants were quick to report suspicious activities. Henry E. Dwight, a visiting American, offered this impression of Berlin in the 1820s:

> When national happiness, or in other words the happiness of every individual
> of the nation, can not with safety be made the topic of conversation, the mind
> will enter with very little ardour into other important subjects. . . . Conscious
> as every Prussian is, that the almost omniscient eye of the government, through
> the medium of its system of *espionage* is fixed upon him, and that a single word
> expressed with boldness, may furnish an occasion for transferring him to [the
> prisons of] Koepnic [Köpenick] or Spandau; he becomes of course, in every
> circle, suspicious of those around him, sustains a negative character in his con-
> versation, advances those indefinite opinions which are harmless, and if he
> does not commend, he takes very good care never to censure the proceedings
> of government.[3]

Conditions were no different in Vienna. Beethoven's conversation books
are laced with references to the watchful eye and heavy hand of government authorities. An entry from 1820, possibly written in a coffee shop,
warns: "Another time—just now the spy Haensl is here." An entry from
later that same year reads: "The man following us knows about everything, he's plainclothes police."[4] The poet Franz Grillparzer, visiting the
composer in 1826, noted with resignation, "[T]he censor has broken me
down." Beethoven's friend Karl Holz, present during that same conversation, observed that in order to voice opinions openly, one would have to
"travel to North America." On another occasion Grillparzer observed to
Beethoven, presumably with some degree of envy, "[T]he censor cannot
hold anything against musicians. If they only knew what you think about
in your music!" Yet we know that at least one of Beethoven's concerts
(on 29 November 1814) was the subject of a report from an anonymous
informant to Baron Franz Hager von Altensteig, head of the government's
secret police.[5]

In German-speaking lands in the 1820s, as in repressive regimes both
before and since, those who wished to speak out against the ruling powers
learned how to camouflage their opinions. These individuals developed
outlets of veiled political expression in seemingly nonpolitical venues,
such as reading societies and associations dedicated to Schiller, Luther,
Gutenberg, Dürer, and other icons of German culture. These largely bourgeois groups cut across professions and social standing, functioned outside church and state, and organized themselves largely on a democratic
basis. Governments kept a watchful eye on the activities of all these
groups but tolerated them on the grounds that they were apolitical, at
least on the surface.[6]

But only on the surface. The many choral societies established in German-speaking lands during the first quarter of the nineteenth century illustrate what Frederick Beiser has called the "cryptopolitical" tendencies of bourgeois German cultural institutions at this time. One of the oldest and most influential of these choral societies was the Berlin Singakademie, a mixed chorus of men and women governed by an executive committee elected by the group's members. Like its many imitators, the Singakademie was a decidedly nationalistic undertaking. It cultivated both sacred and secular music, including arrangements of folk songs and newly composed songs written in a folklike style. Under the guidance of Carl Friedrich Zelter, who led the group from 1800 until his death in 1832, the Singakademie went out of its way to avoid imitating foreign models and manners; its repertory was overwhelmingly German.[7] Choral societies such as the Singakademie could circumvent the prohibition on organized group activities on the grounds that they were pursuing artistic rather than political ends. Song provided an ideal means by which to express political sentiments in an indirect, veiled manner. Although largely regional, singers' festivals—the occasional gathering of multiple choral societies—took on distinctly nationalist overtones. The very act of assembly kept alive the notion of a truly public sphere operating outside the confines of church and court. The rights of association and assembly could be exercised here without fear of reprisals.

Through various public and semi-public associations, then, Germans were able to sublimate political expression through philosophy, literature, and the arts—including, as we shall see, instrumental music. The seemingly insurmountable political fragmentation of German-speaking populations helped to make early German nationalism all the more cultural rather than territorial. Indeed, many German nationalists of the early nineteenth century considered it to be the mission of any future German state to provide a model of cosmopolitanism for the rest of the world, a state based on cultural rather than territorial or military might. Paradoxical as it may seem, particularly in light of German history in the twentieth century, Beethoven's contemporaries for the most part saw no fundamental conflict between the dual beliefs of nationalism and cosmopolitanism: Germany as a nation was to become the cosmopolitan state par excellence, not through its territorial power but through its accomplishments in music, art, philosophy, literature, and the sciences.[8]

The tragedies of later history make such aspirations all the more poignant—and distant. But such feelings were basic to most expressions of German nationalism around 1800. Schiller's poetic fragment known as *Deutsche Größe* (*German Greatness,* ca. 1801) captures the commonplace distinction of the time between the political and cultural nationalism.

The German Empire and the German Nation are two different things. The majesty and honor of the German never rested on the head of his prince. Quite apart from the political, the German has established his own value. Even if the [Holy Roman] Empire disappeared, German greatness would remain untouched. This greatness is one of manners, it resides in culture and in the character of a nation, independent of political destinies. . . .[9]

The cultural character of early German nationalism was reinforced by the emerging idea of the *Volk* in the development of national character. Johann Gottfried Herder placed special emphasis on the centrality of a nation's people in defining nationhood. He called the *Volk* "the invisible, hidden medium that links minds through ideas, hearts through inclinations and impulses, the senses through impressions and forms, civil society through laws and institutions, generations through examples, modes of living and education."[10] Herder viewed language as the single most important element uniting a *Volk*, but he saw all the arts (at least potentially) as the expression of collective aspirations and identity. The concurrent mania for collecting folktales and folk poetry (or at least folklike poetry) was driven in large part by the collective desire of German-speaking peoples to gather and preserve the sources of their cultural identity. Achim von Arnim and Clemens Brentano's *Des Knaben Wunderhorn* (1806–8) and the tales of the Brothers Grimm are the best-known examples of this new phenomenon. In retrospect, such movements can all too easily be seen as having sown the seeds of ominous mentalities that would emphasize the power of the *Volk* in the advancement of racist, xenophobic attitudes. But this was by no means an inevitable path, nor should we allow our knowledge of subsequent history to oversimplify the complexities of an earlier time. Herder, for example, is often identified as the intellectual founder of German nationalism, yet he insisted on a clear distinction between a nation (defined by its *Volk*) and a state (defined by its government). Like many of his Enlightenment contemporaries, he harbored the hope that government of any kind would one day be altogether unnecessary.[11]

Even Herder recognized that such wishful thinking was not to be realized any time soon, however. Events on the ground in the summer and fall of 1806—the advance of French troops into Central Europe, the dissolution of the Holy Roman Empire, the military humiliation of Prussia—gave real immediacy to basic questions of governance. Many inhabitants of German-speaking lands, including Beethoven, welcomed Napoleon's advances, at least initially, because the French brought with them basic institutional reforms that would have otherwise been unattainable. In 1807, for example, the newly established Kingdom of Westphalia, ruled by Napoleon's brother, Jerome, became the first German state to be endowed with a written constitution; no German ruler up to that time had been prepared to define the limits of his power by means of such a document. In direct response to such changes and in an attempt to defuse the threat of revolution at home, Prussian leaders instituted their own legal, educational, and political reforms. King Friedrich Wilhelm III, encouraged by his ministers Wilhelm von Humboldt, Karl August Hardenberg, and Karl vom und zum Stein, abolished serfdom, restricted nobilitary privileges, instituted widespread agrarian reforms, and established the basis for a system of free and universal education.

This "revolution from above" fueled still greater hopes for the idea of Germany as a unified state based on democratic principles. In his *Reden an die deutsche Nation* (*Addresses to the German Nation*, 1808), delivered shortly after the Treaty of Tilsit, which had ceded all Prussian lands west of the Elbe to France, Fichte called for a Germany whose greatness would be driven by the spirit of its philosophy and arts. In his sermons in Halle and Berlin in 1806–10, Schleiermacher made a similar appeal. The political theorist Adam Müller argued that through culture, Germany would gain a leading role among nations, not by virtue of intellectual aggression, but by virtue of the German's capacity and eagerness to absorb and synthesize other cultures. "We find our own happiness not in the suppression but in the highest flowering of the civilization of our neighbors," Müller noted in 1806; "and thus Germany, the fortunate heartland, will not need to deny its respect for others when it will dominate the world by its spirit."[12]

Nationalist sentiment grew stronger still with the defeat of Napoleon at Leipzig in 1813. Joseph Görres declared that "every German, whether he is called Württemberger or Nassauer or whatever . . . belongs not any longer to the particular state in whose borders he happened to be born, but rather to the whole German nation."[13] When a group of some five hundred students from across German-speaking lands gathered at the Wartburg castle in Eisenach in 1817 to celebrate the three hundredth anniversary of the Reformation, their proclamations were far more political than religious. One such declaration deplored the image of the state as a mechanism and called for a more democratic form of government that would replace the long-standing separation of rulers and the ruled: "The will of the princes is not the law of the *Volk*; rather, the law of the *Volk* should be the will of the princes."[14] Karl Follen, a poet and political activist, declared that "each citizen is the head of state, for the just state is like a perfect sphere in which no 'over' or 'under' exists, for each individual point can be and is a summit."[15] Radical as it may seem, this formulation had its roots in Plato and Aristotle, among others, who viewed the state as a macrocosm of the individual.

Not all expressions of the new nationalism were quite so lofty. Friedrich Ludwig Jahn gave physical form to the aspirations of a unified nation through the gymnastics society he established in Berlin in 1811. Tolerated and to some extent even encouraged by the Prussian monarchy in its early years, Jahn's Turnverein emphasized drilled, unified motion en masse. Archery and swordsmanship were soon added to the mix, along with night marches and war games, all with an eye to resistance against the occupying forces of the French. Its two hundred members consisted largely of students in their late teens and early twenties, but over time more and more citizens joined, and branches sprang up in other German cities as well, with an estimated 12,000 members in some 150 different branches by 1818. Gymnastics, according to Jahn, instilled not only bodily strength, but also a sense of individual and collective discipline. As the movement gained followers, Jahn initiated a series of "Gymnastics Days" to be observed throughout German-speaking lands: these commemorated the defeat of the French at Leipzig in 1813 (18 October), the entrance of the allied forces into Paris in 1814 (31 March), and the final allied victory at Waterloo in 1815 (18 June). He designated these occasions as "Memorial Days for the Salvation, Resurrection, and Savior of the German People."[16] As one recent scholar has described it, Jahn's gymnasts "blended paramilitary drills and spurious teutonic symbols with classical ideals of bodily strength."[17] This movement was nevertheless one of the first of its kind in German-speaking lands to establish an open forum of public association with political tendencies. The submission of the individual to a higher authority was central to Jahn's outlook, and his followers were legion. Government authorities recognized—and in post-Napoleonic Europe feared—the power of Jahn's organization. When it was discovered, in 1819, that Kotzebue's assassin, a young student named Karl Sand, had been an active member of Jahn's Turnverein, the society was banned, and Jahn himself was imprisoned for six years on the grounds of "demagogic intrigues."

Increasingly xenophobic forms of nationalism also began to appear during the later stages of the Napoleonic era. Jahn advocated the removal of all foreign words (including even proper names) from German-speaking lands. Ernst Moritz Arndt, in his *Das deutsche Volkstum* (*The German People*) of 1810, attacked the French with particular vehemence. "I hate all Frenchmen without distinction in the name of God and of my people, I teach this hatred to my son, I teach it to the sons of my people. . . ."[18] And Heinrich von Kleist's ode *Germania an ihre Kinder* (*Germania to Her Children*, 1809) was a nationalistic parody of Schiller's cosmopolitan *An die Freude*. In place of Schiller's appeal to universal brotherhood, Kleist called for the extermination of the French by all who call themselves German. In its key concepts, formal design, meter, and rhyme scheme it mocks the idealized fraternalism of Schiller's earlier poem.[19]

The repertories of the crypto-political choral societies became more openly nationalistic during the Napoleonic era, incorporating many of the patriotic songs that had been written during the Wars of Liberation. Ernst Moritz Arndt's *Was ist des deutschen Vaterland?* (*What Is the German's Fatherland?* 1814), set to music by Nägeli, among others, was the most frequently performed of all such songs. It advocated German unity based on a shared language. The text opens with a series of questions following on the central question of the song's title. Is the German's Fatherland Prussia? Swabia? Bavaria? Each of these is rejected with the rejoinder: "Oh, no. The German's Fatherland must be greater." At last the Fatherland is identified as extending "as far as the German tongue is spoken and sings songs to God in heaven."[20] In the end, however, this linguistic community turns against those outside. The penultimate verse of Arndt's text reads:

Das ist des Deutschen Vaterland	This is the German's Fatherland,
Wo Zorn vertilgt den welschen Tand	Where wrath exterminates French frippery,
Wo jeder Franzmann heißet Feind	Where every Frenchman is called an enemy,
Wo jeder Deutsche heißet Freund.	Where every German is called a friend.

Anti-Semitism also increased markedly during the post-Napoleonic era. As the outlines of a German state began to take shape, the need to define national identity by means other than language took on more immediate significance. At the 1817 celebrations marking the three hundredth anniversary of the Reformation, the crowd at the Wartburg castle listened to speeches about German unity, heard Jews denounced, and burned "un-German" books. One of the speakers on this occasion was Jacob Friedrich Fries, professor of philosophy at the University of Jena, who a year earlier had published a pamphlet calling for the exclusion of Jews from German national life.[21]

The conception of Germany based on race and territorial prowess would eventually overwhelm—catastrophically—the ideal of an essentially cultural nationalism. Yet we must resist reading aspirations of cultural nationalism in the early decades of the nineteenth century as doomed to failure. Jahn's emphasis on massive, synchronized movement represented only one approach to the question of how the individual might best relate to the state. Goethe's image of the state as a double orchestra, with each specialized player contributing a distinctive voice to the larger whole and others waiting to join in, reflects an altogether different conception of society, based on the autonomy and cultural development of the individual. Both models would be pursued throughout the nineteenth century and well into the twentieth.

Music played a central role in the model of nationalism based on individual autonomy, for it was during the early nineteenth century that music came to be recognized as an important element in the formation of German national identity.[22] Friedrich Rochlitz, in the first volume (1799) of his newly established *Allgemeine musikalische Zeitung*, expressed his "dreams" for a history of recent music that would be constructed not along the lines of the accomplishments of "worthy individuals" but instead along the lines of the "education [*Bildung*] of a nation, for example, that of the Germans, toward this art."[23] A year later an anonymous author writing in the same journal argued that the state had an obligation to promote the arts, pointing to ancient Greece as an example and maintaining that music, more than any other art, penetrated to the deepest essence of man. Music was far more than "merely a means to fight ennui, or a harmful titillation of the sense"; it was a means of shaping the character (*Charakterbildung*), which in turn carried with it significant benefits for domestic and public life.[24] An advertisement in Berlin's *Vossische Zeitung* on 13 June 1801 announced the publication of quartets by Haydn and Mozart as part of a "patriotic plan" that would present to "the admirers of true music the classical works of our German (and universally acknowledged) fathers of music as monuments to the honor of German art."[25]

Johann Nikolaus Forkel's biography of Johann Sebastian Bach (1802) appeared within this context of growing national consciousness. Early on in his account, Forkel suggested that Bach's "classic" music was immune to changing fashions and that his works could be studied for the benefit of both "learning and good taste" in the same way that the classic authors of Greek and Roman antiquity were studied in the schools of that time. Forkel concluded his biography by reflecting on the fact that "this man—the greatest musical poet and the greatest musical declamator who has ever lived and who will likely ever live—was a German. Be proud of him, Fatherland; be proud of him, but also, be worthy of him!"[26]

Long accustomed to looking toward Italy and France for musical direction, Germans of the early nineteenth century were all too happy to assume a leading role for themselves. "Without being accused of national pride," asserted one writer in 1805, "the German can declare that he deserves first place among all nations in the realm of musical composition." This same observer goes on to call Mozart and Haydn "heroes, or rather, suns from whose spirits poured out harmonies across our Fatherland," who "showed all other composers of the present day the direction they should take and did take." Only since that time has the "German composer found the language in musical works for his feelings, just as in an earlier time the poets and philosophers of our nation found theirs."[27]

Haydn and Mozart were gradually coming to be perceived as national-cultural icons on a par with Goethe, Schiller, and Kant. Beethoven would soon join this elite group.

THE SYMPHONY AS A "GERMAN" GENRE

Notions of distinctively "French" and "Italian" musical styles dominated the musical discourse of seventeenth- and eighteenth-century Europe. Advocates of the two styles clashed from time to time in various political skirmishes around the French court that masqueraded as aesthetic debates, most notably during the *Querelle des Bouffons* that raged in France during the 1750s.[28] But no "German" style arose to compete with the French and Italian; at most, the German style was seen as one that amalgamated those of other nations, a "mixed" style.

German musical identity would eventually establish itself not through a style but rather through a genre: the symphony. This is due in part to the simple fact that the symphony was cultivated far more intensively in German-speaking lands during the late eighteenth and early nineteenth centuries than anywhere else. By the early nineteenth century, the percentage of new works of this kind from England and France had fallen precipitously, and Italian composers had not shown much interest in the genre since the third quarter of the eighteenth century. In a lengthy review of a symphony by Haydn, one anonymous writer noted in 1806 that "the world has the Germans to thank, above all Haydn and Mozart," for "the grand symphony for full orchestra," which "represents the highest and most radiant peak of the latest instrumental music."[29] The critic Ernst Ludwig Gerber, writing in 1813, asserted with pride (if erroneously) that Germany was now "the sole seat of this artistic genre."[30] Another anonymous critic, reviewing the development of music in Germany in the first quarter of the new century, asked: "What other nation has anything to compare with the symphonies of our Haydn and Mozart? Or the even more audacious symphonies of our great hero of instrumental music, our Beethoven?"[31]

By this criterion, the string quartet might also have been considered a German genre: it, too, was dominated by German-speaking composers by the beginning of the nineteenth century, and the triumvirate of Haydn, Mozart, and Beethoven looms equally large in this repertory. Yet the quartet was rarely perceived in national terms, and the reason for this lies in the nature of the music itself. For all its aesthetic prestige, the quartet could never transcend its fundamentally intimate tone and thus could not evoke feelings of breadth that could be described in terms of a national community.

Because of its size and timbral diversity, as noted in chapter 4, the symphony was widely heard as a projection of communal or national aspirations. Composers occasionally acknowledged these associations quite openly. Haydn's proposal to write a "National" Symphony for the French in 1789 has already been noted. Beethoven's incidental music to Goethe's drama *Egmont*, op. 84 (1810), concludes with a "Victory Symphony" (*Siegesymphonie*) that symbolizes the eventual victory of the Dutch over the occupying forces of Spain; Beethoven (following Goethe's cue in the original drama) depicts through the medium of instrumental music that which as yet can only be imagined. And Beethoven concluded the openly programmatic *Wellingtons Sieg*, op. 93 (*Wellington's Victory*, 1813), with yet another "Victory Symphony" (*Sieges-Symphonie*). The *Eroica* Symphony, originally titled *Buonaparte* but then later inscribed, more ambiguously, "To the Memory of a Great Man," leaves more to the imagination. Yet even if the identity of the "great man" remains a matter of speculation, there can be no doubt that Beethoven intended to connect this work to the national and international events unfolding outside the concert hall.

Programmatic works such as these stand outside the symphonic mainstream, however, for the large majority of symphonies from this time convey no hint of any extramusical associations. The telling question, then, is not the extent to which composers suggested the presence of political or nationalistic elements within particular works, but rather the extent to which listeners *heard* such elements in symphonies in general.

The tendency of German-speaking critics to hear the symphony as a distinctively national genre was reinforced by two other factors: its status as a "serious" form of music and its ability to act as a German counterweight to the genre of opera, long dominated by the Italians and the French. Rightly or wrongly, German critics of the late eighteenth century had established a dichotomy between "serious" German music—one that avoided crowd-pleasing displays of instrumental virtuosity and cultivated instead the rigors of polyphony—and the more "frivolous" instrumental music of other nationalities such as France and Italy.[32] Adolf Bernhard Marx, founding editor of the *Berliner Allgemeine musikalische Zeitung*, continued this tradition into the 1820s, calling Beethoven's symphonies "the exclusive property of the German people" and repeatedly distinguishing what he considered the weightiness of German music in general from the supposedly lighter arts of France and Italy.[33]

Part of Marx's motivation in promoting the symphony lay in his desire to encourage the cultivation of a genre that could offset French and Italian dominance in the field of opera. German opera, or rather the *Singspiel*— spoken plays with substantial quantities of singing—had not been without its international successes, most notably Mozart's *Die Zauberflöte*. But not until Weber's *Der Freischütz* (1821) did German musical theater offer a serious challenge to foreign repertories of the day. Still, the public never seemed capable of getting too much Spontini, Cherubini, Méhul, Paer, and above all Rossini.

By the 1820s, then, the claim of the symphony as a quintessentially German genre—indeed, the *only* truly German musical genre—was providing important ammunition in the broader cultural war against other nationalities, particularly the French. In one of many episodes in this ongoing *Kulturkampf*, the critic Gottfried Wilhelm Fink hotly contested the suggestion, put forward by a French journal and translated into German in the *Neue Zeitschrift für Musik* in 1834, that Gossec should take precedence over Haydn as the creator of the modern symphony. Fink was even more indignant that such a view should have been translated and republished without the slightest editorial commentary in a German journal. The modern symphony for large orchestra was an honor that belonged "exclusively to the German, and this honor cannot be taken from us."[34]

Fink was no isolated chauvinist. Robert Schumann would comment a few years later that "when a German speaks of symphonies, he speaks of Beethoven: the two mean one and the same for him and are inseparable. They are his joy, his pride. Just as Italy has its Naples, the Frenchman his Revolution, the Englishman his shipping, etc., so does the German have his Beethovenian symphonies. Beethoven makes him forget that he can point to no great school of painters. With Beethoven, a German has spiritually re-won the battles that Napoleon took from him. He even dares to compare him to Shakespeare."[35] And Richard Wagner would give voice to similar sentiments more than once in his early writings. Instrumental music as a whole is "the exclusive property of the German," he declared in his essay *Über deutsches Musikwesen* (*On the Essence of German Music*, 1840). In the novella *Ein glücklicher Abend* (*A Happy Evening*, 1841), Wagner has one of his characters—identified simply but tellingly as "R"—assert that although Beethoven was "no general," he saw before him, in writing the *Eroica* Symphony, "the territory within which he could accomplish the same thing that Bonaparte had achieved in the fields of Italy."[36]

In retrospect, such aggressive claims of culture can be seen to foreshadow the unfortunate tendency of governments everywhere to employ art of all kinds to political ends. The aestheticization of politics was not a new phenomenon in the twentieth century, of course: rulers had long been using the arts to project a sense of political grandeur and strength. But with the growing participation of the masses in active political life, the ability of art to persuade, mollify, and distract took on increasingly important (and sinister) implications. Walter Benjamin, Theodor Adorno, and others would later expose the perniciousness of art in the service of the state. Adorno was particularly sensitive to the ways in which music could be used to further the ends of democratic and totalitarian regimes alike in ways that were not terribly different, and he urged listeners to resist easy interpretations of any kind.

Cultural and political nationalism did not breed the symphony, nor did the symphony breed nationalism, but the two converged during the first quarter of the nineteenth century to become parts of a larger whole. Vocal forms of massed expression, like the oratorio or the operatic chorus, could also be pressed into the service of political and social causes; but in the face of the censor, texts often had to be ambiguous, settings allegorical.[37] The symphony, by contrast, offered a unique means by which to give voice to communal sentiment outside the medium of language. Without a program or text to be sung, its perceived meanings were at once both opaque and variable. More than any other art form, it provided a malleable object whose power rested in its open-endedness, its refusal to be pigeon-holed into specific boxes of signification. Beethoven's symphonies offer a clear illustration of this multivalent power: every portion of the political spectrum in Germany since the founding of the Second Reich has used these works to further its cause. From the far left to the far right, partisans of almost every persuasion have latched on to the very same works to further their own ends. In the Weimar Republic, leftists celebrated the *Eroica* as a revolutionary work, while rightists heard in it a representation of military might. The National Socialists of the Third Reich declared the Seventh a "Symphony of Nazi Victory," even as the Communists of the German Democratic Republic interpreted this same work as an anticipation of the triumph of the proletariat. And both regimes appropriated the Ninth with equal zeal, if for different reasons.[38]

What all these divergent interpretations share is the conviction that Beethoven's symphonies relate to issues of national significance, transcending any individual or region. In this respect, those who used Beethoven's symphonies to promote the cause of nationalism were continuing a tradition that extended back to the composer's own lifetime.

The symphony, in the end, was the only genre in any of the arts that German critics of the early nineteenth century chose to claim as their own. Literary genres—drama, poetry, the novel—all had their counterparts in other lands and in other tongues. The same held true for all forms of vocal music: song, opera, and oratorio were cultivated throughout Europe. Nor could Germans claim any advantage in the realm of the visual arts, in spite of the individual accomplishments of Dürer, Riemenschneider, Grünewald, and the Cranachs. The symphony alone, in spite of its origins outside Germany, was perceived as a quintessentially German genre. And it enjoyed the added advantage of being able to transcend national boundaries, unencumbered by the barriers of language. It was an art form that at once embodied and transcended nationalism.

THE PERFORMANCE POLITICS OF THE MUSIC FESTIVAL

The German perception of the symphony as a national genre was intensified by the circumstances under which the genre was performed and heard—that is, by a substantial number of musicians assembled in a public space before a large, often heterogeneous audience. In a time and place where the rights of assembly and association were severely limited, these circumstances did not go unnoticed. The concert hall, like the theater and opera house, assumed political overtones, and the symphony, the genre most closely associated with the voice of community, was heard all the more forcefully as an idealized expression of social harmony.

In this respect, the symphony during Beethoven's lifetime was not so much an object as an experience, for in the public mind symphonies existed almost exclusively through the medium of performance. Unlike a novel or even a drama, a symphony could not ordinarily be read or studied at leisure. Published scores were the exception rather than the rule. When Hoffmann wrote his review of the Fifth in 1810, he had to reconcile published parts with a four-hand piano arrangement; the first full scores of the Fifth did not appear in print until 1826. And while transcriptions for piano and various chamber ensembles helped to promulgate the symphonic repertory, no one mistook these reworkings for anything other than arrangements intended to evoke the originals, not replace them. The difference lay not only in the diminished volume and variety of sound—these were obvious enough—but also in the very nature of the listening experience. With so few performers to contemplate, and with these performers in such close proximity, listeners could not help but to associate the sound emanating from the instruments with the individuals producing those sounds. In such a close setting, moreover, performers and listeners often knew one another personally: Whatever was produced was quite visibly the result of only one individual or of a small group of individuals whose physical gestures and personal musical abilities were on ready display for all to see and hear. The collective, communal aspects of both production and reception were altogether lacking in this intimate venue. In the twentieth century, Adorno would argue along similar lines that hearing a symphony on the radio in one's home represented nothing less than the "destruction of the symphony." "No one listening to a symphony in the bourgeois-individual situation of a prviate residence," Adorno declared, "can mistake himself as bodily enfolded within the community."[39]

The social nature of the symphony in performance is captured vividly in a report from Braunschweig published in Schumann's *Neue Zeitschrift für Musik* in 1837:

The first duty of an orchestra is clearly to consider itself as a strongly articulated, united whole. Here no member has significance for himself alone. It is the duty of each to sacrifice his peculiarities insofar as they do not relate to the greater whole. This demands an agreement about the performance of significant instrumental works, be it through the dominating agency of an outstanding director or through a collective agreement of individuals. In any case, nothing purely technical may be left to chance. If this is properly attended to—moreover with great diligence—it is possible that the multitude will appear enlivened as if by *one* spirit. What results then are those unbelievable successes which in recent times have been achieved in the performance of symphonies, and especially *Beethoven's*. The cities of *Paris, Vienna, Berlin,* and *Leipzig* have distinguished themselves above all others in this respect through good performances of great instrumental pieces. The author had the occasion to experience such splendid successes in one of these cities. What inspiring energy was in the orchestra, in the public! A mutual encounter in a shared interest toward a powerful genius brought the most magnificent to light. As the stone sprays sparks when steel touches it, so the fire of inspiration sprang from these tightly packed, listening multitudes. Imagine a public that prepares itself as if for worship in order to grasp the gigantic structure of a Beethovenian symphony. It was completely so during the performance. Here a barely repressed cry of the highest wonderment and joy, or of terror, when Beethoven in his demonic way makes night of day or day of night in the quickest transitions. There experts, with score in hand, making a sign at this or that when it seizes them as with ghostly arms. And no disruption of any sort, everywhere like-minded individuals, brothers in the best sense of the word. This was brought about by an orchestra attentive with its whole soul, from its oldest to its youngest member. The author saw how—in the fourth movement of Beethoven's C-Minor Symphony, when a violin passage traveled down from the highest to the lowest like a rip—the gentlemen of the orchestra entered into a community with the public, that they exchanged glances, forgetting all customary form.[40]

Such feelings of social communion were all the more intense when a symphony was performed within the framework of a music festival—a sometimes annual, sometimes ad hoc series of concerts held over a period of two or three days, centering on the genres of the symphony and the oratorio. The earliest festival of this kind was held in 1810 and their numbers grew steadily over ensuing decades. The typical festival drew on the talents of between 200 and 500 participants and attracted some two to three thousand spectators. Its reach was regional or even transregional, beyond the city or collection of towns that ordinarily provided the musical institutions of any given locale. Aside from a professional conductor and an occasional vocal or instrumental soloist hired specifically for the occasion, the performers at these festivals consisted of amateurs who donated their services voluntarily.[41] The German music festival consciously fostered a sense of diversity among performers and audiences not available through the institution of any standing ensemble. The fact that many of the performers and audience members were strangers to one another—at least initially—gave these events a social aura altogether different from that found in a more narrow, nonfestival setting. The music festival provided a forum in which a geographically diverse citizenry could unite to perform and absorb the works of largely German composers. These events thus created, if only for two or three days, a community of participants united in their devotion to the aesthetic, a microcosm of what an imagined Germany might be, a Germany based on cultural rather than territorial power. Each festival became, in effect, a state in miniature, a multiday gathering of largely amateur musicians in the hundreds and listeners in the thousands. Music acted as both a catalyst and sublimation of the participants' political and social aspirations, and the authorities tolerated these events on the grounds that they were artistic rather than political.

Small wonder, then, that the symphony should figure so prominently in these festivals. In its size and heterogeneous timbres, it provided an aural simulacrum to the assembly itself. The established tendency to hear the symphony as the expression of a broader community strengthened the perception that performances of these works represented ritual enactments of a diverse yet coherent national state, a state that outside the concert hall could only be contemplated. That these events were organized by civic committees of private individuals who had donated their time and energies freely, rather than by the state itself, only enhanced the temporary sense of an autonomous, quasi-national, aesthetic state.

The German music festival was no passive spectacle but rather a collective undertaking whose success rested on the combined participation of its audience and performers. Contemporary accounts of these events make it clear that the social element was in many respects more important than the quality of the music making. The number and enthusiasm of those assembled—performers and listeners alike—was the yardstick by which the success of any given festival was measured. The phrase "lively participation" (*lebhafte Teilnahme*) or some variant of it figures at least once in practically every account of every such festival. The word *Teilnahme* suggests more than mere participation: it carries with it connotations of a collective activity undertaken in sympathetic cooperation. These qualities, moreover, extended beyond the concert hall, for the fact that such large numbers of individuals could gather in a public space over an extended period of time was in many respects the most significant element of these festivals. Every festival concluded with a large banquet whose official toasts offered a rare occasion for public expression on a variety of issues. Less formal social events—picnics, excursions to nearby sights, and smaller gatherings in local establishments—provided the opportunity for individuals to exchange ideas more privately with others who had traveled some distance.

In this sense, the music provided the pretext for large public gatherings that would otherwise have been banned or severely restricted. This is not to say that music making was of merely secondary interest; to the contrary, the oratorio and the symphony provided the central focus of activity for hundreds of performers and thousands of listeners. And of these genres, the symphony was perceived to mirror the ideal structure of the society to which the members of this audience aspired: a heterogeneous union of accomplished individuals, an organic community in which each distinct part contributed equally to a harmonious whole.

Professional critics were not always happy with the musical results. They complained with growing frequency about the monstrous size and poor ensemble of the amateur orchestras, particularly in the performance of symphonies. By the 1840s, musical considerations would begin to take precedence over this sense of a collective spirit, and the festivals would soon come to be dominated by professional musicians, at least in the orchestra. Profit became a driving motive, and with the gradual loosening of laws restricting the rights of assembly, the excitement of taking part in a large, voluntary gathering began to lose its distinctive quality. By the 1850s, these festivals were moving toward an altogether different form, as a series of professional concerts that happened to be held within the span of a few days. The social element remained important, but it was no longer at the core of the music making itself.

But for at least a decade after Beethoven's death, the music festival was an event in which musical and social elements were inextricably intertwined. It was an essentially amateur event, organized as a grass-roots movement, sanctioned by civic authorities but for all practical purposes produced, managed, and executed by private citizens. Organizers, participants, and critics regularly evoked the parallels with the artistic and athletic festivals of ancient Greece. The blending of beauty and a democratic social structure in ancient Greece, at least among its upper class, made the appeal of the Greek past to the German public of the early nineteenth century all the more powerful. Germans recognized that art in the Greek *polis* functioned as a means of building and reinforcing a sense of community.[42] One early commentator noted that as with the Olympics of ancient Greece, the broad base of festival participation from throughout the "fragmented German lands" would one day lead to a *Kunstnationalität*, an "art-nationality."[43] Another critic, writing in 1826, emphasized that like the Olympic and Isthmian Festivals of ancient times, the German music festival transcended circumstances of location and social standing.[44] In his *Berliner Allgemeine musikalische Zeitung*, A. B. Marx published a lengthy spoof on a recently "discovered" ancient scroll written by one Lasus of Hermione, entitled *Das Musikfest zu Ephyrae (Korinth) im dritten Jahre der 16. Olympiade* (*The Music Festival in Ephyrae (Corinth) in the Third Year of the 16th Olympiad*), a lengthy "text" with an even lengthier pseudo-scholarly "commentary." The orchestra, according to this scroll, consisted of some eight hundred performers and included virtually every instrument known to have existed in ancient Greece. From this variety of sound, according to the commentator, "we can conclude that the Greeks, too, had their symphonies."[45]

The inclination of early nineteenth-century Germans to identify themselves with the ancient Greeks played a key role in the formation of their national identity. Like the ancient Greeks, Germans of the time considered themselves a politically fragmented nation whose strength lay in its cultural patrimony. The image of a fractured society held together by its art and striving toward democracy made the appeal of Periclean Athens all the more powerful.[46] Friedrich Engels, in a review of the Lower Rhine Music Festival of 1842, observed that whereas the ancient Greeks knew their dramas only through performance, drama in the present day could be read by anyone and thus experienced individually, without the need of an assembled cast and audience. The repertory of the German music festival, Engels noted, was the only remaining art form that could still be experienced through performance alone. "And thus may the German well celebrate and cultivate music, in which he is king above all other peoples, for he alone has succeeded in bringing to light from its hidden depths the innermost secret of the human spirit and to articulate it in notes. Thus it is given only to him to sense the power of music, to understand thoroughly the language of instruments and of song."[47] Engels's chauvinism, common enough in its time, should not obscure his deeper insight into the social nature of the symphony. The very act of listening to such a work was socially formative.

Other governments had already discovered that music festivals could foster a sense of national unity. The Handel Festival in London in 1784 was very much an instrument of the crown, sponsored with the express intention of promoting a sense of national pride and unity.[48] It combined vocal and instrumental forces over a period of several days in celebration of a national hero who happened to be German by birth. The original event was such a success that a similar festival was held annually every year thereafter until 1791, with the number of participants more than doubling from around five hundred the first year to more than a thousand in the last. The leaders of the French Revolution, in turn, recognized at once the capacity of music to galvanize collective emotions. Festivals in post-revolutionary France, according to Mirabeau, were to serve the same function as in ancient Greece and Rome: to affirm, through ritual, the essential identity of rulers and the ruled. In the heady years between the storming of the Bastille and the death of Robespierre in 1794, the Directorate staged a series of ever more elaborate festivals in which music—primarily choral music—played a central role.[49]

No German ruler of the time availed himself of these models, however. Instead, the earliest German music festivals were the result of shared civic and private initiatives. The first event of this kind, held in Frankenhausen (Thuringia) on 20–21 June 1810, set the tone for later festivals throughout German-speaking lands. The key elements were the participation of leading conductors (Ludwig Spohr and Georg Friedrich Bischoff), the overwhelming predominance of amateur musicians, an audience drawn from well beyond the immediate vicinity, and an emphasis in repertory on the symphony and oratorio. The first day's program opened with Haydn's *Die Schöpfung,* while the second day concluded with a performance of Beethoven's First Symphony. The following year's festival began with Beethoven's Second and concluded with *Die Schöpfung.* After a two-year interruption because of war, the festival resumed in 1815 with a decidedly nationalistic tone under the title "A German Victory Celebration of Music," commemorating the second anniversary of the Allied victory over the French at the Battle of Leipzig in 1813. An advance call for subscriptions was issued in Leipzig's *Allgemeine musikalische Zeitung* by Carl Maria von Weber, assuring prospective attendees that the city magistrate would facilitate the accommodation of all visitors.[50] The centerpiece of the first day's concert was Ludwig Spohr's new cantata, *Das befreite Deutschland* (*Liberated Germany*), for orchestra, vocal soloists, and three choruses representing the German *Volk* and the French and Russian armies. The second day's program included Mozart's Symphony in C Major, K. 551 ("Jupiter"), with an orchestra of more than 150 musicians. The festivities concluded with the singing of a text written especially for the occasion, sung to the tune of the Prussian royal anthem, *Heil dir, im Siegerkranz* (better known in English-speaking lands as *God Save the King*). The audience, according to one contemporary report, joined in the singing on the second half of each strophe, which created a "deeply moving effect, if only by the massive size of some one thousand voices along with the instruments."[51]

The number and breadth of music festivals expanded rapidly in subsequent years, with gatherings in such cities as Nürnberg, Magdeburg, Königsberg, Elbing, Breslau, Münster, Zerbst, and Halle. Bischoff was a fixture at many events, participating in festivals held in Hildesheim (1817), Hannover (1817), Helmstedt (1820), Quedlinburg (1820, 1824), Bückeburg (1821), Pyrmont (1825), and Halberstadt (1833). But by far the largest, most successful, and longest-running of all such undertakings was the Lower Rhine Music Festival. First held in 1818 and continuing to the present day, it rotated during its early decades among the cities of Düsseldorf, Cologne, Aachen, and Elberfeld. The program and participants were set each year by a governing board consisting of municipal authorities and private citizens, a cross-section of merchants, bankers, industrialists, attorneys, and other leading members of the affluent bourgeoisie. The number of performers rose steadily, from roughly 300 in the early years (125 orchestra players, 168 choristers) to more than 400 by the mid-1830s (153 orchestra players, 266 choristers).[52]

The 1821 festival, held in Cologne, attracted 1,550 spectators for the first day's program, which featured Friedrich Schneider's oratorio *Das Weltgericht* (*The Last Judgment*) and 1,782 for the second day's concert, which included Beethoven's Fifth Symphony.[53] A pamphlet published for the festival held in Elberfeld in June 1827 (three months after Beethoven's death) lists at least some of the audience members by name, profession, and place of residence.[54] While most of the guests came from nearby locales in the Rhine-Ruhr region, a substantial number traveled considerable distances to take part in the festivities. The large majority of these individuals are identified as "merchants," coming from as far away as Hamburg, Frankfurt, Braunschweig, Fulda, Nürnberg, Gera (Saxony), Brandenburg, and Tyrolia, with half a dozen from Berlin and more than a dozen from distant Bohemia. The audience also included students from Bremen, Lübeck, Harburg, Trier, and Altenburg (Saxony); a lawyer from Frankfurt; painters from Magdeburg, Berlin, and Vienna; an architect from Trier; a postal inspector from Münster; a musical instrument dealer from Saxony; a notary from Koblenz; a wagoner ("Fuhrmann") from Montjoie, another from Gladbach; and half a dozen representatives of the nobility—barons and counts—mostly local, but one from Berlin.

The social, professional, and geographic diversity of this gathering is striking. Few if any collective enterprises outside the church could claim such variety. The qualitative difference between music festival concerts and ordinary concerts becomes all the more pronounced when we remind ourselves that at the beginning of the nineteenth century the German-speaking populace was mostly rural, its urban centers not very large. In 1800, Berlin had a population of about 173,000, only a fraction of the size of Paris (581,000) or London (1.1 million). At the beginning of the nineteenth century, only sixty-four cities in all of German-speaking Europe could boast a population of more than 10,000.[55]

Single performances could at times be enormous. Ferdinand Ries's production of Beethoven's Ninth in 1825 drew on a combined orchestra and chorus of some four hundred musicians.[56] Because of inadequate rehearsal time, the scherzo could not be performed. But on the basis of the work's other three movements, one anonymous critic heard in this performance a reflection of society as a whole:

> It seems to us that the master wanted to represent in these instrumental movements . . . disorder, the forces and impulses of great multitudes—for example, at a popular festival [*Volksfest*]—in which at times a powerful voice clears a path here and there, but soon all collapses in confusion, frenzy, and wild jubilation, until at last the singer succeeds in calming this tumult. All follow his summons, and now begins the Song of Joy, to which the whole populace [*Volk*] adds its voice in agreement [*einstimmt*]. The melody of this song can make its effect only when it is sung by the greatest possible multitude.[57]

Within this context, it is scarcely surprising that the Ninth would soon become the ne plus ultra of the music festival's symphonic repertory. This is not merely because the finale introduces a chorus, thereby uniting instrumental and vocal forces, but also, as the anonymous reviewer suggests, because of the way in which these forces are brought together. The "Ode to Joy" melody emerges only after themes from all three previous movements have been rejected. It is first heard in the lower strings and gradually draws other instruments in, one by one, moving higher and higher in range, persuading each to join forces, as it were, in the common cause of the theme. But only after yet another hurdle—the intensified return of the dissonant fanfare that had opened the movement—do the voices finally enter, vanquishing once and for all the doubts and torments of what had gone before. This process of confrontation (the dissonant fanfare), rejection (of the earlier themes), counterproposal (the "Ode to Joy" melody in its instrumental form), and fulfillment (the addition of the voices) reflects the kind of struggle for social unity that dominated German society at the time. The "Ode to Joy" melody itself was perceived as a folk song or "social song" (*geselliges Lied*)—that is, as a song to be sung in a sociable setting and of a character designed to promote feelings of fraternity. One review of a performance of the Ninth in 1827, under the direction of Felix Mendelssohn, notes that the double fugue combining the "chorale-like" melody of "Seid umschlungen, Millionen" with the "folk song" to "Freude, schöner Götterfunken" manifests the "increasing participation of society" within an ever-larger whole—manifests, in effect, the very creation of a state.[58]

The Symphony as Democracy

The tendencies to interpret both music festivals and symphonies in political terms are readily evident in Wolfgang Robert Griepenkerl's fictional *Das Musikfest, oder Die Beethovener* (*The Music Festival, or The Beetho-*

venians) of 1838. Griepenkerl (1810–68) was a novelist, journalist, and music critic, one of Berlioz's earliest and most enthusiastic champions in Germany.[59] He based *Das Musikfest* loosely on the program and participants of the music festival held in his native Braunschweig in July of 1836. The conductors on that occasion had included Friedrich Schneider, Heinrich Marschner, and Ludwig Spohr; the festival had opened with Handel's *Messiah* (sung in German) and concluded with Beethoven's *Eroica* Symphony. In Griepenkerl's fictional festival, the first day's program was to have presented Beethoven's Third and Ninth symphonies (conducted by Spontini and Mendelssohn, respectively), the second day Handel's *Messiah* (conducted by Friedrich Schneider). But the festival never gets that far. Two merchants and a journalist—all philistines—successfully conspire to undermine the affair, and the rehearsals of Beethoven's symphonies lead to a series of tragi-comic events that derail the festival altogether. In the end, one of the musicians, a bass player, goes mad and kills himself, driven over the edge by the impact of the rehearsal of Beethoven's Ninth. Pfeiffer, the town's organist and clandestine radical, dies while improvising on themes from Beethoven's symphonies. The local authorities arrest or drive into flight the remaining principal characters who had set the festival in motion in the first place—which is to say, those who had sought to promote Beethoven's symphonies.

Griepenkerl's novel was successful enough to merit a second edition in 1841, with an engraved song written especially for the occasion by no less a figure than Giacomo Meyerbeer. The song's text is from an inscription that figures in the novel itself, extolling the hope of future times. Meyerbeer's setting moves from slow gloom ("The past is a deep trough," in G minor) to faster hope ("The present") and concludes ("The future") with the opening theme transformed to G major on the words "Hope dawns red in the morning." The novel itself lies squarely in the tradition of Jean Paul: Buffoonery and tragedy interweave through multiple subplots, and we hear many narrative voices, the identities of which are at times purposefully obscure. The tone of *Das Musikfest* veers unpredictably from the grotesquely comic to the deeply serious. Running through all this are a series of substantive discussions on the nature of music and contemporaneous musical culture. For all its ribald humor, the novel conveys an intense and immediate relationship between the culture of music and the culture of the state. Beethoven's symphonies, particularly the Third and Ninth, are viewed as politically revolutionary works. The novel's central figure, a count named Adalbert, at one point calls music festivals "national festivals" and discourses on their social import, using the same terminology that was being widely applied at the time to both the symphony and the state. The individual participating in such an event "learns to subordinate himself to the great whole. The proud feeling of a self-conquered egoism unites thousands. Is this not something beautiful, a true blossoming of humanity?" Elsewhere, Adalbert argues that the different instruments of a symphony can be imagined to represent "many different voices of the *Volk*, united in their grand understanding of sounds, but further yet through the common interest in a powerful, circumpolar idea (the theme)."[60] An open rehearsal of the first movement of Beethoven's Third Symphony must be stopped in the middle of the development section because of the music's overwhelming effect on the audience, which gives voice to its collective ecstasy. Responding to the extended passage of syncopation (measures 248–83), Pfeiffer, the organist-radical, loudly proclaims that "this was not Shakespeare, . . . this was Pindar, the dithyrambic, storming Pindar of the nineteenth century. He sings of the struggles of his brothers, struggles that have not yet achieved their goal." Elsewhere, we learn that Pfeiffer has marked this passage in his copy of the score with the words "Neunzehntes Jahrhundert" ("Nineteenth Century").[61]

The Ninth Symphony elicits even more intense reactions. Pfeiffer, while listening to a rehearsal, declares the first movement to be "the struggle of Old and New, the portentous battle of giants and titans in our day." And at the moment in the finale when the chorus first intones the words "Freude, schöner Götterfunken," the Vicar—a mordant, cynical character—leaps to his feet and shouts, enigmatically: "Whoever knows what an open whore this disguised 'Freude' of Schiller's was by birth, let him seize it!"[62] A terse footnote provides the answer: "It was freedom [*Freiheit*]." Censorship, the Vicar implies with his bizarre outburst, had prevented Schiller from expressing the true object of this ode and still compels the Vicar to speak in enigmatic terms. Thus was born the persistent and seemingly ineradicable myth that Schiller's *An die Freude* was at heart an ode to freedom rather than joy. Not a shred of evidence exists to support any such intention on Schiller's part, but the idea would continue to circulate, culminating in Leonard Bernstein's historic performance of the Ninth Symphony shortly after the fall of the Berlin Wall in 1989, in which the word *Freude* was indeed replaced with *Freiheit*.[63]

That a radical (Pfeiffer), an aristocrat (Adalbert), and a cleric (the Vicar) could share a common view of Beethoven's symphonies testifies to capacity of this music to elicit such cosmically synthesizing interpretations. All three consider these works to have ushered in an era in which art is a matter no longer for the individual, but for society as a whole. These symphonies, according to Adalbert, are "nine awesome movers of thundering time," and they "express the hidden, wild mainsprings of the century." Beethoven's symphonies anticipated the Revolution of 1830 in France, "the first battlecry" of a great social transformation. With Beethoven, Adalbert declares, "art has ceased to be a matter of play."

There was a time when lonely dreams by the murmuring brook, the boring chatter of the turtle-doves, and a tortured form created by the sweat of the brow all passed for true art. This time has passed. That ridiculous artistic absolutism of the individual has reached its endpoint. The great public life . . . is now the true studio of the artist. Here he should follow the pulse of a significant crisis. . . . Art is thus no longer the little bell that tolls for the isolated, condemned individual, but rather the great bell of the nations that resonates through the centuries.[64]

Pfeiffer comes to much the same conclusion on his own. For the second edition of his novel, Griepenkerl added a prefatory selection of "Papers from the Estate of the Organist Pfeiffer." These texts have little to do with music; instead, they return again and again to the imperative of bridging the divide between the individual and society. Mankind can do this through the agencies of (in ascending order) religion, philosophy, and art—a reshuffling of Hegel's hierarchy that now privileges art over philosophy and religion. And it is music that is most readily capable of realizing the ideals of art.

The novel's several discussions of Beethoven's symphonies repeatedly return to the quality of "humor"—what we today would now be more inclined to call irony. Pfeiffer and Adalbert both emphasize the ability of this music to juxtapose seemingly incompatible elements in a compelling manner. Such juxtapositions, according to Pfeiffer, mirror "the great panorama of the world," in which "all things great and small, fast and slow, weak and strong" take on a unified, tangible form. Adalbert finds in such contrasts "the true goal of art," a synthesis (or at least a temporary illusion of a synthesis) of the finite and the infinite.[65] He goes on to compare Beethoven to Shakespeare and Jean Paul, both of whose writings were renowned for their sudden and striking contrasts. Haydn is a dove, Beethoven an eagle, and the difference in hearing their music is comparable to the sensation of ascending into the clouds on two very different sets of wings. In the case of Haydn, musical contrasts are not presented with sufficient abruptness: "One holds on anxiously to illusory boundaries, one wants to smooth things out and build bridges across those chasms over which one should be floating on the wings of an eagle."[66]

In Griepenkerl's *Das Musikfest*, these idealized views of Beethoven's symphonies all lead to disaster in the realm of actual life. The novel's plot is in effect the story of a failed revolution, one that incorporates a critique of its very premise: that instrumental music could serve as a catalyst for social change. Things end just as badly for the philistines plotting against "the Beethovenians." The merchants are both sentenced to prison for six months and compelled to bear the costs of the festival they had successfully scuttled. The journalist is left unpunished, "in consideration of his stupidity and harmlessness." Adalbert and the Vicar go into exile. In the briefest of epilogues, we learn that nothing is heard of the pair for many years, and only later are they said to have been sighted in France and England, "under the most mysterious of circumstances." But their trace, as the final sentence of the novel informs us, "disperses—wherever the reader wishes it." The spirit of the Beethovenians is at once nowhere and everywhere. The revolution, if it is to continue, must be carried forward by listeners.

By the end of Beethoven's lifetime, the composer's admirers had invested his music—and specifically, his symphonies—with a national significance he had neither sought nor cultivated. Beethoven's funeral oration, written by his friend the poet Franz Grillparzer, opens with these words:

> Standing by the grave of him who has passed away we are in a manner the representatives of an entire nation, of the whole German people, mourning the loss of the one highly acclaimed half of that which was left us of the departed splendor of our native art, of the fatherland's full spiritual bloom. There yet lives—and may his life be long!—the hero of verse in German speech and tongue [i.e., Goethe]; but the last master of tuneful song, the organ of soulful concord, the heir and amplifier of Handel and Bach's and Haydn and Mozart's immortal fame is now no more, and we stand weeping over the riven strings of the harp that is hushed.[67]

The idea that an artist should be capable of uniting an entire people was remarkable enough in its time. That this artist should also be one whose principal metier was not language but instrumental music makes this public reaction all the more remarkable.

Listening to Form: The Refuge of Absolute Music

THE POLITICIZATION of instrumental music—or, to be more precise, the politicization of listening to instrumental music—was a new phenomenon during Beethoven's lifetime, and it intensified steadily over the decades that followed. The symphony, heard as an idealized expression of social unity and political democracy, came to be perceived in increasingly wider circles as a means by which to criticize the inherently particularistic and authoritarian nature of a politically fractured Germany dominated by the nobility and aristocracy. With a gradual loosening of censorship and surveillance in practice if not in principle, critics felt increasingly emboldened to communicate their interpretations of these works through the prism of politics. That Griepenkerl's novel could make its way into an expanded second edition in 1841 says much about the growing readiness of critics to speak out against the political status quo.

Not coincidentally, it was during the 1830s that critics first began to use political metaphors to describe the musical landscape. Robert Schumann, in an unsigned review published in 1834, proposed multiple ways of conceiving of the musical "factions" and "parties" he considered so characteristic of the day. He proposed dividing the musical spectrum in various ways: "Liberal, Moderate, and Legitimist," "Romantic, Modern, and Classic," or "Right, Middle, and Left." "On the right sit the elders," he observed, "the contrapuntists, the antiquarians and folklorists, the antichromaticists. On the left sit the youths, the Phrygian caps, the despisers of form [*Formenverächter*], and the genially cheeky [*Genialitäts-frechen*], among whom the Beethovenians stand out as a faction in their own right. In the *juste-milieu* waver young and old alike."[1] Schumann's vocabulary is thoroughly political: the "Phrygian caps" are the hats worn by liberated slaves in ancient Greece; more recently the term had been used by extension to indicate enthusiasts of the French Revolution. The term *juste-milieu* evokes even more recent events in France: it was the rallying cry for the supporters of Louis-Philippe, the new king who had come to power in the wake of the July Revolution and was seeking to negotiate a political strategy between the extremes of left and right.

By the early 1850s, such metaphors had become commonplace. Ernst Gottschald's lengthy review-essay on Schumann's Second Symphony, for example, teems with political terminology and innuendo. He calls the fundamental idea of the work "the victory-crowned struggle of a particularized individuality" that has achieved an "inward coalescence with the spiritual generality in which all egoistical limitations are destroyed." By the end of the symphony, this individuality, which had once been separated from the world by self-absorption, now dwells in "the empire of liberty, equality, and fraternity." Gottschald acknowledges that some readers might be repulsed by such "radical-democratic-political-musical criticism," but he proceeds to argue, through a close analysis of the score, just how the symphony reveals this fundamental idea.[2]

Differences in musical ideology could be traced at least in part to matters of musical style. The "antichromaticists," as Schumann suggested, were more inclined toward the conservative, chromaticists toward the progressive. But the more basic distinction between right and left centered on assumptions about the very function of music and its relationship to the world beyond it. Franz Brendel, editor of the progressive *Neue Zeitschrift für Musik*, described the "reform" party as one that sought to make art an "expression and mirror" of its time, an agency of change in real life. The great composers of the past, from this perspective, were "superseded," significant only insofar as they had "prepared the way for the present." The conservatives, by contrast, insisted that art was immune to the vicissitudes of time, untouched by what Brendel called "the storms of history." This party was interested only in the "eternal and infinite," whereas reformists saw the development of "all fields of life, of the state, of science, as a great Whole."[3] Brendel argued that the musician had become "too accustomed to regarding his art as a separate sphere," giving insufficient attention to "progress" and "freedom." As an instance of this, Brendel cites the tendency to view music as an "international language" as having fostered a sense of indifference toward the national state and its people; political change could not be promoted through cosmopolitanism. Brendel considered music to be threatened by "empty formalism" and looked forward to a new approach to issues of musical content, the outpouring of "fully formed individuals" who happened to express themselves through the medium of music.[4]

The belief that art in general and music in particular could function as a vehicle of political and social change permeates the writings of Richard Wagner, especially those written in the wake of the revolutions of 1848–49: *Die Kunst und die Revolution* (*Art and Revolution*, 1849), *Das Kunstwerk der Zukunft* (*The Artwork of the Future*, 1850), and *Oper und Drama* (*Opera and Drama*, 1851). For Wagner, art was the only genuine means by which humanity could be guided toward its "true direction," an image of its future.[5] Beethoven's symphonies represented a series of steps toward the realization of a complete synthesis of all arts, though Wagner would of course reserve to himself the ultimate realization of the all-embracing *Gesamtkunstwerk*. The important point for our purposes here, however, is his readiness—and the readiness of his followers—to hear Beethoven's symphonies within the context of the struggle for social and political reform.

Wagner furthered his agenda by sharpening the distinction between politically engaged and disengaged instrumental music, calling the former the "music of the future" (*Zukunftsmusik*), the latter "absolute music" (*absolute Musik*), a brilliant turn of phrase that plays on the multiple meaning of "absolute."[6] The term evokes at once the traditions of the idealist aesthetic, with its notions of an all-embracing, infinite Absolute, even while implicitly disparaging a music that could also be considered isolated, remote, and disengaged from the world of the here and now.

Like Hoffmann, who some forty years before had struggled to distinguish Beethoven from his predecessors even while acknowledging their accomplishments, Wagner was compelled to acknowledge the stature of an existing body of music (the symphonies of Beethoven) even while laying the groundwork for a new and even greater repertory (the Wagnerian *Gesamtkunstwerk*). Unable to deny Beethoven supremacy in the realm of the symphony, Wagner declared that Beethoven himself had promulgated the end of the genre with the Ninth Symphony. Through his incorporation of words into a traditionally wordless form of music, Beethoven (so Wagner argued) had acknowledged that instrumental music had exhausted its expressive potential. Composers who continued to write symphonies were ignoring history and its inevitable dialectic:

> As soon as Beethoven had written his last symphony, every musical guild could patch and stuff as much as it liked in its effort to create a man of absolute music. But it was just this and nothing more: a shabby, patched and stuffed bogeyman. No sensate, natural man could come out of such a workshop any longer. After Haydn and Mozart, a Beethoven could and had to appear. The spirit of music necessarily demanded him, and without waiting, there he was. Who would now be to Beethoven that which he was to Haydn and Mozart in the realm of absolute music? The greatest genius would be capable of nothing more here, precisely because the spirit of absolute music no longer has need of him.[7]

Ideas of the inaccessible infinite held no appeal for Wagner. In his discussion of Beethoven's Fifth Symphony, in fact, he explicitly evokes E.T.A. Hoffmann's notion of "infinite longing" in order to reverse it. Comparing Beethoven to Columbus, who in seeking a passage to India discovered a new world, Wagner praises the composer for his ability to "steer his ship out of the ocean of infinite longing into the harbor of fulfillment" in the Fifth Symphony, even if this particular work does not represent what would eventually prove to be the pinnacle of the composer's symphonic achievements.[8] Whereas Hoffmann had sought truth in a striving for the infinite, the Absolute, Wagner embraces a more Hegelian approach that traces the realization of the Absolute through the progressively higher accomplishments of the human mind.

Proclamations about the end of the symphony and the growing politicization of music criticism elicited sharp responses from traditionalists. Given the long-standing association of the symphony with the voice of the masses, the political right had little choice but to deny altogether the premise that instrumental music and politics could be so closely connected. "Is there a republican or monarchical harmony or melody?" asked the composer and critic Eduard Krüger in 1848. Musicians, Krüger conceded, were influenced by the revolutionary events of the day along with everyone else, but did this mean that the "republican in a republican state will blow the trombone better than a monarchist?" For Krüger, art would inevitably reflect life, but not necessarily its ephemeral vacillations.[9] Other conservative critics joined in the attempt to insulate music even from the turbulence of the political world. For the critic and theorist Johann Christian Lobe, the listening public wished to "forget the present for at least a few hours in 'true' music" and "save itself" from "the fight, the vicissitudes, partisanship, cares, and troubles of the day." Lobe wanted nothing to do with "so-called democratic or political music of any kind." He took Griepenkerl to task for wanting to "amputate the wings of Pegasus" in order to "turn him into a cavalry horse" leading a band of "democratic irregulars." He further criticized Wagner as a "republican," as someone "more passionate about politics than art" and whose art, as a consequence, suffered from "one-sidedness" and "lack of perspective."[10]

But by far the most eloquent and influential of all appeals against the politicization of listening came from the pen of Eduard Hanslick (1825–1904). He was not yet thirty years old and still a relatively obscure jurist and part-time music critic when he published his *Vom Musikalisch-Schönen: Ein Beitrag zur Revision der Ästhetik der Tonkunst* (*On the Musically Beautiful: A Contribution to the Revision of the Aesthetics of Music*) in 1854. He would revise this treatise through no fewer than ten subsequent editions over the next forty-eight years. The argument is brief and engagingly presented. Hanslick maintains that beauty in music resides not in any presumed emotional content, but rather in its form alone. He acknowledges that music is readily capable of arousing emotions, and even allows that these emotions can be described metaphorically, but he insists that "sounding forms in motion constitute the sole and exclusive content and object of music."[11] Although he uses the term "absolute music" only once in this treatise (*reine, absolute Tonkunst*), he embraces the very idea that Wagner had scorned: an autonomous music clearly separated from all that lies outside it, including all other arts. Beauty in music, Hanslick insists, is intrinsically and specifically musical. And music is unique among all the arts in its fusion of form and content: Its form *is* its content. Hanslick likens music in its purest manifestation to the arabesque, an abstract and often highly intricate design that makes no attempt to represent any object outside of itself.[12]

Hanslick's approach is in some respects similar to that of Kant, who more than sixty years before had assigned instrumental music and wallpaper to the same aesthetic category of abstract patterns without representational qualities. But whereas Kant struggled with the question of whether music belonged to the "agreeable" or the "fine" arts—he finally declared that music was either the highest of the agreeable arts or the lowest of the fine arts—Hanslick associates it squarely with *Geist*, that is, with the mind, the spirit, and thus squarely with the fine arts, the arts of beauty. He carefully avoids the question of just how this could be so, falling back repeatedly on the notion of music's material uniqueness and insisting that the forms of music (melody, harmony, rhythm) are *geistfähiges Material*, material capable of being engaged by the *Geist*.

Hanslick's treatise soon became the manifesto of musical formalism, the rallying point for all those who sought to protect instrumental music—above all, Beethoven's symphonies—against encroachments from the world of politics. The musical work, by this line of thought, is autonomous and nonreferential; while it may be susceptible to differing interpretations, these perceptions have nothing to do with the work's true essence. Listening, Hanslick repeatedly reminds, is a "merely" subjective activity that is itself shaped by the subjectivity of performance. Listening is thus twice removed from the essence of the fixed object, the musical work: first by the interpretation of the performers, and second by the interpretation of the listener's own mind.[13] The only immutable object (and thus the only object worthy of our attention) is the musical work itself, presumably in the form of the composer's score. Most listening, Hanslick insists, is "pathological," based on physiological responses to the sensuous immediacy of the music. The notion of active ("aesthetic") listening is granted in passing in chapter 5 of the treatise but not developed in any detail. He maintains that "truly aesthetic listening is an art," yet he characterizes it primarily in terms of what it is not, that is, pathological.[14]

But Hanslick could not entirely avoid confronting the role of the listener in the construction of musical beauty, and he addresses the issue, albeit obliquely, in the very last paragraph of the entire treatise. The "spiritual content" of the musical work "unites the beautiful in music with all other great and beautiful ideas" in the *Gemüth* of the listener.[15] Hanslick carefully avoids using the term *Geist* here: *Gemüth* is a close synonym but does not enjoy the same philosophical pedigree, and it connotes a rather less active force than *Geist*. An individual's *Gemüth* encompasses the mind but also includes elements of disposition and feeling. As long as he was talking about composers, Hanslick had no hesitation to speak of *Geist*; but this was not a faculty he was prepared to acknowledge in the listener. And in this particular passage, Hanslick ascribes agency to the "spiritual content" of the music rather than to the listener. Just how this transpires, just how musical beauty ultimately connects to other forms of beauty, is never explained: it seems to occur within the *Gemüth* of the listener, yet the listener's role in the process remains largely passive.

What makes this particular assertion all the more remarkable is that it served as the concluding pronouncement of the entire treatise in its second edition. Having ignored or minimized the role of the listener up until this point, Hanslick suddenly brings the listener onto center stage in the treatise's final sentence. Small wonder, then, that he should delete this sentence altogether and close the third and all subsequent editions with a reiteration of his conviction that music is "a free creation of the *Geist* using *geistfähiges Material.*" Composers used *Geist* in composing music, but Hanslick assiduously sidesteps the question of whether audiences might do the same in listening to it.

The original ending of the first edition is even more curious. It followed immediately after Hanslick's pronouncements on the *Gemüth* of the listener and strengthened still further the connections of musical beauty with beauty in general. Hanslick cut this entire passage for the second (1858) and all later editions of his book:

> It is not merely and absolutely through its own intrinsic beauty that music affects the listener, but rather at the same time as a sounding image of the great motions of the universe. Through profound and secret connections to nature, the meaning of tones is elevated high above the tones themselves, allowing us to perceive at the same time the infinite in works of human talent. Because the elements of music—sound, tone, rhythm, loudness, softness—are to be found throughout the entire universe, so does one find anew in music the entire universe.[16]

The significance of this passage and its subsequent deletion can scarcely be overestimated. Hanslick's affirmation of the idealist aesthetic might easily have been written half a century before by Schelling, yet it provides the climax of his entire "revision" of the aesthetics of music. Deleting this passage was no minor editorial change, no mere tightening up of the text. In canceling the peroration of his argument, Hanslick would in effect change the nature of the argument itself.

Nor was this deletion a sudden change of heart. Hanslick canceled other appeals to idealism in preparing the second edition of *Vom Musikalisch-Schönen*. Immediately before the work's most frequently quoted assertion, that "sounding forms in motion constitute the sole and exclusive content and object of music," he had originally offered a line of thought directly connecting his argument to the traditions of aesthetic idealism. The passage in question (with the later deletions shown below in italics) reads:

> If we now ask what is to be expressed with this tone-material, then the answer is: musical ideas. A musical idea brought to its appearance is already autonomous beauty; it is already an end in itself and in no way primarily a medium or material for the representation of feelings and thoughts, *even if it is capable of possessing, at the same time, a high degree of symbolic significance in its reflection of the great laws of the world, which is something we find in all artistic beauty.* Sounding forms in motion are the sole and exclusive content and object of music.[17]

In its original form, Hanslick's pronouncement implicitly sanctions—or at the very least does not preclude—the validity of programmatic and even political interpretations of "absolute" works. At least one important early reader of *Vom Musikalisch-Schönen* sensed a fundamental incompatibility between even this oblique empowerment of the listener and the treatise's underlying premise of aesthetic autonomy. At the end of an otherwise laudatory review that appeared shortly after the book's original publication, Hanslick's friend Robert Zimmerman asked why the author should have concluded his treatise by "invalidating" the "golden truth" of his central thesis with the idea that music might also be a sounding reflection of the motions of the universe. Zimmerman surmised that in characterizing the opinions he sought to discredit, Hanslick had been unconsciously overwhelmed by those very ideas.[18] Hanslick would later dedicate the second and most subsequent editions of *Vom Musikalisch-Schönen* to Zimmerman, and he took his friend's closing criticism to heart in making revisions for that second edition.

But Zimmerman was too quick to equate idealism with the aesthetic of expressive content. The idealist aesthetic, after all, does not preclude the use of programs, programmatic titles, or programmatic interpretations of any kind, on the grounds that the specific is invariably a manifestation of some broader, more general idea. Conversely, the reflection of an abstract ideal is not inconsistent with the representation of a specific object or event. But this kind of approach validated program music, including the dreaded notion of political interpretation even of works that presented the listener with no program of any kind.

By this point, however, musical (and political) discourse had become so polarized that both the musical "left" and "right" either failed to see or chose to ignore the essential compatibility of formalist and idealist theories of content. Without citing Hanslick by name, A. B. Marx, for example, conceded in 1859 that the "interplay of tones is the primordial essence of music [*Urmusik*]; it has always been and will always be the mother earth from which everything that lives in music draws its life's power, its existence." Marx went on to insist, however, that man cannot

> play endlessly and without a goal. Above all, he seeks himself in the play, the play should be *his* play; it should have the imprint, the expression of *his* being. Even in the play of tones, his fantasy seeks the feeling of his being. . . . It is precisely because man gives artistic form to the constraining relationships and moods of real life that he feels himself to be master of this self-created world. And in this transfigured reflection of the real world, he considers himself redeemed and free.[19]

Marx's comments are entirely consistent with Hanslick's own observation in the first edition of his treatise that the fantasy of the listener "gladly relates the ideas of art to its own human life of the soul" and perceives the motions of music in such a way that this fantasy can "ascend from there onward to an intimation of the Absolute."[20] But most writers of the day—including Hanslick himself—seem to have been more interested in polemics than in rapprochement, and many of Hanslick's opponents drew on idealism to attack his formalism.[21] It was surely with some malice that Gotthold Kunkel, reviewing Joachim Raff's thoroughly programmatic *Lenore* Symphony in 1875, quoted Hanslick's idealistic (and by now deleted) final paragraph in its entirety as a justification for programmatic titles in works of purely instrumental music.[22]

Had Hanslick's opponents known his earlier music criticisms, they would have taken even greater glee in attacking his later position. His writings from the late 1840s are at times indistinguishable from those being written at the same time by Brendel. Hanslick openly acknowledged the political element not only in the operatic repertory of his day—he cites Auber's *La Muette de Portici*, Meyerbeer's *Les Hugenots*, and Wagner's *Rienzi* as cases in point—but in instrumental music as well. "Do not Hungarian sabers rattle in the finale of Schubert's C-Major Symphony? And when you play Chopin's mazurkas, do you not feel the mournful, oppressive air of Ostrolenka?"[23] At the height of the Viennese insurrection in March 1848, Hanslick had declared music, religion, and philosophy to be "merely different refractions of the same ray of light," asserting that "the works of great composers are more than mere music; they are mirror images of the *philosophical*, *religious*, and *political* world views of their time. Does not the proud majesty and the tormented skepticism of German philosophy suffuse the late works of Beethoven and the works of Berlioz?"[24]

In and of themselves, such observations are unremarkable because they are so thoroughly typical of their time and place. Only later, in the wake of the Revolutions of 1848–49, would Hanslick embrace the formalism with which he would become so closely identified. The motivation for this change was not entirely abstract. Hanslick's memoirs, published in 1894, are quite revealing in this regard. He portrays himself at one point as being "swept up" in a moment of mob violence in the streets of Vienna in October of 1848 and witnessing the corpse of the assassinated minister of war, Latour, hung up on a lamppost.

> The mob had lighted the gas flame above the head of the murder victim and shouted and hooted around the corpse, at times setting it swinging back and forth with a push. Shuddering inwardly, I forced my way out of the crowd, which by now filled the entire square, and I ran almost unconsciously back to my abode. There I lighted my lamp and opened a volume of Goethe, in order to wash myself clean from what had happened.[25]

For Hanslick, art offered a refuge from politics, and his later aesthetic theory would shore up the bulwark of that refuge. By placing "purity" at the center of his aesthetics, he could effectively limit music to an entirely self-referential sphere. No compositional "intentions" could be read into or out of music. "Whatever does not appear in the music," the Hanslick flatly declared in *Vom Musikalisch-Schönen*, "is simply not there, and whatever appears there has ceased to be an intention."[26] By focusing his attention almost exclusively on the composer and the work, Hanslick effectively ignored the long-standing issues of how the mind might overcome the gulf between subjectivity and objectivity. The perceiving mind, the listener, has been eliminated from the picture.

With Hanslick's treatise, the notion of instrumental music as a vehicle of ideas had come full circle since its emergence in the 1790s. In the span of little more than sixty years, this art had gone from being perceived as a vague "language of emotions" to being perceived as a vehicle—*the* vehicle—for the apprehension of the Absolute and, back again, by the middle of the nineteenth century, to an art form whose significance was entirely self-contained and self-referential.

The vast majority of Hanslick's contemporaries, however, dismissed his theories. The perception of music as a vehicle of transcendent ideas—and not merely musical ones—would continue to flourish throughout the remainder of the nineteenth century and well into the twentieth. Most of the early published responses to *Vom Musikalisch-Schönen* were negative, not because the musical "left" held a monopoly on the press, but because Hanslick's separation of music from the act of listening was so extreme.[27] Yet Hanslick is conventionally portrayed as a musical conservative, fighting a rearguard action against the progressive notions of Liszt, Wagner, and their followers. In point of fact he assumed a far more radical stance in the realm of aesthetics than anyone of his generation. His deletions at the end of both the first and second editions of *Vom Musikalisch-Schönen* reflect the emergence of a new and quite radical attitude toward listening.

Music was no longer revelation, a means of glimpsing the Absolute, but an art whose self-contained beauty defied connections to anything and everything other than itself. While the idea of musical formalism can be traced back to Schiller and beyond, *Vom Musikalisch-Schönen* proposed a far more aggressive and comprehensive application of this principle than had ever been proposed before. Hanslick himself called his treatise "a contribution to the *revision* of musical aesthetics," conceding and even calling attention to its contrarian status in musical thought.

In time, Hanslick's ideas would gain the status of orthodoxy. The doctrine of "art for art's sake" and the growing prestige of formalist criticism helped to pave the way for a mode of listening in which "absolute" music, unburdened by the demands of representation, came to be invested with a quality of formal purity lacking in all other kinds of music. By 1877, Walter Pater could famously declare that "all art constantly aspires towards the condition of music."[28] Hanslick's notion of formalism, an autonomous beauty that exists in and of itself, would enjoy still greater prestige in the middle decades of the twentieth century. By 1950, the aestheticization of politics had become so extreme that many in the world of music—listeners as well as composers—embraced the idea of a music transcending all time and place, existing beyond the reach of manipulation, distortion, and ideology. So much music had been appropriated, abused, or suppressed in the recent past—one need think only of Nazi Germany's attitudes toward Wagner, Mendelssohn, and Bruckner, or the Soviet Union's shameful treatment of Prokofiev and Shostakovich—that the perception of instrumental music as a domain transcending the all-too-worldly realm of politics became the standard mode of listening, at least in the Western world. Writing in the wake of World War II, the eminent composer and critic Virgil Thomson pointed with no small degree of irritation to Beethoven's Third, Fifth, and Ninth Symphonies as having given rise to what he called the "editorial symphony," works with a "point of view."[29] And we can understand the longevity of the apocryphal anecdote about Arturo Toscanini, who, asked during the war years if the first movement of the *Eroica* Symphony had any connection to dictators past or present, is said to have replied: "Some say this is Napoleon, some Hitler, some Mussolini. For me it is simply Allegro con brio." The delight with which this pronouncement would be repeated reflects a genuine and widespread (if naïve) pride in music's ability to rise above even the most powerful figures of world history.

The Cold War enhanced the prestige of "absolute" music still further. Eastern bloc regimes denounced "empty formalism" in all the arts, including music, and the West embraced the idea of "pure" music with corresponding zeal. The 1970 bicentennial celebrations of Beethoven's birth illustrate these competing ideologies with special clarity. Willi Stoph,

President of the State Council of the German Democratic Republic and de facto head of state, declared that Beethoven's music "culminates in he future image of a creative society, freed from exploitation and repression." The ideas Beethoven "shaped musically in his compositions" would ultimately be realized with the "victorious struggle of the working class" in a socialistic society. The West, Stoph maintained, had sought to remove the connection between Beethoven and the *Volk*, exploiting his music for purely commercial gain and ignoring the social implications of his creations.[30] Celebrations in the West, by contrast, emphasized Beethoven the cosmopolitan, Beethoven the universalist. Politicians had little to say on the occasion, ceding center stage to academics unconcerned with the composer's relationship to the competing ideologies of East and West.[31]

These contrasting celebrations are eerily parallel to the dispute between Brendel and Hanslick a hundred years before. The communist East decried the same "empty formalism" Brendel had ridiculed, and it embraced, like Brendel, the banners of "progress" and "the future," chastising "conservatives" for their enduring allegiance to the "absolute" music of the past. The capitalist West, in turn, rejected the appropriation of art for political purposes, advocating instead, like Hanslick, an approach to music in its "pure" form, transcending the events of the moment.

Brendel and Hanslick, East and West—these polarizations remind us of the enduring truth of one of Goethe's most celebrated aphorisms: "One cannot escape the world more certainly than through art, and one cannot bind oneself to it more certainly than through art."[32] In the end, art is both a refuge *and* a vehicle of change, and the very same work can function in both ways—or rather, the very same work can be *heard* in both ways. For interpretations, in the end, depend on each listener's predisposition to hear (or not to hear) philosophical and social implications in purely instrumental music. What Lydia Goehr has called the inherently double nature of music—connected to the world and yet separate from that world—is precisely what makes music such a potent vehicle and simulacrum of ideas and objects outside itself. The term "extramusical," as Goehr argues, might better be used not as a synonym for the nonmusical, but rather as a term that captures the essence of that which mediates between the nonmusical and the purely musical.[33] This concept is particularly useful in helping us to understand today the ways in which Beethoven's contemporaries heard music in general and symphonies in particular.

Listeners today remain divided. Many continue to resist the appropriation of purely instrumental, nonprogrammatic symphonies toward political ends, particularly in the case of works created some two centuries before. From a historical perspective, however, such an attitude is thoroughly anachronistic. Beethoven's contemporaries would have had great difficulty imagining such a strictly formalistic, apolitical attitude toward the symphony.

In the end, any idea of a neutral mode of listening—free of values, time, or place—is a chimera. Every individual and every generation listens in a manner shaped by personal and collective circumstances. Rather than lament, with Hanslick, the inherently subjective nature of listening, we can follow the lead of Beethoven's contemporaries and embrace these individual and collective perspectives, striving to integrate them, however imperfectly, into a higher synthesis of subject and object, of the particular and the universal, of the listener and the work.

Notes

INTRODUCTION

1. See Christopher Reynolds, *Motives for Allusion: Context and Content in Nineteenth-Century Music* (Cambridge, Mass.: Harvard University Press, 2003).

2. On the question of musical ciphers, see John Daverio, *Crossing Paths: Schubert, Schumann, and Brahms* (New York: Oxford University Press, 2002), chapters 3–5.

3. Theodor Adorno, *Beethoven: Philosophie der Musik*, ed. Rolf Tiedemann (Frankfurt/Main: Suhrkamp, 1993), p. 36; the translation here is from *Beethoven: The Philosophy of Music*, ed. Rolf Tiedemann, trans. Edmund Jephcott (Stanford: Stanford University Press, 1999), p. 14.

4. Scott Burnham, *Beethoven Hero* (Princeton: Princeton University Press, 1995); Berthold Hoeckner, *Programming the Absolute: Nineteenth-Century German Music and the Hermeneutics of the Moment* (Princeton: Princeton University Press, 2002); Michael P. Steinberg, *Listening to Reason: Culture, Subjectivity, and Nineteenth-Century Music* (Princeton: Princeton University Press, 2004).

5. Reinhold Brinkmann, "In the Time(s) of the *Eroica*," in *Beethoven and His World*, ed. Scott Burnham and Michael P. Steinberg (Princeton: Princeton University Press, 2000), pp. 1–26; Lewis Lockwood, "Beethoven, Florestan, and the Varieties of Heroism," ibid., pp. 27–47; Maynard Solomon, *Late Beethoven: Music, Thought, Imagination* (Berkeley and Los Angeles: University of California Press, 2003), pp. 135–78; Stephen Rumph, *Beethoven after Napoleon: Political Romanticism in the Late Works* (Berkeley and Los Angeles: University of California Press, 2004).

6. Mark Evan Bonds, *After Beethoven: Imperatives of Originality in the Symphony* (Cambridge, Mass.: Harvard University Press, 1996).

7. James H. Johnson, *Listening in Paris: A Cultural History* (Berkeley and Los Angeles: University of California Press, 1995).

PROLOGUE
AN UNLIKELY GENRE: THE RISE OF THE SYMPHONY

1. Jan LaRue, *A Catalogue of 18th-Century Symphonies*, vol. 1: *Thematic Identifier* (Bloomington: Indiana University Press, 1988).

2. See Neal Zaslaw, *Mozart's Symphonies: Context, Performance Practice, Reception* (Oxford: Clarendon, 1989), pp. 510–13.

3. J.A.P. Schulz, "Sinfonie" and "Instrumentalmusik," in Johann Georg Sulzer, *Allgemeine Theorie der schönen Künste*, 2 vols. (Leipzig, 1771–74; reprint of second edition, 1792–99, 5 vols., Hildesheim: Olms, 1994); Heinrich Christoph Koch, *Versuch einer Anleitung zur Composition*, 3 vols. (Leipzig, 1782–93; re-

print, Hildesheim: Olms, 1969). On the idea of instrumental music as untexted vocal music, see Michael Broyles, "Organic Form and the Binary Repeat," *MQ* 66 (1980): 348–49.

4. Adolph Bernhard Marx's concert review of 13 December 1824, *BAmZ* 1 (29 December 1824): 444 ("ein wahrer Prüfstein für Publikum und Komponisten"). For other comments of a similar nature, see the anonymous review of Joachim Hoffmann's Symphony in A Major, *Wiener Allgemeine musikalische Zeitung* 3 (30 June 1819): 415–16; Oswald Lorenz's review of W. Attern, Symphony no. 1, op. 14, *NZfM* 13 (16 December 1840): 193–94; and anonymous, "Gedanken über die Symphonie," in *Großes Instrumental- und Vocal-Concert*, 16 vols., ed. Ernst Ortlepp (Stuttgart: Köhler, 1841), XVI, 57.

5. Max Kalbeck, *Johannes Brahms*, 4 vols. (Vienna and Leipzig: Wiener Verlag; Berlin: Deutsche Brahms-Gesellschaft, 1904–14), I, 171–72.

6. See Ernst Ludwig Gerber, "Eine freundliche Vorstellung über gearbeitete Instrumentalmusik, besonders über Symphonien," *AmZ* 15 (14 July 1813): 457–63; *Cäcilia* 3 (1825): 241–47; Gottfried Wilhelm Fink, Review of Adolph Hesse, Symphony no. 5, *AmZ* 42 (25 November 1840): 985–88; anonymous, Review of Friedrich Müller, Symphony, op. 54, *AmZ* 46 (30 October 1844): 729.

7. Jon Finson, "'To Our Sincere Regret': New Documents on the Publication of Robert Schumann's D-Minor Symphony," paper delivered at the annual meeting of the American Musicological Society, Columbus, Ohio, November, 2002. I am grateful to Jon Finson for sharing a copy of this paper with me.

8. On the culture of piano transcriptions in general, see Thomas Christensen, "Four-Hand Piano Transcription and Geographies of Nineteenth-Century Musical Reception," *JAMS* 52 (1999): 255–98.

9. F. E. Kirby, "The Germanic Symphony of the Nineteenth Century: Genre, Form, Instrumentation, Expression," *Journal of Musicological Research* 14 (1995): 197.

10. See Otto Biba, "Concert Life in Beethoven's Vienna," in *Beethoven, Performers, and Critics: The International Beethoven Congress, Detroit, 1977*, ed. Robert Winter and Bruce Carr (Detroit: Wayne State University Press, 1980), pp. 77–93; see also Stefan Weinzierl, *Beethovens Konzerträume: Raumakustik und symphonische Aufführungspraxis an der Schwelle zum modernen Konzertwesen* (Frankfurt/Main: E. Bochinsky, 2002), appendix I (pp. 220–45), for a chronological listing of all documented performances of Beethoven's symphonies in Vienna during his lifetime.

CHAPTER ONE
LISTENING WITH IMAGINATION: THE REVOLUTION IN AESTHETICS

1. E. M. Forster, *Howards End* (1910), chapter 5. Other writers who have commented on this passage include Peter Kivy, *Music Alone: Philosophical Reflections on the Purely Musical Experience* (Ithaca: Cornell University Press, 1990), and Scott Burnham, "How Music Matters: Poetic Content Revisited," in *Rethinking Music*, ed. Nicholas Cook and Mark Everist (New York: Oxford University Press, 1999), pp. 204–8. For the broader context of this passage in For-

ster's writing in general, see Michelle Fillion, "E. M. Forster's Beethoven," *Beethoven Forum* 9 (2002): 171–203. For a more detailed and systematic typology of listeners, see Theodor W. Adorno, *Einleitung in die Musiksoziologie* (Frankfurt/Main: Suhrkamp, 1962), pp. 14–34.

2. For accounts of listening practices in the late eighteenth and early nineteenth centuries, see Johnson, *Listening in Paris*; Peter Gay, *The Naked Heart* (New York: Norton, 1995), pp. 11–35; William Weber, "Did People Listen in the 18th Century?" *Early Music* 25 (1997): 678–91; and Matthew Riley, *Musical Listening in the German Enlightenment: Attention, Wonder and Astonishment* (Aldershot: Ashgate, 2004). Leon Botstein succinctly summarizes the methodological difficulties of reconstructing listening practices in "Toward a History of Listening," *MQ* 82 (1998): 427–31.

3. E.T.A. Hoffmann, review of Beethoven's Fifth Symphony, *AmZ* 12 (4 and 11 July 1810): 630–42, 652–59; published in modern edition in Hoffmann's *Schriften zur Musik: Aufsätze und Rezensionen,* ed. Friedrich Schnapp (Darmstadt: Wissenschaftliche Buchgesellschaft, 1979), pp. 34–51. When Hoffmann turned portions of this review into an essay in 1813, he dropped the review's musical examples and its discussion of the Fifth's more technical elements, combined the remainder with portions of another review he had written in the meantime on Beethoven's Piano Trios, op. 70, and published the revised work as "Beethovens Instrumentalmusik" within the collection entitled *Kreisleriana.* In this form, Hoffmann's ideas gained even wider exposure. On the immediate and enormous resonance of Hoffmann's commentary, see Klaus Kropfinger, "Klassik-Rezeption in Berlin (1800–1830)," in *Studien zur Musikgeschichte Berlins im frühen 19. Jahrhundert,* ed. Carl Dahlhaus (Regensburg: Bosse, 1980), pp. 354–56. One anecdote may suffice here to illustrate the esteem in which contemporaries held Hoffmann's criticism. In 1824, August Kuhn, editor of *Der Freimüthige,* announced that his general-interest journal would soon transform itself into one dealing exclusively with music and that the new journal would be edited by the young and still almost entirely unknown Adolph Bernhard Marx, whom Kuhn recommended as a "an intelligent young man who has penetrated deep into the manner of presentation and the aesthetic views of E.T.A. Hoffmann." Quoted in Elisabeth Eleonore Bauer, *Wie Beethoven auf den Sockel kam: Die Entstehung eines musikalischen Mythos* (Stuttgart: J. B. Metzler, 1992), p. 60.

4. Kant, *Kritik der Urteilskraft,* ed. Heiner F. Klemme (Hamburg: Felix Meiner, 2001), B218. Following standard practice, citations to this work will be to the pagination of the second ("B") edition (Berlin, 1793).

5. Jean-Jacques Rousseau, "Essai sur l'origine des langues" (first published posthumously in 1781), in his *Écrits sur la musique,* ed. Catherine Kintzler (Paris: Stock, 1979), p. 229.

6. Jean-Jacques Rousseau, "Sonate," in his *Dictionnaire de musique* (Paris, 1768; reprint, Hildesheim: Olms, 1969), p. 452: "Je n'oublierai jamais la saillie du célèbre Fontenelle, qui se trouvant excédé des ces éternelles Symphonies, s'écria tout haut dans un transport d'impatience: *sonate, que me veux-tu?*" See Maria Rika Maniates, "'Sonate, que me veux-tu?' The Enigma of French Musical Aesthetics in the 18th Century," *Current Musicology,* no. 9 (1969): 117–40. On the resonance of Fontenelle's reputed exclamation, particularly in Germany, see Mary

Sue Morrow, *German Music Criticism in the Late Eighteenth Century: Aesthetic Issues in Instrumental Music* (Cambridge: Cambridge University Press, 1997), pp. 4–13. The critic August Kahlert was still referring to Fontenelle's epigram as late as 1832 in his *Blätter aus der Brieftasche eines Musikers* (Breslau: C. G. Förster, 1832), p. 179.

7. Sulzer, *Allgemeine Theorie der schönen Künste*, "Musik": "In die letzte Stelle setzen wir die Anwendung der Musik auf Concerte, die blos zum Zeitvertreib und etwa zur Übung im Spielen angestellt werden. Dazu gehören die Concerte, die Symphonien, die Sonaten, die Solo, die insgemein ein lebhaftes und nicht unangenehmes Geräusch, oder ein artiges und unterhaltendes, aber das Herz nicht beschäftigendes Geschwätz vorstellen."

8. E.T.A. Hoffmann, review of Beethoven's Fifth Symphony (1810), *Schriften zur Musik*, p. 36: "Haydn faßt das Menschliche im menschlichen Leben romantisch auf; er ist kommensurabler für die Mehrzahl. Mozart nimmt mehr das Übermenschliche, das Wunderbare, welches im innern Geiste wohnt, in Anspruch. Beethovens Musik bewegt die Hebel des Schauers, der Furcht, des Entsetzens, des Schmerzes, und erweckt jene unendliche Sehnsucht, die das Wesen der Romantik ist."

9. Hans Heinrich Eggebrecht, *Zur Geschichte der Beethoven-Rezeption*, 2nd ed. (Laaber: Laaber-Verlag, 1994), p. 75, and Burnham, *Beethoven Hero*, p. 67. See also Daniel K. L. Chua, *Absolute Music and the Construction of Meaning* (Cambridge: Cambridge University Press, 1999), p. 276.

10. Eduard Hanslick, *Vom Musikalisch-Schönen: Ein Beitrag zur Revision der Aesthetik* (1854), ed. Dietmar Strauß, 2 vols. (Mainz: Schott, 1990), chapter 1.

11. F. E. Sparshott, "Aesthetics of Music," in *The New Grove Dictionary of Music and Musicians*, 20 vols., ed. Stanley Sadie (London: Macmillan, 1980), I, 127. Carl Dahlhaus, *Die Idee der absoluten Musik* (Kassel: Bärenreiter, 1978), p. 29; translated by Roger Lustig as *The Idea of Absolute Music* (Chicago: University of Chicago Press, 1989), pp. 23–24.

12. See Hugo Goldschmidt, *Die Musikästhetik des 18. Jahrhunderts* (Zurich and Leipzig: Rascher, 1915), pp. 210, 221, where Wackenroder is called "a prophet" whose theories "do not fit any music of the time" and the "apologist for Beethoven's late style" twenty years before the fact. Martin Geck makes a similar claim in his *Von Beethoven bis Mahler: Die Musik des deutschen Idealismus* (Stuttgart: J. B. Metzler, 1993), pp. 96, 129. I shall return to Tieck's essay later in this chapter.

13. Dahlhaus, *The Idea of Absolute Music*, pp. 90, 65; see also p. 103. See also idem, "Romantische Musikästhetik und Wiener Klassik," *AfMw* 29 (1972): 167–81; idem, "E.T.A. Hoffmanns Beethoven-Kritik und die Ästhetik des Erhabenen," *AfMw* 38 (1981): 79–92.

14. Elements of idealist thought have been recognized in the writings of the early romantics on music on many occasions, but the application of idealist vocabulary and premises to the aesthetics of instrumental music has never been addressed in any systematic fashion. The entry for Schelling in *Die Musik in Geschichte und Gegenwart*, for example, makes no reference at all to the implications of idealism for contemporary perceptions of instrumental music. Hans Heinrich Eggebrecht, in turn (*Musik im Abendland: Prozesse und Stationen vom Mittelalter*

bis zur Gegenwart [Munich: Piper, 1991], pp. 592–621), rightly emphasizes the importance of the idea of music existing in its own separate world for early Romantic aesthetics but does not relate this outlook to idealism. Many recent scholars, moreover, seem oddly reluctant to recognize the presence of idealist concepts in writings from the turn of the nineteenth century: Sparshott, for example ("Aesthetics of Music"), begins his account of idealism with Hegel, while Dahlhaus (*The Idea of Absolute Music,* pp. 10, 129) attributes an "aesthetic of essences" to Schopenhauer, Nietzsche, and the late Wagner, but not to earlier writers. Dahlhaus and others, as I argue in the epilogue of the present book, also blur the crucial distinction between idealist aesthetics and the later doctrine of "absolute" music. Historians of philosophy have on the whole been better attuned to the close connections of music and idealist philosophy in the late eighteenth and early nineteenth centuries. Andrew Bowie's work is particularly important in this regard; see his *Aesthetics and Subjectivity: From Kant to Nietzsche,* 2nd ed. (Manchester: Manchester University Press, 2003) and *From Romanticism to Critical Theory: The Philosophy of German Literary Theory* (London: Routledge, 1997).

15. Introductions to the earlier history of idealism in aesthetics may be found in Erwin Panofsky, *Idea: A Concept in Art Theory,* trans. Joseph J. S. Peake (Columbia: University of South Carolina Press, 1968); Hans Zeller, *Winckelmanns Beschreibung des Apollo im Belvedere* (Zurich: Atlantis, 1955), pp. 130–34; and Giorgio Tonelli, "Ideal in Philosophy: From the Renaissance to 1780," in *The Dictionary of the History of Ideas,* ed. Philip P. Wiener, 4 vols. (New York: Charles Scribner's Sons, 1973), II, 549–52.

16. Kant's *Kritik der Urteilskraft* (1790) was particularly important in this regard. Recent accounts of the growing role of imagination in the eighteenth century include Lillian Furst, *Romanticism in Perspective,* 2nd ed. (London: Macmillan, 1979), pp. 119–209; James Engell, *The Creative Imagination: Enlightenment to Romanticism* (Cambridge: Harvard University Press, 1981); and Mark Johnson, *The Body in the Mind: The Bodily Basis of Meaning, Imagination, and Reason* (Chicago: University of Chicago Press, 1987), pp. 139–72.

17. Christian Gottfried Körner, "Ueber Charakterdarstellung in der Musik," in Wolfgang Seifert, *Christian Gottfried Körner: Ein Musikästhetiker der deutschen Klassik* (Regensburg: Gustav Bosse, 1960), p. 151: "Wir *schätzen* die Erscheinung nach demjenigen, was in ihr nicht *erscheint,* sondern *gedacht* werden muß." Emphasis in the original.

18. Jean-Jacques Rousseau, "Imitation," in his *Dictionnaire de musique* (1768), p. 251: "Il ne représentera pas directement ces choses; mais il excitera dans l'âme les mêmes mouvemens qu'on éprouve en les voyant."

19. On the relationship between mimesis and "expressive" theories, see John Neubauer, *The Emancipation of Music from Language: Departure from Mimesis in Eighteenth-Century Aesthetics* (New Haven: Yale University Press, 1986), pp. 149–67; Hans Heinrich Eggebrecht, "Das musikalische Ausdrucksprinzip im 'Sturm und Drang,'" *Deutsche Vierteljahrsschrift für Literaturwissenschaft und Geistesgeschichte* 29 (1955): 323–49; and Bellamy Hosler, *Changing Aesthetic Views of Instrumental Music in 18th-Century Germany* (Ann Arbor: UMI Research Press, 1981). The best survey of theories of mimesis and expression in all

the arts of this period remains M. H. Abrams, *The Mirror and the Lamp: Romantic Theory and the Critical Tradition* (New York: Oxford University Press, 1953).

20. See Hosler, *Changing Aesthetic Views;* Neubauer, *Emancipation of Music;* and Mark Evan Bonds, *Wordless Rhetoric: Musical Form and the Metaphor of the Oration* (Cambridge, Mass.: Harvard University Press, 1991), pp. 61–68.

21. Idealism is an extremely broad phenomenon, and the outline of its application to musical aesthetics presented here should not convey the impression that this mode of thought developed in a clear or linear fashion. Fichte and Schelling—to name only two of the more prominent philosophers associated with this movement—each developed his own distinctive brand of idealism, and in the account that follows, I have made no attempt to distinguish among idealism's various manifestations, such as subjective, objective, transcendental, and absolute, preferring instead to focus on the underlying similarities of these views as applied to instrumental music.

22. Johann Joachim Winckelmann, "Vorläufige Abhandlung zu den Denkmalen der Kunst des Altertums" (1767), in his *Sämtliche Werke,* ed. Joseph Eiselein, 12 vols. (Donaueschingen: Verlag deutscher Classiker, 1825–35), VII, 110.

23. See Frederic Will, *Intelligible Beauty in Aesthetic Thought, from Winckelmann to Victor Cousin* (Tübingen: Max Niemeyer, 1958), chapter 6, "Winckelmann and the Ideal of Beauty."

24. Johann Gottfried Herder, *Erstes Kritisches Wäldchen* (1769), in his *Schriften zur Ästhetik und Literatur, 1767–1781,* ed. Gunter E. Grimm (Frankfurt/Main: Deutscher Klassiker Verlag, 1993), p. 66.

25. Sulzer, *Allgemeine Theorie der schönen Künste,* "Ideal": "Man kann überhaupt von jedem Gegenstand der Kunst, der nicht nach einem in der Natur vorhandenen abgezeichnet worden, sondern sein Wesen und seine Gestalt von dem Genie des Künstlers bekommen hat, sagen, er sey nach einem Ideal gemacht."

26. Karl Philipp Moritz, "Versuch einer Vereinigung aller schönen Künste und Wissenschaften unter dem Begriff des in sich selbst Vollendeten" (1785), in his *Schriften zur Ästhetik und Poetik,* ed. Hans Joachim Schrimpf (Tübingen: Max Niemeyer, 1962), p. 3: "Ich betrachte ihn [the beautiful object], als etwas, nicht in mir, sondern *in sich selbst Vollendetes,* das also in sich ein Ganzes ausmacht, und mir *um sein selbst willen* Vergnügen gewährt; indem ich dem schönen Gegenstande nicht sowohl eine Beziehung auf mich, als mir vielmehr eine Beziehung auf ihn gebe." Emphasis in the original.

27. Moritz, "Versuch," p. 5: "[D]ies Verlieren, dies Vergessen unsrer selbst, ist der höchste Grad des reinen und uneigennützigen Vergnügens, welches uns das Schöne gewährt. Wir opfern in dem Augenblick unser individuelles eingeschränktes Dasein einer Art von höherem Dasein auf."

28. Quoted in Otto Erich Deutsch, ed., *Schubert: Die Dokumente seines Lebens* (Kassel: Bärenreiter, 1964), pp. 42–43: "Die Zaubertöne von Mozarts Musik . . . zeigen uns in den Finsternissen dieses Lebens eine lichte, helle, schöne Ferne, worauf wir mit Zuversicht hoffen." On the early nineteenth-century idea of music as a utopian realm, see Max Becker, *Narkotikum und Utopie: Musik-Konzepte in Empfindsamkeit und Romantik* (Kassel: Bärenreiter, 1996).

29. Wilhelm Heinrich Wackenroder, *Das merkwürdige musikalische Leben des Tonkünstlers Joseph Berglinger,* in his *Sämtliche Werke und Briefe: Historisch-*

kritische Ausgabe, ed. Silvio Vietta and Richard Littlejohns, 2 vols. (Heidelberg: Carl Winter Universitätsverlag, 1991), I, 132: "Die Gegenwart versank vor ihm; sein Inneres war von allen irdischen Kleinigkeiten, welche der wahre Staub auf dem Glanze der Seele sind, gereinigt."

30. Tieck, *Phantasien,* "Symphonien," in Wackenroder, *Sämtliche Werke,* I, 241: "aus dem Streit der irrenden Gedanken in ein stilles, heiteres, ruhiges Land erlöst zu werden." Hoffman, review of Beethoven's Fifth Symphony (1810), in his *Schriften zur Musik,* p. 37: "das wundervolle Geisterreich des Unendlichen."

31. Carl Friedrich Zelter, letter to Haydn of 16 March 1804, in Joseph Haydn, *Gesammelte Briefe und Augzeichnungen,* ed. Dénes Bartha (Kassel: Bärenreiter, 1965), p. 438: "Ihr Geist ist in das Heiligthum göttlicher Weisheit eingedrungen; Sie haben das Feuer vom Himmel geholt, womit Sie irdische Herzen erwärmen und erleuchten und zu dem Unendlichen leiten. Das Beste, was wir Andern können, besteht bloß darin: mit Dank und Freude Gott zu verehren, der Sie gesandt, damit wir die Wunder erkennen, die er durch Sie in der Kunst geoffenbart hat."

32. Letter of 17 July 1812 to "Emilie M. in H[amburg]," in Beethoven, *Briefwechsel: Gesamtausgabe,* 7 vols., ed. Sieghard Brandenburg (Munich: G. Henle, 1996–2001), II, 274 (letter no. 585); *The Letters of Beethoven,* ed. Emily Anderson, 3 vols. (London: Macmillan, 1961), I, 381; letter no. 376): "[Ü]be nicht allein die Kunst, sondern dringe auch in ihr Inneres; sie verdient es, denn nur die Kunst und die Wissenschaft erhöhen den Menschen bis zur Gottheit." No autograph of the letter survives. Note the similarity to Goethe's *Zahme Xenien IX,* first published in 1827: "Wer Wissenschaft und Kunst besitzt, / Hat auch Religion; / Wer jene beiden nicht besitzt, / Der habe Religion."

33. Letter of 28 February 1812 to Breitkopf & Härtel (*Briefwechsel,* II, 246, letter no. 555; *Letters,* I, 360, letter no. 351). Letter of 17 September 1824 to Bernhard Schotts Söhne (*Briefwechsel,* V, 368, letter no. 1881; *Letters,* III, 1141, letter no. 1308). For a fuller discussion of these and similar passages, see Maynard Solomon, *Late Beethoven,* pp. 92–101.

34. Letter to Archduke Rudolph, July–August 1821 (*Briefwechsel,* IV, 446, letter no. 1438; *Letters,* III, 1095, letter no. 1248): "Höheres gibt es nichts, als der Gottheit sich mehr nähern als andere Menschen und von hier aus die Strahlen der Gottheit unter das Menschengeschlecht verbreiten."

35. Anonymous, "Musikzustand und musikalisches Leben in Wien," *Cäcilia* 1 (1824): 200; translated in David Gramit, *Cultivating Music: The Aspirations, Interests, and Limits of German Musical Culture, 1770–1848* (Berkeley and Los Angeles: University of California Press, 2002), p. 159.

36. Kant, *Kritik der Urteilskraft,* B192–93: "[U]nter einer ästhetischen Idee ... verstehe ich diejenige Vorstellung der Einbildungskraft, die viel zu denken veranlaßt, ohne daß ihr doch irgendein bestimmter Gedanke d. i. Begriff adäquat sein kann, die folglich keine Sprache völlig erreicht und verständlich machen kann. Man sieht leicht, daß sie das Gegenstück (Pendant) von einer Vernunftidee sei, welche umgekehrt ein Begriff ist, dem keine Anschauung (Vorstellung der Einbildungskraft) adäquat sein kann." Translation from Immanuel Kant, *The Critique of Judgement,* trans. James Creed Meredith (Oxford: Clarendon, 1952), pp. 175–76.

37. Ibid., B214; Meredith translation, slightly modified, p. 191.

38. Ibid., B218. Philip Alperson points out certain ambiguities in the treatment of instrumental music in the *Kritik der Urteilskraft*, suggesting that Kant may well have held "higher" forms (as opposed to mere *Tafelmusik*; see B178) in greater esteem, even while conceding that Kant never states this position explicitly. See Alperson, "The Arts of Music," *Journal of Aesthetics and Art Criticism* 50 (1992): 221–23.

39. Friedrich Schiller, "Über Matthissons Gedichte" (1794), in his *Werke und Briefe*, ed. Klaus Harro Hilzinger et al., 12 vols. (Frankfurt/Main: Deutscher Klassiker Verlag, 1988–2004), VIII, 1023: "Zwar sind Empfindungen, *ihrem Inhalte nach*, keiner Darstellung fähig; aber *ihrer Form nach* sind sie es allerdings, und es existiert wirklich eine allgemein beliebte und wirksame Kunst, die kein anderes Objekt hat, als eben diese Form der Empfindungen. Diese Kunst ist die *Musik*." Emphasis in the original.

40. Ibid., VIII, 1024–25: "Kurz wir verlangen, daß jede poetische Komposition neben dem, was ihr Inhalt ausdrückt, zugleich durch ihre Form Nachahmung und Ausdruck von Empfindungen sei, und als Musik auf uns wirke. . . .

"Nun besteht aber der ganze Effekt der Musik (als schöner und nicht bloß angenehmer Kunst) darin, die inneren Bewegungen des Gemüts durch analogische äußere zu begleiten und zu versinnlichen. . . . Dringt nun der Tonsetzer und der Landschaftmaler in das Geheimnis jener Gesetze ein, welche über die innern Bewegungen des menschlichen Herzens walten, und studiert er die Analogie, welche zwischen diesen Gemütsbewegungen und gewissen äußern Erscheinungen statt findet, so wird er aus einem Bildner gemeiner Natur zum wahrhaften Seelenmaler. Er tritt aus dem Reich der Willkür in das Reich der Notwendigkeit ein, und darf sich, wo nicht dem plastischen Künstler, der den *äußern* Menschen, doch dem Dichter, der den *innern* zu seinem Objekte macht, getrost an die Seite stellen." Emphasis in the original. Schiller's review was widely discussed in its time and quoted extensively: see the editorial comments in Schiller, *Werke und Briefe*, VIII, 1543–46.

41. Ibid., VIII, 1026: "Andeuten mag er jene Ideen, anspielen jene Empfindungen; doch ausführen soll er sie nicht selbst, nicht der Einbildungskraft seines Lesers vorgreifen. Jede nähere Bestimmung wird hier als eine lästige Schranke empfunden, denn eben darin liegt das Anziehende solcher *ästhetischen Ideen*, daß wir in den Inhalt derselben wie in eine grundlose Tiefe blicken. Der wirkliche und ausdrückliche Gehalt, den der Dichter hineinlegt, bleibt stets eine endliche; der mögliche Gehalt, den er uns hinein zu legen überläßt, ist eine unendliche Größe."

42. Schiller, "Über naive und sentimentalische Dichtung" (1795), in his *Werke und Briefe*, VIII, 786: "Das sentimentale Genie hingegen verläßt die Wirklichkeit, um zu Ideen aufzusteigen und mit freier Selbsttätigkeit seinen Stoff zu beherrschen." On the category of the infinite in early romantic aesthetics in general, see Ursula Leitl-Zametzer, "Der Unendlichkeitsbegriff in der Kunstauffassung der Frühromantik bei Friedrich Schlegel und W. H. Wackenroder," Ph.D. diss., Munich, 1955, a work whose scope extends well beyond the two writers named in its title.

43. Schiller, "Über das Pathetische" (1793), in his *Werke und Briefe*, VIII, 427.

44. Körner, "Ueber Charakterdarstellung," p. 147: "Über das Darstellungswürdige in der Musik herrschten lange Zeit seltsame Vorurtheile. Auch hier wurde

der Grundsatz mißverstanden, daß Nachahmung der Natur die Bestimmung der Kunst sey; und Nachäffung alles Hörbaren vom Rollen des Donners bis zum Krähen des Hahns galt manchem für das eigenthümliche Geschäft des Tonkünstlers. Ein besserer Geschmack fängt an, allgemeiner sich auszubreiten. Ausdruck menschlicher Empfindung tritt an die Stelle eines seelenlosen Geräusches. Aber ist dieß der Punkt, wo der Tonkünstler stehen bleiben darf, oder giebt es für ihn noch ein höheres Ziel?"

45. Ibid., p. 148: "Was wir in der Wirklichkeit bei einer einzelnen Erscheinung vermissen, soll uns der Künstler ergänzen; er soll seinen Stoff *idealisieren.* In den Schöpfungen seiner Phantasie soll die Würde der menschlichen Natur erscheinen. Aus einer niedern Sphäre der Abhängigkeit und Beschränktheit soll er uns zu sich emporheben, und das Unendliche, was uns außerhalb der Kunst nur zu denken vergönnt ist, in einer Anschauung darstellen." Emphasis in the original.

46. See Wolfgang Seifert, *Christian Gottfried Körner: Ein Musikästhetiker der deutschen Klassik* (Regensburg: Gustav Bosse, 1960), pp. 114–15. On the connections between idealism and the concept of the characteristic, see Jacob de Ruiter, *Der Charakterbegriff in der Musik: Studien zur deutschen Ästhetik der Instrumentalmusik, 1740–1850* (Stuttgart: Franz Steiner, 1989), pp. 284–98.

47. On Schelling's philosophy of music, see August Steinkrüger, *Die Aesthetik der Musik bei Schelling und Hegel: Ein Beitrag zur Musikästhetik der Romantik* (Bonn: Verein Studentenwohl, 1927), esp. pp. 150–64.

48. Manfred Frank, *Einführung in die frühromantische Ästhetik* (Frankfurt/Main: Suhrkamp, 1989), pp. 16, 171. Although not published until 1859, Schelling's lectures circulated widely in manuscript from the first decade of the nineteenth century onward.

49. Friedrich Wilhelm Joseph Schelling, *Philosophie der Kunst,* in his *Sämmtliche Werke,* ed. K.F.A. Schelling, 14 vols. (Stuttgart and Augsburg: J. G. Cotta, 1856–61), V, 386: "Durch die Kunst wird die göttliche Schöpfung objektiv dargestellt, denn diese beruht auf derselben Einbildung der unendlichen Idealität ins Reale, auf welcher auch jene beruht. Das treffliche deutsche Wort Einbildungskraft bedeutet eigentlich die Kraft der Ineinsbildung, auf welcher in der That alle Schöpfung beruht. Sie ist die Kraft, wodurch ein Ideales zugleich auch ein Reales, die Seele Leib ist, die Kraft der Individuation, welche die eigentlich schöpferische ist."

50. Ibid., V, 501–3: "Die Formen der Musik sind Formen der ewigen Dinge, inwiefern sie von der realen Seite betrachtet werden. . . . [S]o bringt die Musik die Form der Bewegungen der Weltkörper, die reine, von dem Gegenstand oder Stoff befreite Form in dem Rhythmus und der Harmonie als solche zur Anschauung. Die Musik ist insofern diejenige Kunst, die am meisten das Körperliche abstreift, indem sie die reine Bewegung selbst als solche, von dem Gegenstand abgezogen, vorstellt und von unsichtbaren, fast geistigen Flügeln getragen wird. . . . Wir können jetzt erst die höchste Bedeutung von Rhythmus, Harmonie und Melodie festsetzen. Sie sind die ersten und reinsten Formen der Bewegung im Universum. . . . Auf den Flügeln der Harmonie und des Rhythmus schweben die Weltkörper. . . . Von denselben Flügeln erhoben schwebt die Musik im Raum, um aus dem durchsichtigen Leib des Lauts und Tons ein hörbares Universum zu weben."

51. August Wilhelm Schlegel, *Vorlesungen über schöne Literatur und Kunst* (1801–2). Erster Teil: *Die Kunstlehre*, in his *Kritische Ausgabe der Vorlesungen,* vol. 1: *Vorlesungen über Ästhetik I (1798–1803),* ed. Ernst Behler (Paderborn: Schöningh, 1989), p. 209: "etwas worauf unser Geist mit einem unendlichen Bestreben gerichtet ist." Ibid., p. 381: "eine Ahndung [*sic*] der harmonischen Vollendung, der Einheit alles Daseyns, welche die Christen sich unter dem Bilde der himmlischen Seligkeit denken."

52. Ibid., p. 375: "[S]o muß man der Musik den Vorzug zugestehn, ihrem ganzen Wesen nach idealisch zu seyn. Sie reinigt die Leidenschaften gleichsam von dem materiellen ihnen anhängenden Schmutz, indem sie selbige ohne Bezug auf Gegenstände bloß nach ihrer Form in unserm innern Sinn darstellt; und läßt sie nach Abstreifung der irdischen Hülle in reinerem Aether athmen." Ibid., p. 381: "[E]in einziges unwandelbares durchaus unendliches Streben, die Andacht, bleibt übrig."

53. Friedrich Schlegel, *Die Entwicklung der Philosophie in zwölf Büchern* (1804–5), in his *Kritische Friedrich-Schlegel-Ausgabe,* ed. Ernst Behler (Paderborn, Munich, Vienna: Ferdinand Schöningh, 1958–), XII, 346; ibid., XIII, 57.

54. Rudolf Köpke, *Ludwig Tieck: Erinnerungen aus dem Leben des Dichters* (Leipzig, 1855; reprint, Darmstadt: Wissenschaftliche Buchgesellschaft, 1970), p. 183.

55. See Wackenroder's letter of 23 July 1793 to his parents, in his *Sämtliche Werke,* II, 196.

56. On the troublesome questions of authorship in the collaborative publications of Wackenroder and Tieck, see the commentary to Wackenroder's *Sämtliche Werke,* I, 283–88 and 368–72.

57. Wackenroder, *Herzensergiessungen,* "Von zwey wunderbaren Sprachen, und deren geheimnißvoller Kraft," in his *Sämtliche Werke,* I, 97. Published in December 1796, the title page of Wackenroder's work bears the date 1797.

58. Wackenroder, *Phantasien,* "Die Wunder der Tonkunst," in his *Sämtliche Werke,* I, 207: "Die Musik aber halte ich für die wunderbarste dieser Erfindungen [the fine arts], weil sie menschliche Gefühle auf eine übermenschliche Art schildert, weil sie uns alle Bewegungen unsers Gemüths unkörperlich, in goldne Wolken luftiger Harmonieen eingekleidet, über unserm Haupte zeigt."

59. Ibid., I, 208: "Sie ist die einzige Kunst, welche die mannigfaltigsten und widersprechendsten Bewegungen unsres Gemüths auf dieselben schönen Harmonieen zurückführt."

60. Wackenroder, *Phantasien,* "Das eigentümliche innere Wesen der Tonkunst, und die Seelenlehre der heutigen Instrumentalmusik," in his *Sämtliche Werke,* I, 220: "[I]n diesen Wellen strömt recht eigentlich nur das reine, *formlose* Wesen, der Gang und die Farbe, und auch vornehmlich der tausendfältige Übergang der Empfindungen; die idealische, engelreine Kunst weiß in ihrer Unschuld weder den Ursprung noch das Ziel ihrer Regungen, kennt nicht den Zusammenhang ihrer Gefühle mit der wirklichen Welt." Emphasis in the original.

61. Tieck, *Phantasien,* "Die Töne," in Wackenroder's *Sämtliche Werke,* I, 236: "[D]iese Töne . . . ahmen nicht nach, sie verschönern nicht, sondern sie sind eine abgesonderte Welt für sich selbst."

62. See, e.g., Carl Dahlhaus, "Romantische Musikästhetik und Wiener Klassik," pp. 174–75. Note, too, the invitation to Wackenroder to perform one of Haydn's keyboard concertos; see above, note 55.

63. The enduring popularity of Reichardt's incidental music to *Macbeth* was remarkable: A. B. Marx was still writing enthusiastically about it as late as 1824. See Walter Salmen, *Johan Friedrich Reichardt* (Zurich: Atlantis, 1963), pp. 281–83. Tieck and Reichardt also happened to be close friends.

64. Tieck, *Phantasien*, "Symphonien," in Wackenroder's *Sämtliche Werke*, I, 244. For more on Reichardt's music to *Macbeth*, see Ursula Kramer, "Auf den Spuren des Häßlichen: Zur ästhetischen und musikalischen Bedeutung von J. F. Reichardts *Hexenszenen zu Shakespeares Macbeth*," in *Aspekte historischer und systematischer Musikforschung*, ed. Christoph-Hellmut Mahling and Kristina Pfarr (Mainz: Are Edition, 2002), pp. 349–66.

65. Letter of 27 October 1809 in Johann Wolfgang Goethe, *Sämtliche Werke*, ed. Karl Richter (Munich: Hanser, 1985–98), XX/1, 219: "Es gibt gewisse Sinfonieen [*sic*] von Haydn, die durch ihren losen liberalen Gang mein Blut in behagliche Bewegung bringen und den freien Teilen meines Körpers die Neigung und Richtung geben wohltätig nach außen zu wirken. Meine Finger werden dann weicher und länger, meine Augen möchten etwas ersehn [*sic*] das noch kein Blick berührt hat, die Lippen öffnen sich, mein Inneres will heraus ins Freie."

66. Johann Gottfried Herder, "Ob Malerei oder Tonkunst eine grössere Wirkung gewähre? Ein Göttergespräch" (1785), in his *Sämmtliche Werke*, ed. Bernhard Suphan, 33 vols. (Berlin: Weidmann, 1877–1913), XV: "Das Dunkle und Verworrene ihrer Empfindungen liegt an ihrem Organ, nicht an meinen Tönen: diese sind rein und helle, das höchste Muster einer zusammenstimmenden Ordnung. Sie sind, wie schon ein von mir begeisterter sterblicher Weise gesagt hat, die Verhältnisse und Zahlen des Weltalls im angenehmsten, leichtesten, wirkendsten aller Symbole. Du hast mich also, Schwester, gelobt, indem du mich tadelst. Du hast das Unendliche meiner Kunst und ihrer innigsten Wirkung gepriesen" (p. 228). "Du wirst mir aber zugeben, daß ohne meine Worte, ohne Gesang, Tanz und andre Handlung, für Menschen deine Empfindungen immer im Dunkeln bleiben. Du sprichst zum Herzen; aber bei wie wenigen zum Verstande!" (p. 231).

67. Herder, *Kalligone*, Part Two, in his *Sämmtliche Werke*, XXII, 187: "[D]enn sie [music] ist Geist, verwandt mit der großen Natur innersten Kraft, der Bewegung. Was anschaulich dem Menschen nicht werden kann, wird ihm in *ihrer* Weise, in ihrer Weise allein, mittheilbar, die Welt des Unsichtbaren."

68. *Andacht* has been translated in a variety of ways: as "reverence" (Edward Lippman, ed., *Musical Aesthetics: A Historical Reader,* 3 vols. [New York: Pendragon, 1986–90], II, 40), as "devotion" (Lustig's translation of Dahlhaus, *The Idea of Absolute Music,* p. 78), and as "religious awe" (Peter le Huray and James Day, eds., *Music and Aesthetics in the Eighteenth and Early-Nineteenth Centuries* [Cambridge: Cambridge University Press, 1981], p. 257). I prefer "reverent contemplation" because it combines both humility and active thought (-*dacht* derives from *denken*, "to think"), whereas "devotion" overemphasizes the religious element, and "awe" connotes a stunning of the senses, as if they were incapable of operating actively in the process of aesthetic perception.

69. Herder, *Kalligone*, in his *Sämmtliche Werke*, XXII, 187.

70. Christian Friedrich Michaelis, *Über den Geist der Tonkunst,* 2 vols. (Leipzig, 1795–1800; reprint, Brussels: Culture et Civilisation, 1970), I, 11, 12 (idealism); I, 25, II, 30 (pleasure vs. culture).

71. Christian Friedrich Michaelis, "Noch einige Bemerkungen über den Rang der Tonkunst unter den schönen Künsten," *AmZ* 6 (15 August 1804): 772: "In ihr [music] scheint sich am leichtesten und innigsten das Individuelle mit dem Idealen zu verbinden, in ihr drückt sich vielleicht am lebendigsten (wie die modernen Aesthetiker sagen) das Unendliche durch das Endliche aus."

72. Christian Friedrich Michaelis, "Ueber das Idealische der Tonkunst," *AmZ* 10 (13 April 1808): 449.

73. Review of *Phantasien über die Kunst. ... von Ludwig Tieck* (Hamburg: Perthes, 1799), *AmZ* 2 (5 March 1800): 401–7.

74. [Johann] Triest, "Bemerkungen über die Ausbildung der Tonkunst in Deutschland im achtzehnten Jahrhundert," *AmZ* 3 (1801): 300–301, 297. Triest's essay has been translated by Susan Gillespie as "Remarks on the Development of the Art of Music in Germany in the Eighteenth Century," in *Haydn and His World*, ed. Elaine Sisman (Princeton: Princeton University Press, 1997), pp. 321–94.

75. Franz Horn, "Musikalische Fragmente," *AmZ* 4 (24 March 1802): 422.

76. Heinrich Christoph Koch, *Kurzgefasstes Handwörterbuch der Musik* (Leipzig, 1807; reprint, Hildesheim: Olms, 1981); idem, *Musikalisches Lexikon* (Frankfurt/Main, 1802; reprint, Kassel: Bärenreiter, 2001).

77. Amadeus Wendt, "Von dem Einfluss der Musik auf den Character," *AmZ* 11 (1808): 103.

78. E.T.A. Hoffmann, review of Beethoven's Fifth Symphony (1810), in his *Schriften zur Musik,* 34: "Die Musik [specifically, instrumental music] schließt dem Menschen ein unbekanntes Reich auf; eine Welt, die nichts gemein hat mit der äußern Sinnenwelt, die ihn umgibt, und in der er alle durch Begriffe bestimmbaren Gefühle zurückläßt, um sich dem Unaussprechlichen hinzugeben."

79. Hoffmann, *Die Serapionsbrüder,* "Der Dichter und der Komponist" (1813), in his *Sämtliche Werke,* ed. Hartmut Steinecke and Wulf Segebrecht, 6 vols. (Frankfurt/Main: Deutscher Klassiker Verlag, 1993), IV, 103: "Ist nicht die Musik die geheimnisvolle Sprache eines fernen Geisterreichs, deren wunderbare Akzente in unserm Innern widerklingen, und ein höheres, intensives Leben erwecken? Alle Leidenschaften kämpfen, schimmerned und glanzvoll gerüstet, mit einander und gehen unter in einer unaussprechlichen Sehnsucht, die unsere Brust erfüllt. Dies ist die unnennbare Wirkung der Instrumentalmusik. Aber nun soll die Musik ganz in's Leben treten, sie soll seine Erscheinungen ergreifen, und Wort und Tat schmückend, von bestimmten Leidenschaften und Handlungen sprechen. . . . Kann denn die Musik etwas anderes verkünden als die Wunder jenes Landes, von dem sie zu uns herübertönt?"

80. Hoffmann, "Alte und neue Kirchenmusik" (1814), in his *Schriften zur Musik,* p. 215: "[U]nd so wird der Akkord, die Harmonie, Bild und Ausdruck der Geistergemeinschaft, der Vereinigung mit dem Ewigen, dem Idealen, das über uns thront und doch uns einschließt."

81. Hoffmann, Review of Friedrich Witt's Symphony no. 5 (1809), in his *Schriften zur Musik,* p. 19.

CHAPTER TWO
LISTENING AS THINKING: FROM RHETORIC TO PHILOSOPHY

1. Johann Mattheson, *Der vollkommene Capellmeister* (Hamburg, 1739; reprint, Kassel: Bärenreiter, 1954), pp. 208–9: "Vernehme ich in der Kirche eine feierliche Symphonie, so überfällt mich ein andächtiger Schauder; arbeitet ein starcker Instrumenten-Chor in die Wette, so bringt mir solches eine hohe Verwunderung zu Wege; fängt das Orgelwerck an zu brausen und zu donnern, so entstehet eine göttliche Furcht in mir; schließt sich denn alles mit einem freudigen Hallelujah, so hüpfft mir das Hertz im Leibe." Mattheson goes on to note that the effect of a vocal work would still be powerful even if for some reason he did not know the meaning of the words being sung.

2. Wackenroder to Tieck, letter of 5 May 1792, in his *Sämtliche Werke,* II, 29: "Wenn ich in ein Konzert gehe, find' ich, daß ich immer auf zweyerley Art die Musik genieße. Nur die eine Art des Genußes ist die wahre: sie besteht in der aufmerksamsten Beobachtung der Töne u[nd] ihrer Fortschreitung; in der völligen Hingebung der Seele, in diesen fortreißenden Strohm von Empfindungen; in der Entfernung und Abgezogenheit von jedem störenden Gedanken und von allen fremdartigen sinnlichen Eindrücken. Dieses geizige Einschlürfen der Töne ist mir einer gewissen Anstrengung verbunden, die man nicht allzulange aushält. Eben daher glaub' ich behaupten zu können, daß man höchstens eine Stunde lang Musik mit Theilnehmung zu empfinden vermöge." In the same letter, Wackenroder describes another way of listening, in which he allows the music to provoke images in his mind, without paying such close attention to the actual course of the notes themselves—in other words, to use the music as a stimulus to the fantasy, rather than to use the fantasy as a stimulus to the "quaffing" of the music. Ironically, this less satisfactory mode of listening is the one that has been most often ascribed to writers such as Wackenroder.

3. In his *Das musikalische Hören der Neuzeit* (Berlin: Akademie-Verlag, 1959), Heinrich Besseler recognizes that what he calls "active-synthetic" listening peaked in the late eighteenth and early nineteenth centuries, but he characterizes Wackenroder's views here as a break with tradition, ignoring the more fundamental philosophical continuity between Wackenroder and figures such as Kant and Fichte before him.

4. Rousseau, "Sonate," in his *Dictionnaire de musique* (1768); see above, p. 7.

5. Rousseau, "Air," in his *Dictionnaire de musique* (1768).

6. Charles Batteux, *Les beaux-arts réduits à un même principe* (Paris: Durand, 1746), pp. 263–64: "La parole nous instruit, nous convainc, c'est l'organe de la raison: mais le Ton & le Geste sont ceux du coeur: ils nous émeuvent, nous gagnent, nous persuadent. La Parole n'exprime la passion que par le moyen des idées auxquelles les sentimens sont liés, & comme par réflexion. Le Ton & le Geste arrivent au coeur directement & sans aucun détour."

7. See Bonds, *Wordless Rhetoric*.

8. Karl Philipp Moritz, *Andreas Hartknopf: Eine Allegorie* (1786), in his *Werke*, ed. Horst Günther, 3 vols. (Frankfurt/Main: Insel, 1981), I, 458, 459:

> Hartknopf nahm seine Flöte aus der Tasche, und begleitete das herrliche Rezitativ seiner Lehren, mit angemeßnen Akkorden—er übersetzte, indem er phantasierte, die Sprache des Verstandes in die Sprache der Empfindungen: denn dazu diente ihm
>
> *die Musik.*
>
> Oft, wenn er den Vordersatz gesprochen hatte, so blies er den Nachsatz mit seiner Flöte dazu.
>
>   Er atmete die Gedanken, so wie er sie in die Töne der Flöte hauchte, aus dem Verstande ins Herz hinein. . . .
>
> Daß durch gleiche Taktteile Ernst und Würde—durch ungleiche lebhafte Empfindungen—durch drei oder vier kurze Töne zwischen zwei längern, Fröhlichkeit—duch einen oder zwei kurze Töne vor einem langen Wildheit, Ungestüm—durch ♭♭♭ das Schwerfällige ausgedruckt wird—wie geht das zu? Worin liegt hier die Ähnlichkeit zwischen den Zeichen und der bezeichneten Sache?
>
>   Wer das herausbringt, der ist im Stande ein Alphabet der Emfindungssprache zu verfertigen, woraus sich tausend herrliche Werke zusammen setzen lassen. — Ist nicht die Musik der Sterblichen eine Kinderklapper, sobald sie sich nicht an die große Natur hält, sobald sie die nicht nachahmt?

9. Both examples are taken from Riley, *Musical Listening in the German Enlightenment,* pp. 7–8, 17, 130.

10. Ernst Ludwig Gerber, *Historisch-biographisches Lexikon der Tonkünstler,* vol. 1 (Leipzig: J.G.I. Breitkopf, 1790), p. 610; Johann Ferdinand Ritter von Schönfeld, *Jahrbuch der Tonkunst Wien und Prag 1796;* translated by Kathrine Talbot as "A Yearbook of Music in Vienna and Prague, 1796," in *Haydn and His World,* ed. Elaine Sisman (Princeton: Princeton University Press, 1997), pp. 289–320; the passage cited here is from p. 299.

11. Triest, "Bemerkungen über die Ausbildung der Tonkunst in Deutschland," *AmZ* 3 (1801): 300–301 (C.P.E. Bach) and 407 (Haydn).

12. Ignaz Theodor Ferdinand Arnold, *Gallerie der berühmtesten Tonkünstler des achtzehnten und neunzehnten Jahrhunderts* (Erfurt, 1810; reprint, Buren: Knuf, 1984), p. 110; Giuseppe Carpani, *Le Haydine, ovvero Lettere sulla vita e le opere del celebre maestro Giuseppe Haydn* (Milan: Candido Buccinelli, 1812), pp. 11–12.

13. Stendhal, *Lives of Haydn, Mozart and Metastasio* (1814), ed. and trans. Richard N. Coe (New York: Calder & Boyars, 1972), pp. 57–58; Joseph Fröhlich, *Joseph Haydn,* ed. Adolf Sandberger (Regensburg: Gustav Bosse, 1936), pp. 22–24, 27–29. Fröhlich's biographical sketch was originally published in the *Allgemeine Encyklopädie der Wissenschaften und Künste* (Leipzig, 1828).

14. In his *Musical Listening in the German Enlightenment,* Matthew Riley rightly emphasizes the growing importance of attentiveness (*Aufmerksamkeit*) in eighteenth-century aesthetics. These same sources, however, also testify to

the composer's even greater responsibility to engage and sustain the attention of their listeners.

15. Friedrich Schlegel, *Philosophische Lehrjahre*, in his *Kritische Friedrich-Schlegel-Ausgabe*, XVIII, 361 (no. 494); idem, *Athenäums-Fragmente*, in his *Kritische Friedrich-Schlegel-Ausgabe*, II, 254 (no. 444). On the historical context of the last of these aphorisms, see Bonds, *Wordless Rhetoric*, pp. 166–67.

16. Count Waldstein's earlier prophecy of Beethoven going to Vienna to "receive the spirit of Mozart from Haydn's hands" had been written in a private notebook, and it reflects Beethoven's status at the time (1792) as a pupil of the two earlier composers, not as their equal or superior; see Elaine Sisman, "'The Spirit of Mozart from Haydn's Hands': Beethoven's Musical Inheritance," in *The Cambridge Companion to Beethoven*, ed. Glenn Stanley (Cambridge: Cambridge University Press, 2000), pp. 45–63. The novelist Johann Ernst Wagner, writing in a Viennese newspaper in 1807, had compared Haydn to Wieland, Mozart to Schiller, and Beethoven to Jean Paul, without, however, suggesting a hierarchy of value among the three composers or writers; see Charles Rosen, *The Frontiers of Meaning: Three Informal Lectures on Music* (New York: Hill and Wang, 1994), pp. 41–42. Johann Friedrich Reichardt's letter of 16 December 1808, published in 1810 in his *Vertraute Briefe geschrieben auf einer Reise nach Wien und den österreichischen Staaten zu Ende des Jahres 1808 und zu Anfang 1809*, is the only antecedent to Hoffmann's review that situates Beethoven's music as part of a progression beyond the works of Haydn and Mozart; see H. C. Robbins Landon, *Haydn: Chronicle & Works*, 5 vols. (Bloomington: Indiana University Press, 1976–80), V, 409.

17. Hoffmann, *Schriften zur Musik*, p. 35: "Der Ausdruck eines kindlichen, heitern Gemüts herrscht in Haydns Kompositionen. Seine Symphonie *führt uns* in unabsehbare, grüne Haine, in ein lustiges, buntes Gewühl glücklicher Menschen. Jünglinge und Mädchen schweben in Reihentänzen vorüber. . . . Ein Leben voll Liebe, voll Seligkeit wie vor der Sünde, in ewiger Jugend; kein Leiden, kein Schmerz, nur ein süßes, wehmütiges Verlangen nach der geliebten Gestalt, die in der Ferne im Glanz des Abendrotes daher schwebt. . . ." (Emphasis added here and in all subsequent citations from Hoffmann's review.)

18. Hoffmann, *Schriften zur Musik*, pp. 35–36: "In die Tiefen des Geisterreichs *führt uns* Mozart. Furcht umfängt uns: aber, ohne Marter, ist sie mehr Ahnung des Unendlichen. Liebe und Wehmut tönen in holden Stimmen; die Nacht der Geisterwelt geht auf in hellem Purpurschimmer, und in unaussprechlicher Sehnsucht *ziehen wir* den Gestalten nach, die, *freundlich uns* in ihre Reihen *winken*, im ewigen Sphärentanze durch die Wolken fliegen. (Z. B. Mozarts Sinfonie in Es dur, unter dem Namen des Schwanengesanges bekannt.)"

19. Hoffmann, *Schriften zur Musik*, p. 36: "So *öffnet uns* auch Beethovens Instrumentalmusik das Reich des Ungeheueren und Unermeßlichen. Glühende Strahlen schießen durch dieses Reiches tiefe Nacht, und wir werden Riesenschatten gewahr, die auf- und abwogen, enger und enger uns einschließen, und alles in uns vernichten, nur nicht den Schmerz der unendlichen Sehnsucht. . . ."

20. Hoffmann, *Schriften zur Musik*, p. 36. The original German is given in chapter 1, note 8.

21. Hoffmann, "Beethovens Instrumentalmusik," *Kreisleriana* (1813), in his *Sämtliche Werke*, II/1, 55, 59–60: "Wie ist es aber, wenn nur *Eurem* schwachen Blick der innere tiefe Zusammenhang jeder Beethovenschen Komposition entgeht? Wenn es nur an *Euch* liegt, daß ihr des Meisters, dem Geweihten verständliche Sprache nicht versteht, wenn Euch die Pforte des innersten Heiligtums verschlossen blieb? . . . und mitten in diesem aufgeschlossenen Geisterreiche horcht die entzückte Seele der unbekannten Sprache zu und versteht alle die geheimsten Ahndungen, von denen sie ergriffen. . . . Es ist, als meinte der Meister, man könne von tiefen, geheimnisvollen Dingen . . . nie in gemeinen, sondern nur in erhabenen, herrlichen Worten reden." Emphasis in the original.

22. Kant, *Kritik der Urteilskraft*, B181: "Genie ist das Talent (Naturgabe), welches der Kunst die Regel gibt. Da das Talent, als angebornes produktives Vermögen des Künstlers, selbst zur Natur gehört, so könnte man sich auch so ausdrücken: Genie ist die angeborne Gemütsanlage (*ingenium*), durch welche die Natur der Kunst die Regel gibt."

23. Kant, *Kritik der Urteilskraft*, B183–84.

24. Kant, *Kritik der Urteilskraft*, B192–93; Meredith translation, pp. 175–76.

25. See Andrew Bowie, *From Romanticism to Critical Theory*, chapters 1–3; Cristina Lafont, *The Linguistic Turn in Hermeneutic Philosophy*, trans. José Medina (Cambridge, Mass.: MIT Press, 1999), chapters 1–2; Kurt Mueller-Vollmer, "Romantic Language Theory and the Art of Understanding," in *The Cambridge History of Literary Criticism,* vol. 5: *Romanticism,* ed. Marshall Brown (Cambridge: Cambridge University Press, 2000), pp. 162–84.

26. Kant, *Kritik der Urteilskraft*, B215; Meredith translation, p. 191.

27. Kant, *Kritik der Urteilskraft*, B218–21.

28. On the connections between fiction and philosophy in this era, see Nicholas Saul, "The Pursuit of the Subject: Literature as Critic and Perfecter of Philosophy, 1790–1830," in *Philosophy and German Literature, 1700–1990,* ed. Nicholas Saul (Cambridge: Cambridge University Press, 2002), pp. 57–101.

29. Jean Paul, *Das Kampaner Tal* (1797), in his *Werke*, 10 vols., ed. Norbert Miller (Munich: Hanser, 1959–85), IV, 563.

30. "The Oldest Systematic Programme of German Idealism," in *The Early Political Writings of the German Romantics*, ed. Frederick C. Beiser (Cambridge: Cambridge University Press, 1996), p. 4.

31. Schlegel, "Ideen," originally published in *Athenäum* (1800), in *Kritische Friedrich-Schlegel-Ausgabe*, II, 261 (no. 38): "Wo die Philosophie aufhört, muß die Poesie anfangen." Idem, *Athenäums-Fragment* 116 ("progressive Universalpoesie"), in his *Kritische Friedrich-Schlegel-Ausgabe*, II, 182.

32. Friedrich Schlegel, *Die Entwicklung der Philosophie in zwölf Büchern*, in his *Kritische Friedrich-Schlegel-Ausgabe*, XII, 214; translation from Bowie, *From Romanticism to Critical Theory*, p. 85.

33. Friedrich Wilhelm Joseph Schelling, *System des transzendentalen Idealismus* (1800), ed. Horst D. Brandt and Peter Müller (Hamburg: Felix Meiner, 1992), p. 299.

34. Schelling, *System des transzendentalen Idealismus*, pp. 296–97. "Das Kunstwerk nur reflektiert mir, was sonst durch nichts reflektiert wird, jenes absolut Identische, was selbst im Ich schon sich getrennt hat; was also der Philosoph schon

im ersten Akt des Bewußtseins sich trennen läßt, wird, sonst für jede Anschauung unzugänglich, durch das Wunder der Kunst aus ihren Produkten zurückgestrahlt."

35. Schelling, *System des transzendentalen Idealismus*: "Der Grundcharakter des Kunstwerks ist also eine *bewußtlose Unendlichkeit* [Synthesis von Natur und Freiheit]. Der Künstler scheint in seinem Werk außer dem, was er mit offenbarer Absicht darein gelegt hat, instinktmäßig gleichsam eine Unendlichkeit dargestellt zu haben, welche ganz zu entwickeln kein endlicher Verstand fähig ist" (p. 290). "So ist es mit jedem wahren Kunstwerk, indem jedes, als ob eine Unendlichkeit von Absichten darin wäre, einer unendlichen Auslegung fähig ist, wobei man doch nie sagen kann, ob diese Unendlichkeit im Künstler selbst gelegen habe, oder aber bloß im Kunstwerk liege" (p. 291).

36. Schelling, *System des transzendentalen Idealismus*, p. 298: "Es ist nichts ein Kunstwerk, was nicht ein Unendliches unmittelbar oder wenigstens im Reflex darstellt."

37. See Andrew Bowie, "German Idealism and the Arts," in *The Cambridge Companion to Idealism,* ed. Karl Ameriks (Cambridge: Cambridge University Press, 2000), p. 246.

38. Novalis, *Schriften*, 3rd ed., ed. Paul Kluckhohn and Richard Samuel (Stuttgart: Kohlhammer, 1977–), III, 685–86 (no. 671). See Manfred Frank's commentary on this and related passages in Novalis's writings in Frank, *Einführung in die frühromantische Ästhetik*, pp. 248–86.

39. Schelling, *System des transzendentalen Idealismus*, p. 299: "Die Kunst ist eben deswegen dem Philosophen das Höchste, weil sie ihm das Allerheiligste gleichsam öffnet, wo in ewiger und ursprünglicher Vereinigung gleichsam in einer Flamme brennt, was in der Natur und Geschichte gesondert ist. . . ."

40. Schelling, *System des transzendentalen Idealismus*, p.299: "das Land der Phantasie, nach dem wir trachten."

41. See Frank, *Einführung in die frühromantische Ästhetik*, pp. 127, 233–34, 312.

CHAPTER THREE
LISTENING TO TRUTH: BEETHOVEN'S FIFTH SYMPHONY

1. Johann Nikolaus Forkel, *Über die Theorie der Musik insofern sie Liebhabern und Kennern nothwendig und nützlich ist* (Göttingen: Wittwe Vandenhöck, 1777). This prospectus for a series of public lectures was later re-issued in Carl Friedrich Cramer's *Magazin der Musik* 1 (1783): 855–912. For a discussion of these lectures, see Riley, *Musical Listening in the German Enlightenment,* chapter 4.

2. Leon Botstein, "Listening through Reading: Musical Literacy and the Concert Audience," *19th-Century Music* 16 (1992): 129–45.

3. For examples of discussions of Kantian philosophy in the pages of the *Allgemeine musikalische Zeitung,* see Christian Friedrich Michaelis, "Ein Versuch, das innere Wesen der Tonkunst zu entwickeln," *AmZ* 8 (23 July 1806): 673–83, 691–96; idem, "Ueber das Idealische in der Tonkunst," *AmZ* 10 (13 April 1808): 449–52; Amadeus Wendt, "Von dem Einfluss der Musik auf den Charakter,"

AmZ 11 (1808): 81–90, 97–103; Georg August Griesinger, "Biographische Notizen über Joseph Haydn," *AmZ* 11 (23 August 1809): 740 (with an extended quotation from the *Critique of Judgment* on the unconscious nature of artistic genius); and von Weiler, "Ueber den Begriff der Schönheit, als Grundlage einer Ästhetik der Tonkunst," *AmZ* 13 (13 February 1811): 117–24. Kant's views on the relationship of genius and sublime as presented in the *Critique of Judgment* also figure prominently in chapter 11 of Johann Nicolaus Forkel's *Ueber Johann Sebastian Bachs Leben, Kunst und Kunstwerke* (1802), ed. Walther Vetter (Berlin: Henschelverlag, 1966), even though Forkel never cites the philosopher by name.

4. See Frieder Zaminer, "Über die Herkunft des Ausdrucks 'Musik verstehen,' " in Peter Faltin and Hans-Peter Reinecke, eds., *Musik und Verstehen: Aufsätze zur semiotischen Theorie, Ästhetik und Soziologie der musikalischen Rezeption* (Cologne: Arno Volk/Hans Gerig, 1973), pp. 314–19.

5. This point is emphasized with special clarity in Ronald Taylor's brief but insightful *Hoffmann* (New York: Hillary House, 1963).

6. Schelling, *System des transzendentalen Idealismus*, p. 299.

7. Edmund Burke, *A Philosophical Enquiry into the Origin of Our Ideas of the Sublime and Beautiful* (1757, rev. 1759), ed. James Boulton (Notre Dame: University of Notre Dame Press, 1958), p. 39 (section VII: "Of the Sublime"). Burke's treatise was translated into German in 1773.

8. On the aesthetics of the symphonic sublime, see Carl Dahlhaus, "E.T.A. Hoffmanns Beethoven-Kritik und die Ästhetik des Erhabenen"; Nicolas Waldvogel, "The Eighteenth-Century Esthetics of the Sublime and the Valuation of the Symphony," Ph.D. diss., Yale University, 1992, chapters 3 and 4; and Elaine Sisman, *Mozart: The "Jupiter" Symphony* (Cambridge: Cambridge University Press, 1993), pp. 13–20.

9. See Mark Evan Bonds, "The Symphony as Pindaric Ode," in *Haydn and His World*, ed. Elaine Sisman. (Princeton: Princeton University Press, 1997), pp. 131–53.

10. Franz Xaver Niemetschek, *Leben des k. k. Kapellmeisters Wolfang Gottlieb Mozart* (1798), quoted in Sisman, *Mozart's "Jupiter" Symphony,* p. 10.

11. John Baillie, *Essay on the Sublime* (London: R. Dodsely, 1747), p. 7.

12. Kant, *Kritik der Urteilskraft*, B77.

13. Kant, *Kritik der Urteilskraft*, B124; B197.

14. See Solomon, *Late Beethoven*, pp. 67–70, 146–50.

15. Schiller, "Über das Erhabene" (1795?), in his *Werke und Briefe*, VIII, 838: "Die Fähigkeit, das Erhabene zu empfinden, ist also eine der herrlichsten Anlagen in der Menschennatur, die sowohl wegen ihres Ursprungs aus dem selbstständigen Denk- und Willensvermögen unsre *Achtung*, als wegen ihres Einflusses auf den moralischen Menschen, die vollkommenste Entwickelung verdient. Das Schöne macht sich bloß verdient um den *Menschen*, das Erhabene um den *reinen Dämon* in ihm; und weil es einmal unsre Bestimmung ist, auch bei allen sinnlichen Schranken uns nach dem Gesetzbuch reiner Geister zu richten, so muß das Erhabene zu dem Schönen hinzukommen, um die *ästhetische Erziehung* zu einem vollständigen Ganzen zu machen, und die Empfindungsfähigkeit des menschlichen Herzens, nach dem ganzen Umfang unsrer Bestimmung, und also auch über die Sinnenwelt hinaus, zu erweitern."

16. Ibid., VIII, 830: "Das Erhabene verschafft uns also einen Ausgang aus der sinnlichen Welt, worin uns das Schöne gern immer gefangen halten möchte. Nicht allmählich (denn es gibt von der Abhängigkeit keinen Übergang zur Freiheit), sondern plötzlich und durch eine Erschütterung, reißt es den selbstständigen Geist aus dem Netze los, womit die verfeinerte Sinnlichkeit ihn umstrickte, und das um so fester bindet, je durchsichtiger es gesponnen ist. Wenn sie durch den unmerklichen Einfluß eines weichlichen Geschmacks auch noch so viel über die Menschen gewonnen hat—wenn es ihr gelungen ist, sich in der verführerischen Hülle des geistigen Schönen in den innersten Sitz der moralischen Gesetzgebung einzudrängen, und dort die Heiligkeit der Maximen an ihrer Quelle zu vergiften, so ist oft eine einzige erhabene Rührung genug, dieses Gewebe des Betrugs zu zerreißen, dem gefesselten Geist seine ganze Schnellkraft auf einmal zurückzugeben, ihm eine Revelation über seine wahre Bestimmung zu erteilen, und ein Gefühl seiner Würde, wenigstens für den Moment aufzunötigen. Die Schönheit unter der Gestalt der Göttin Calypso hat den tapfern Sohn des Ulysses bezaubert, und durch die Macht ihrer Reizungen hält sie ihn lange Zeit auf ihrer Insel gefangen. Lange glaubt er einer unsterblichen Gottheit zu huldigen, da er doch nur in den Armen der Wollust liegt—aber ein erhabener Eindruck ergreift ihn plötzlich unter Mentors Gestalt, er erinnert sich seiner bessern Bestimmung, wirft sich in die Wellen und ist frei."

17. Friedrich Schleiermacher, *Über die Religion: Reden an die Gebildeten unter ihren Verächtern* (1799) (Hamburg: Felix Meiner, 1958), p. 92.

18. Friedrich Schlegel, *Transzendentalphilosophie* (1800–1801), in his *Kritische Friedrich-Schlegel-Ausgabe*, XII, 7: "Dies ist ein Sehnen, die Sehnsucht nach dem Unendlichen. Etwas Höheres gibt es im Menschen nicht." Idem, *Philosophische Lehrjahre* (1798–1801), in his *Kritische Friedrich-Schlegel-Ausgabe* XVIII, 418 (no. 1168): "Das Wesen der Philosophie besteht in d[er] Sehnsucht nach d[em] Unendlichen und in d[er] Ausbildung d[es] Verstandes." See also Schlegel, "Ideen," originally published in *Athenäum* (1800), in *Kritische Friedrich-Schlegel-Ausgabe*, II, 256 (no. 3): "Only in relationship to the infinite can there be substance and use; whatever is not directed toward it [the infinite] is simply empty and useless."

19. Friedrich Schlegel, *Transzendentalphilosophie* (1800–1801), in his *Kritische Friedrich-Schlegel-Ausgabe*, XII, 8: "Die Sehnsucht nach dem Unendlichen muß immer Sehnsucht seyn. Unter der Form der Anschauung kann es nicht vorkommen. Das Ideal läßt sich nie anschauen. Das Ideal wird durch Spekulazion erzeugt."

20. Jean Paul, *Vorschule der Ästhetik*, in his *Sämtliche Werke*, V, 106–9.

21. Schelling, in his *Philosophie der Kunst* (*Sämmtliche Werke*, V, 462), distinguishes between the apparent and the truly infinite; Burke, in his chapter on "Infinity" in *A Philosophical Enquiry into the Origin of Our Ideas of the Sublime and Beautiful*, had made a similar distinction.

22. In his *Grammatisch-kritisches Wörterbuch der hochdeutschen Mundart*, 4 vols. (Vienna: Pichler, 1808), Johann Christoph Adelung defines *Marter* as "the highest degree, or at the least a very high degree of pain, especially bodily pain; also, figuratively, pain of the spirit" ("der höchste Grad, oder doch ein sehr hoher

Grad der Schmerzen, besonders körperlichen Schmerzen, figürlich aber auch der Schmerzen des Geistes").

23. Jean Paul, *Vorschule der Ästhetik*, in his *Sämtliche Werke*, V, 467: "Das Reich des Romantischen teilt sich eigentlich in das Morgenreich des Auges und in das Abendreich des Ohrs und gleicht darin seinem Verwandten, dem Traum."

24. Jean Paul, *Das Kampaner Thal* (1797), in his *Sämtliche Werke*, IV, 563.

25. Frank, *Einführung in die Frühromantische Ästhetik*, p. 295; Georg Wilhelm Friedrich Hegel, "*Phänomenologie des Geistes* (1807), ed. Eva Moldenhauer and Karl Markus Michel (Frankfurt/Main: Suhrkamp, 1970), p. 19. Frank points out that Friedrich Schlegel also used this metaphor for *Witz*, the sudden and unexpected connection of opposites. Frank also notes (pp. 318, 339) that lightning was a favorite epistemological metaphor of Karl Wilhelm Ferdinand Solger in the years around 1815.

26. In his *Vorschule der Ästhetik* (*Sämtliche Werke*, V, 100–101), Jean Paul compares romanticism to the Greek concept of the "music of the spheres." This passage appears shortly before a statement Hoffmann would thinly paraphrase in his review of Beethoven's Fifth. Jean Paul: "Ebenso selten als das romantische Talent ist daher der romantische Geschmack." Hoffmann: "Der romantische Geschmack ist selten, noch seltner das romantische Talent."

27. Once again, Jean Paul's *Vorschule der Ästhetik* provided a model for Hoffmann. Under the rubric "The Essence of Romantic Poetry" (*Sämtliche Werke*, V, 88–89), Jean Paul explicitly evokes the image of Plato's cave and its shadows.

28. See Leon Botstein, "The Consequences of Presumed Innocence: The Nineteenth-Century Reception of Joseph Haydn," in *Haydn Studies*, ed. W. Dean Sutcliffe (Cambridge: Cambridge University Press, 1998), pp. 1–34.

29. See my discussion of Beethoven's symphonic shadow in *After Beethoven*, chapter 1.

30. Whether Hoffmann knew Hegel's *Phenomenology of Spirit* directly cannot be documented, but the treatise had already attracted intense attention by the time Hoffmann set to work on his review of Beethoven's Fifth Symphony. On the early reception of Hegel's treatise, see Terry Pinkard, *Hegel: A Biography* (Cambridge: Cambridge University Press, 2000), pp. 256–65. Jean Paul was one of the work's most enthusiastic early reviewers. Hoffmann's knowledge of this work can be reasonably inferred for a person of his education and professional training as a jurist. The biographical connections are tantalizing. For a brief time—three months in 1808—Hegel and Hoffmann both lived in Bamberg. We do not know whether the *Capellmeister* ever crossed paths with the newly appointed editor of the *Bamberger Zeitung*, though such a meeting seems entirely plausible in a city of little more than 18,000 inhabitants. (The population in 1811–1812 was 18,143, according to a personal communication of 26 May 2005 from Dr. Robert Zink, Archivdirektor of the Stadtarchiv Bamberg; I am grateful to Dr. Zink for providing this information.) Years later, Hegel and Hoffmann were also in Berlin at the same time and even belonged to the same fraternal order, the "Gesetzlose Gesellschaft," Hegel from 1818 onward, Hoffmann from 1820 until his death in 1822. This latter connection is of course too late to have exercised any influence on Hoffmann's earlier writings, but it does illustrate the relatively small circles of intellectual life at the time, even in a city the size of Berlin.

31. Herder, a decade earlier, had similarly pointed out that Orpheus had moved the gods of the underworld through "the language of his playing on the strings" of his lyre, adding that "the Eumenides would not have obeyed the words of a mortal" (*Kalligone,* in his *Sämmtliche Werke,* XXII, 185–86).

32. Hoffmann, *Schriften zur Musik,* p. 34.

33. A. B. Marx, "Etwas über die Symphonie und Beethovens Leistungen in diesem Fach," *BAmZ* 1 (1824): 165–68, 173–76, 181–84; Robert Schumann, review of Hector Berlioz's *Symphonie fantastique, NZfM* 3 (1835): 33–34. This approach is even more openly evident in Marx's later *Ludwig van Beethoven: Leben und Schaffen* (Berlin, 1859; reprint, Hildesheim: Olms, 1979).

34. C. Hubert H. Parry, "Symphony," in *A Dictionary of Music and Musicians,* 4 vols., ed. George Grove (London: Macmillan, 1880–89), IV, 27–28: "It might seem almost superfluous to trace the history of [the] Symphony after Beethoven. Nothing since his time has shown, nor in the changing conditions of the history of the race is it likely anything should show, any approach to the vitality and depth of his work. But it is just these changing conditions that leave a little opening for composers to tread the same path with him."

35. *AmZ* 2 (9 October 1799): 25. Note the parallel formulation to Triest's later praise of Haydn's art as *kunstvolle Popularität* ("artful popularity") or *populäre Kunstfülle* ("popular richness of art"). For similar reactions to Beethoven's music, see Robin Wallace, *Beethoven's Critics: Aesthetic Dilemmas and Resolutions during the Composer's Lifetime* (Cambridge: Cambridge University Press, 1986), pp. 8, 16, 18.

36. See, e.g., the generally positive review of a concert performance of the Fifth Symphony in Leipzig, "Musik in Leipzig," *AmZ* 11 (12 April 1809): 434–35.

37. See Schelling, *System des transzendentalen Idealismus,* p. 289.

38. Jean Paul, *Vorschule der Ästhetik,* in his *Werke,* V, 57–58, 73, 135, 179, and *passim.*

39. Ibid., V, 57: "Nun gibt es eine höhere Besonnenheit, die, welche die innere Welt selber entzweit und entzweiteilt in ein Ich und in dessen Reich, in einen Schöpfer und dessen Welt."

40. Hoffmann's review (*Schriften zur Musik,* p. 37) reads: "Nichtsdestoweniger ist er, rücksichts der Besonnenheit, Haydn und Mozart ganz an die Seite zu stellen. Er trennt sein Ich von dem innern Reich der Töne und gebietet darüber als unumschränkter Herr." Martyn Clarke's translation in *E.T.A. Hoffmann's Musical Writings,* ed. David Charlton (Cambridge: Cambridge University Press, 1989), p. 238 ("He is nevertheless fully the equal of Haydn and Mozart in rational awareness, his controlling self detached from the inner realm of sounds and ruling it in absolute authority"), does not convey the sense of purposeful, self-conscious agency expressed in the original.

41. Friedrich Schlegel, "Über die Unverständlichkeit" (1800), in his *Kritische Friedrich-Schlegel-Ausgabe,* II, 363–72; translated as "On Incomprehensibility," in *Classic and Romantic German Aesthetics,* ed. J. M. Bernstein (Cambridge: Cambridge University Press, 2003), pp. 297–307.

42. Jean Paul, *Vorschule der Ästhetik,* in his *Werke,* V, 72.

43. On the relationship of organic form and thought in Kant's *Critique of Judgment,* see Manfred Frank, *Der kommende Gott: Vorlesungen über die neue My-*

thologie (Frankfurt/Main: Suhrkamp, 1982), pp. 162–64. On the broader relationship of organicism and aesthetics in the late eighteenth and early nineteenth centuries, see Abrams, *The Mirror and the Lamp,* chapter 7; Charles I. Armstrong, *Romantic Organicism: From Idealist Origins to Ambivalent Afterlife* (New York: Palgrave Macmillan, 2003), esp. chapters 2 and 3.

44. Hegel, *Phänomenologie des Geistes,* p. 24; translated by A. V. Miller as *Phenomenology of Spirit* (Oxford: Clarendon, 1977), p. 11.

45. Hegel, *Phänomenologie des Geistes,* p. 19; *Phenomenology of Spirit,* p. 7.

46. Hoffmann, *Schriften zur Musik,* p. 37: "Wie ästhetische Meßkünstler im Shakespeare oft über gänzlichen Mangel wahrer Einheit und inneren Zusammenhanges geklagt haben, und nur dem tiefern Blick ein schöner Baum, Knospen und Blätter, Blüten und Früchte aus einem Keim treibend, erwächst: so entfaltet auch nur ein sehr tiefes Eingehen in die innere Struktur Beethovenscher Musik *die* hohe Besonnenheit des Meisters, welche von dem wahren Genie unzertrennlich ist und von dem anhaltenden Studium der Kunst genährt wird." Emphasis in the original.

47. Hoffmann, "Beethovens Instrumentalmusik," in his *Sämtliche Werke,* II/1, 55–56: "Nichts kann einfacher sein, als der nur aus zwei Takten bestehende Hauptgedanke des ersten Allegro's, der, Anfangs im Unisono, dem Zuhörer nicht einmal die Tonart bestimmt. . . . Wie einfach—noch einmal sei es gesagt—ist das Thema, das der Meister dem Ganzen zum Grunde legte, aber wie wundervoll reihen sich ihm alle Neben- und Zwischensätze durch ihr rhythmisches Verhältnis so an, daß sie nur dazu dienen, den Charakter des Allegros, den jenes Hauptthema nur andeutete, immer mehr und mehr zu entfalten. Alle Sätze sind kurz, beinahe alle nur aus zwei, drei Takten bestehend, und noch dazu verteilt in beständigem Wechsel der Blas- und der Saiteninstrumente; man sollte glauben, daß aus solchen Elementen nur etwas zerstückeltes, unfaßbares entstehen könne, aber statt dessen ist es eben jene Einrichtung des Ganzen sowie die beständige aufeinander folgende Wiederholung der Sätze und einzelner Akkorde, die das Gefühl einer unnennbaren Sehnsucht bis zum höchsten Grade steigert."

48. See Broyles, "Organic Form and the Binary Repeat," 341.

49. For further commentary on Haydn's Symphony no. 46 and other works in which Haydn integrates movements of a cycle, see James Webster, *Haydn's "Farewell" Symphony and the Idea of Classical Style: Through-Composition and Cyclic Integration in His Instrumental Music* (Cambridge: Cambridge University Press, 1991), esp. chapter 6, "Integration of the Cycle."

50. Cf. the figure at the beginning of Variation 5 (starting at m. 95), which reappears toward the end of the third movement (m. 174) with the figure that features prominently throughout the finale (measures 23–38, 50–53, etc.).

51. Burnham, *Beethoven Hero.*

52. Schelling, *System des transzendentalen Idealismus,* chapter 6, section 2 ("Charakter des Kunstprodukts"), subsection c; August Wilhelm Schlegel, *Vorlesungen über schöne Literatur und Kunst* (1801–2), part one: *Die Kunstlehre,* pp. 209, 234, 248. On the broader reluctance of many early romantics to distinguish between the sublime and the beautiful, see Dietrich Mathy, "Zur frühromantischen Selbstaufhebung des Erhabenen im Schönen," in *Das Erhabene: Zwischen Grenzerfahrung und Größenwahn,* ed. Christine Pries (Weinheim: VCH, 1989), pp. 143–60.

53. Jean Paul, *Vorschule der Ästhetik*, in his *Werke*, V, 88: "Das Romantische ist das Schöne ohne Begrenzung, oder das *schöne* Unendliche, so wie es ein *erhabenes* gibt." Emphasis in the original. On the gradual decline of distinction between the sublime and the beautiful over the course of the nineteenth century, see Corina Caduff, *Die Literarisierung von Musik und bildender Kunst um 1800* (Munich: Wilhelm Fink, 2003), pp. 128–50.

54. E.T.A. Hoffmann, review of Beethoven's Piano Trios, op. 70, in *AmZ* (1813), in his *Schriften zur Musik*, pp. 118–44.

55. Friedrich Schlegel, *Athenäums-Fragmente*, in his *Kritische Friedrich-Schlegel-Ausgabe*, II, 173 (no. 53).

56. Novalis, *Schriften*, II, 269–70 (no. 566).

57. Joseph Kerman, *The Beethoven Quartets* (New York: Knopf, 1967), p. 367.

58. These positions are summarized and evaluated in Richard Kramer, "Between Cavatina and Overture: Opus 130 and the Voices of Narrative," *Beethoven Forum* 1 (1992): 165–89, and Lewis Lockwood, *Beethoven: The Music and the Life* (New York: Norton, 2003), pp. 458–68.

59. Friedrich Schlegel, *Athenäums-Fragmente*, in his *Kritische Friedrich-Schlegel-Ausgabe*, II, 184 (no. 121).

60. See Maynard Solomon, "The Sense of an Ending: The Ninth Symphony," *Critical Inquiry* 17 (1991): 289–305; republished in Solomon, *Late Beethoven*, pp. 213–28.

61. Lockwood, "Beethoven, Florestan, and the Varieties of Heroism," p. 40.

62. Theodor Adorno, *Aesthetic Theory*, ed. Gretel Adorno and Rolf Tiedemann, trans. Robert Hullot-Kentor (Minneapolis: University of Minnesota Press, 1997), pp. 126–33. See also Lambert Zuidervaart, *Adorno's Aesthetic Theory: The Redemption of Illusion* (Cambridge, Mass.: MIT University Press, 1991), pp. 194–97; idem, *Artistic Truth: Aesthetics, Discourse, and Imaginative Disclosure* (Cambridge: Cambridge University Press, 2004); Albrecht Wellmer, *The Persistence of Modernity: Essays on Aesthetics, Ethics and Postmodernism*, trans. David Midgley (Cambridge, Mass.: MIT Press, 1991), pp. 1–35; and Simon Jarvis, *Adorno: A Critical Introduction* (New York: Routledge, 1998), pp. 90–123.

63. Jerrold Levinson, "Truth in Music," in his *Music, Art, and Metaphysics: Essays in Philosophical Aesthetics* (Ithaca: Cornell University Press, 1990), pp. 279–305.

64. Georg Wilhlelm Friedrich Hegel, *Aesthetics: Lectures on Fine Art*, trans. T. M. Knox, 2 vols. (Oxford: Clarendon, 1975), II, 1236.

CHAPTER FOUR
LISTENING TO THE AESTHETIC STATE: COSMOPOLITANISM

1. Cosima Wagner, *Die Tagebücher*, 2 vols., ed. Martin Gregor-Dellin and Dietrich Mack (Munich: R. Piper, 1977), II, 1103 (entry for 30 January 1883): "Dort (in Sonaten etc.) musiziere er, in der Symphonie musiziere die Welt durch ihn."

2. François Jean de Chastellux, *Essai sur l'union de la poësie et de la musique* (The Hague and Paris, 1765; reprint, Geneva: Slatkine, 1970), p. 49.

3. For other contemporary references to the synthesis of timbres and voices, see Bonds, "The Symphony as Pindaric Ode," pp. 141–46. The perception of a cantabile tone as antithetical to the nature of the symphony is still evident in Hans Georg Nägeli's *Vorlesungen über Musik, mit Berücksichtigung der Dilettanten* (Stuttgart and Tübingen, 1826; reprint, Darmstadt: Wissenschaftliche Buchgesellschaft, 1983), p. 156. On the stylistic distinctions between symphonies and sonatas in the eighteenth century, see Michael Broyles, "The Two Instrumental Styles of Classicism," *JAMS* 36 (1983): 210–42.

4. See Elaine Sisman, "Haydn's Theater Symphonies," *JAMS* 43 (1990): 304–6.

5. Bernard Germain Etienne de La Ville sur Illon, Comte de La Cépède, *La poëtique de la musique*, 2 vols. (Paris: Author, 1785), II, 333; Koch, *Musikalisches Lexikon*, "Sinfonie oder Symphonie"; Jérôme-Joseph de Momigny, *Cours complet d'harmonie et de composition*, 3 vols. (Paris: Author, 1806), II, 584.

6. Anonymous, review of two symphonies by J. Küffner, *AmZ* 22 (19 April 1820): 273. Other comparisons of the symphony to the chorus are found in August F. C. Kollmann, *An Essay on Practical Musical Composition* (London, 1799; reprint, New York: Da Capo, 1973), p. 15; Marx, "Etwas über die Symphonie," *BAmZ* 1 (1824): 168, 175; Robert Schumann, "Die 7te Symphonie von Franz Schubert," *NZfM* 12 (1840): 81–83; Richard Wagner, *Oper und Drama* (1851, rev. 1868), in his *Gesammelte Schriften und Dichtungen*, 10 vols., ed. Wolfgang Golther (Berlin: Deutsches Verlagshaus Bong & Co., n.d.), IV, 190–91; and Wagner, "Zukunftsmusik" (1860), in his *Gesammelte Schriften und Dichtungen*, VII, 130.

7. Momigny, *Cours complet*, II, 586–606 (Haydn); III, 109–56 (Mozart). For other examples of analyses illustrating the difference between individual and group emotions, see Bonds, *Wordless Rhetoric*, pp. 169–76.

8. See Thomas S. Grey, "Metaphorical Modes in Nineteenth-Century Music Criticism: Image, Narrative, and Idea," in *Music and Text: Critical Inquiries*, ed. Steven Paul Scher (Cambridge: Cambridge University Press, 1992), pp. 99–110.

9. See Landon, *Haydn: Chronicle & Works*, II, 726; the original German is given in H. C. Robbins Landon, "Haydniana (II)," *Haydn Yearbook* 7 (1970): 317.

10. Alexander Wheelock Thayer, *Thayer's Life of Beethoven*, rev. ed., ed. Elliot Forbes (Princeton: Princeton University Press, 1969), p. 889.

11. K.B., "Miscellen," *AmZ* 17 (11 October 1815): 694.

12. Marx, "Etwas über die Symphonie," *BAmZ* 1 (1824): 168.

13. Gottfried Wilhelm Fink, "Ueber die Symphonie, als Beitrag zur Geschichte und Aesthetik derselben," *AmZ* 37 (1835): 559.

14. Ernst Gottschald, "Robert Schumann's zweite Symphonie. Zugleich mit Rücksicht auf andere, insbesondere Beethoven's Symphonien. Vertraute Briefe an A. Dörffel," *NZfM* 32 (1850): 157.

15. A. B. Marx, *Die Musik des neunzehnten Jahrhunderts und ihre Pflege* (Leipzig: Breitkopf & Härtel, 1855), pp. 162–63.

16. August Reissmann, "Symphonie," in Hermann Mendel and August Reissmann, *Musikalisches Conversations-Lexikon*, 11 vols. (Berlin: L. Heiman & Robert Oppenheimer, 1870–79), X, 38–39.

17. See, esp., his *Die Symphonie von Beethoven bis Mahler* (Berlin: Schuster & Loeffler, 1918).

18. Burnham, *Beethoven Hero*, p. 121 (emphasis in the original).

19. Friedrich Schlegel, *Athenäums-Fragmente*, in his *Kritische Friedrich-Schlegel-Ausgabe*, II, 198 (no. 216): "Die Französische Revolution, Fichtes Wissenschaftslehre, und Goethes Meister sind die größten Tendenzen des Zeitalters. Wer an dieser Zusammenstellung Anstoß nimmt, wem keine Revolution wichtig scheinen kann, die nicht laut und materiell ist, der hat sich noch nicht auf den hohen weiten Standpunkt der Geschichte der Menschheit erhoben."

20. Frederick Beiser, "The Enlightenment and Idealism," in *The Cambridge Companion to German Idealism*, ed. Karl Ameriks (Cambridge: Cambridge University Press, 2000), p. 31.

21. Although the term *Bildungsroman* did not emerge until the nineteenth century, *Wilhelm Meisters Lehrjahre* was immediately and widely recognized as a novel about *Bildung*, a word that appears in the very first sentence of Friedrich Schlegel's extended review-essay (1798) on Goethe's novel.

22. Johann Wolfgang Goethe, *Wilhelm Meisters Lehrjahre*, Book 5, Chapter 3: "Ich habe nun einmal gerade zu jener harmonischen Ausbildung meiner Natur, die mir meine Geburt versagt, eine unwiderstehliche Neigung." Translation from *Wilhelm Meister's Apprenticeship*, ed. and trans. Eric A. Blackall (New York: Suhrkamp, 1989), p. 175.

23. Friedrich Schlegel, "Über Goethes Meister" (1798), in his *Kritische Friedrich-Schlegel-Ausgabe*, II, 143: "die Kunst aller Künste, die Kunst zu leben."

24. See Saul, "The Pursuit of the Subject," pp. 57–58.

25. See Terry Pinkard, *German Philosophy, 1760–1800: The Legacy of Idealism* (Cambridge: Cambridge University Press, 2002), pp. 1–15, and Frederick Beiser, *Enlightenment, Revolution, and Romanticism: The Genesis of Modern German Political Thought, 1790–1800* (Cambridge, Mass.: Harvard University Press, 1992).

26. Beethoven to Breitkopf & Härtel, 2 November 1809 (*Briefwechsel*, II, 88, letter no. 408; *Letters*, I, 246, letter no. 228). On the *Tagebuch*, see Maynard Solomon, "Beethoven's *Tagebuch*," in his *Beethoven Essays* (Cambridge, Mass.: Harvard University Press, 1988), pp. 233–95; idem, *Late Beethoven*, chapters 7 and 8.

27. Reinhold Brinkmann ("In the Time(s) of the *Eroica*," pp. 4, 21) has suggested that Beethoven's symphonies could be rightly added to the trio of characteristic tendencies of the age cited by Friedrich Schlegel in his Athenäums Fragment no. 216. While I endorse this sentiment entirely, I would expand the connection to embrace the symphony as a genre, and not Beethoven's alone.

28. Quoted in Paul Kluckhohn, *Persönlichkeit und Gemeinschaft: Studien zur Staatsauffassung der deutschen Romantik* (Halle: Max Niemeyer, 1925), p. 27. On the mechanistic concept of the state in the late eighteenth century, see Ulrich Scheuner, *Der Beitrag der deutschen Romantik zur politischen Theorie* (Opladen: Westdeutscher Verlag, 1980), pp. 7–8.

29. For useful anthologies of contemporary writings advocating the organic concept of the state, see H. S. Reiss, ed., *The Political Thought of the German Romantics, 1793–1815* (Oxford: Basil Blackwell, 1955), and Frederick Beiser, ed., *The Early Political Writings of the German Romantics* (Cambridge: Cambridge University Press, 1996). See also Ahlrich Meyer, "Mechanische und organische

Metaphorik politischer Philosophie," *Archiv für Begriffsgeschichte* 13 (1969): 128–99; Reinhold Aris, *History of Political Thought in Germany from 1789 to 1815* (London: George Allen & Unwin, 1936), pp. 266–319; Frank, *Der kommende Gott*, pp. 153–244; and Beiser, *Enlightenment, Revolution, and Romanticism*, pp. 236–39.

30. Novalis, *Pollen* (1798), in his *Schriften*, 4 vols., ed. J. Minor (Jena: Eugen Diederichs, 1923), II, 272: "Um Mensch zu werden und zu bleiben, bedarf er eines Staates. . . . Ein Mensch ohne Staat ist ein Wilder. Alle Kultur entspringt aus den Verhältnissen eines Menschen mit dem Staate." The translation here is from Beiser, *The Early Political Writings*, p. 26.

31. Fichte, *Der geschlossene Handelsstaat* (1800), as quoted in James J. Sheehan, *German History, 1770–1866* (Oxford: Clarendon, 1989), p. 376.

32. Fichte, "unzertrennliches organisches Ganzes," quoted in Franz Schnabel, *Deutsche Geschichte im neunzehnten Jahrhundert*, vol. 1: *Die Grundlagen* (Freiburg im Breisgau: Herder, 1929), p. 296.

33. On Schelling's views of the state as organism, see Reiss, ed., *The Political Thought of the German Romantics,* p. 23; Schnabel, *Deutsche Geschichte,* I, 295–301.

34. Schelling, *Vorlesungen über die Methode des akademischen Studiums* (1802, published 1803), in *Die Idee der deutschen Universität: Die fünf Grundschriften aus der Zeit ihrer Neubegründung durch klassischen Idealismus und romantischen Realismus,* ed. Ernst Anrich (Darmstadt: Wissenschaftliche Buchgesellschaft, 1964), p. 61 (unity in variety); p. 19: "Jeder Staat ist in dem Verhältnis vollkommen, in welchem jedes einzelne Glied, indem es Mittel zum Ganzen, zugleich in sich selbst Zweck ist."

35. Beiser, *Enlightenment, Revolution, and Romanticism,* p. 58. Fichte's principal texts in this regard are his *Beiträge zur Berichtigung der Urteile des Publikums über die französische Revolution* (1793), *Einige Vorlesungen über die Bestimmung des Gelehrten* (1794), and *Der geschlossene Handelsstaat* (1800).

36. Josef Chytry, *The Aesthetic State: A Quest in Modern German Thought* (Berkeley and Los Angeles: University of California Press, 1989), p. 26; Marchand, *Down from Olympus,* p. 9.

37. Novalis, "Faith and Love," in *The Early Political Writings of the German Romantics,* pp. 45, 48.

38. Friedrich Schiller, *Über die ästhetische Erziehung des Menschen,* ed. Käte Hamburger (Stuttgart: Reclam, 1965), Seventh Letter, p. 27; *On the Aesthetic Education of Man,* ed. and trans. E. M. Wilkinson and L. A. Willoughby (Oxford: Clarendon, 1967), p. 45.

39. Schiller, *Über die ästhetische Erziehung des Menschen,* Second Letter, pp. 5–7; *On the Aesthetic Education of Man,* pp. 7–9.

40. Schiller, *Über die ästhetische Erziehung des Menschen,* Fifteenth Letter, p. 59; *On the Aesthetic Education of Man,* p. 101.

41. Schiller, *Über die ästhetische Erziehung des Menschen,* Fourth Letter, p. 14; *On the Aesthetic Education of Man,* p. 21.

42. Schiller, *Über die ästhetische Erziehung des Menschen,* Twenty-seventh Letter, p. 126; *On the Aesthetic Education of Man,* p. 215.

43. Schiller, *Was kann eine gute stehende Schaubühne eigentlich wirken?* in his *Werke und Briefe,* VIII, 199.

44. Letter to Christian Gottfried Körner, quoted in Aris, *History of Political Thought in Germany,* p. 201.

45. Schiller, *Über die ästhetische Erziehung des Menschen,* Twenty-seventh Letter, p. 128; *On the Aesthetic Education of Man,* p. 219.

46. Goethe, *Wilhelm Meisters Wanderjahre,* chapter 10 (1821 version); book II, chapter 1 (1829 version).

47. Goethe, *Wilhelm Meisters Wanderjahre,* chapter 13 (1821 version); book II, chapter 8 (1829 version).

48. Goethe, *Wilhelm Meisters Wanderjahre,* 1829 version, book I, chapter 4, in his *Sämtliche Werke,* ed. Karl Richter, 34 vols. (Munich: Hanser, 1985–98), XVII, 270: "Übe dich zum tüchtigen Violinisten und sei versichert, der Kapellmeister wird dir deinen Platz im Orchester mit Gunst anweisen." This passage does not appear in the 1821 version.

49. On the choral movement in Germany, see Henry Raynor, *Music and Society since 1815* (New York: Schocken, 1976), chapter 6; Dieter Düding, *Organisierter gesellschaftlicher Nationalismus in Deutschland (1808–1847): Bedeutung und Funktion der Turner- und Sängervereine für die deutsche Nationalbewegung* (Munich: R. Oldenbourg, 1984).

50. Quoted in Cornelia Schröder, ed., *Carl Friedrich Zelter und die Akademie: Dokumente und Briefe zur Entstehung der Musik-Sektion in der Preußischen Akademie der Künste* (Berlin: Akademie der Künste, 1959), p. 121.

51. See Celia Applegate, "How German Is It? Nationalism and the Idea of Serious Music in the Early Nineteenth Century," *19th-Century Music* 21 (1988): 293–96.

52. Quoted in John Spitzer, "Metaphors of the Orchestra—The Orchestra as Metaphor," *MQ* 80 (1996): 240.

53. Heinrich Christoph Koch, "Über den Charakter der Solo- und Ripienstimmen," *Journal der Tonkunst* 2 (1795): 154: "Die Ripienstimme stellt ein Glied einer Gesellschaft vor, die, von einer bestimmten Empfindung belebt, diese Empfindung äußert. . . ."

54. Schumann, "Schwärmerbriefe: Eusebius an Chiara," *NZfM* 3 (20 October 1835): 127.

55. Gottfried Wilhelm Fink, "Symphonie," in *Encyclopädie der gesammten musikalischen Wissenschaften,* ed. Gustav Schilling, vol. 6 (Stuttgart: Köhler, 1838).

56. On the concept of joy as a synthetic emotion, see James Parsons, "*Deine Zauber binden wieder*: Beethoven, Schiller, and the Joyous Reconciliation of Opposites," *Beethoven Forum* 9 (2002): 1–53.

CHAPTER FIVE
LISTENING TO THE GERMAN STATE: NATIONALISM

1. Jon Vanden Heuvel, *A German Life in the Age of Revolution: Joseph Görres, 1776–1848* (Washington, D.C.: Catholic University of America Press, 2001),

p. 222, identifies various other publications shut down by the Prussian government in 1816.

2. For an overview of the politics of repression in the decades after 1815, see Sheehan, *German History, 1770–1866*, pp. 441–50.

3. Henry E. Dwight, *Travels in the North of Germany* (New York: G. & C. & H. Carvill, 1829), p. 166.

4. Ludwig van Beethoven, *Konversationshefte*, ed. Karl-Heinz Köhler and Grita Herre (Leipzig: Deutscher Verlag für Musik, 1972–), I, 333; II, 229.

5. Beethoven, *Konversationshefte*, IX, 168; ibid., III, 288; Maynard Solomon, *Beethoven*, 2nd ed. (New York: Schirmer, 1998), p. 291. For an overview of censorship in Vienna as it related to music, see Alice M. Hanson, *Musical Life in Biedermeier Vienna* (Cambridge: Cambridge University Press, 1985), chapter 2.

6. Marlies Stützel-Prüsener, "Die deutschen Lesegesellschaften im Zeitalter der Aufklärung," in *Lesegesellschaften und bürgerliche Emanzipation: Ein europäischer Vergleich*, ed. Otto Dann (Munich: C. H. Beck, 1981), pp. 75–76. On sublimated forms of political expression during the 1820s, see Sheehan, *German History, 1770–1866*, pp. 444–47; David Blackbourn, *The Long Nineteenth Century: A History of Germany, 1780–1918* (Oxford: Oxford University Press, 1998), pp. 124–28.

7. See Düding, *Organisierter gesellschaftlicher Nationalismus*, pp. 45–46; idem, "The Nineteenth-Century German Nationalist Movement as a Movement of Societies," in *Nation-Building in Central Europe*, ed. Hagen Schulze (Leamington Spa: Berg, 1987), pp. 19–49. On the democratic organization of choral societies, see Raynor, *Music and Society since 1815*, pp. 90–92.

8. On the intermixture of cosmopolitanism and nationalism in the late eighteenth and early nineteenth centuries, see Friedrich Meinecke, *Cosmopolitanism and the National State*, trans. Robert B. Kimber (Princeton: Princeton University Press, 1970); George Armstrong Kelly, *Idealism, Politics and History: Sources of Hegelian Thought* (Cambridge: Cambridge University Press, 1969), pp. 248–68; Levinger, *Enlightened Nationalism*.

9. Friedrich Schiller, *Deutsche Größe* (1801), in his *Werke und Briefe*, I, 735–36.

10. Herder, quoted in Sheehan, *German History, 1770–1866*, p. 165.

11. Beiser, *Enlightenment, Revolution, Romanticism*, p. 212. See also David Aram Kaiser, *Romanticism, Aesthetics, and Nationalism* (Cambridge: Cambridge University Press, 1999).

12. Adam Müller, *Vorlesungen über die deutsche Wissenschaft und Literatur* (Dresden, 1806), quoted in Hans Kohn, "Romanticism and the Rise of German Nationalism," *Review of Politics* 12 (1950): 467.

13. *Rheinischer Merkur*, 3 September 1814, quoted in Vanden Heuvel, *A German Life in the Age of Revolution*, p. 203.

14. Quoted in Gary D. Stark, "The Ideology of the German *Burschenschaft* Generation," *European Studies Review* 8 (1978), p. 335.

15. Quoted in Richard Pregizer, *Die politischen Ideen des Karl Follen: Ein Beitrag zur Geschichte des Radikalismus in Deutschland* (Tübingen: J.C.B. Mohr, 1912), p. 23.

16. Düding, *Organisierter gesellschaftlicher Nationalismus*, pp. 67, 118.

17. Sheehan, *German History, 1770–1866*, p. 383.

18. Quoted in Liah Greenfeld, *Nationalism: Five Roads to Modernity* (Cambridge, Mass.: Harvard University Press, 1992), p. 376.

19. See Ernst Weber, *Lyrik der Befreiungskriege (1812–1815): Gesellschaftspolitische Meinungs- und Willensbildung durch Literatur* (Stuttgart: J. B. Metzler, 1991), p. 103.

20. Joachim Raff would later incorporate Gustav Reichardt's well-known melody for this text into the fourth and fifth movements of his Symphony no. 1 (1861), subtitled "An das Vaterland."

21. On the confluence of German nationalism and anti-Semitism in the early nineteenth century, see Greenfeld, *Nationalism*, pp. 378–86; on the anti-Semitic events at the Wartburg Festival, see Pinkard, *German Philosophy, 1760–1860*, p. 210.

22. Celia Applegate and Pamela Potter, eds., *Music and German National Identity* (Chicago: University of Chicago Press, 2002) provides a valuable survey of the topic. See also Erich Reimer, "Nationalbewußtsein und Musikgeschichtsschreibung in Deutschland, 1800–1850," *Die Musikforschung* 46 (1993): 20–24; and Applegate, "How German Is It?"

23. Friedrich Rochlitz, "Vorschläge zu Betrachtungen über die neueste Geschichte der Musik," *AmZ* 1 (3 July 1799): 626–27: "[S]oll eine solche Geschichte der Musik und der Bildung einer Nation, z.B. der Deutschen, für diese Kunst, nicht wie gewöhnlich, Geschichte einzelner verdienter Männer werden: so muss sie, wie mich dünkt, mit der Geschichte der Bildung der Nation überhaupt; oder, wenn dies ja allzuweitaussehend schiene, wenigstens mit der Geschichte der Kultur aller Künste und der Nation für dieselben, fortschreiten." Rochlitz would later commission and publish Johann Triest's "Bemerkungen über die Ausbildung der Tonkunst in Deutschland" (1801), an overview very much in keeping with the wishes he expresses here.

24. Anonymous, "Etwas über den Werth der Musik überhaupt, und die Mittel, ihn zu erhöhen," *AmZ* 2 (3 September 1800): 837–38.

25. Quoted in Kropfinger, "Klassik-Rezeption," p. 318.

26. Forkel, *Ueber Johann Sebastian Bachs Leben*, p. 124: "Und dieser Mann— der größte musikalische Dichter und der größte musikalische Declamator, den es je gegeben hat, und den es wahrscheinlich je geben wird—war ein Deutscher. Sey stolz auf ihn, Vaterland; sey auf ihn stolz, aber, sey auch seiner werth!"

27. D. Hohnbaum, "Gedanken über den Geist der heutigen deutschen Setzkunst," *AmZ* 7 (20 March 1805): 397–98, 399.

28. On the political underpinnings of this debate, see Philippe Vendrix, "La reine, le roi et sa maîtresse: Essai sur la représentation de la différence pendant la Querelle des Bouffons," *Il Saggiatore musicale* 5 (1998): 219–44.

29. Anonymous, "Merkwürdige Novität," *AmZ* 8 (25 June 1806): 616.

30. Gerber, "Eine freundliche Vorstellung," p. 458.

31. Anonymous, "Teutschland im ersten Viertel des neuen Jahrhunderts. Betrachtungen eines Musikfreundes," *Cäcilia* 4 (1825): 109–10.

32. These qualities were perceived as distinctively "German" already in the second half of the 18th century. See Mary Sue Morrow, "Building a National Identity with Music: A Story from the Eighteenth Century," in *Searching for Com-*

mon Ground: Diskurse zur deutschen Identität, 1750–1871, ed. Nicholas Vazsonyi (Cologne: Böhlau, 2000), pp. 255–68, and Bernd Sponheuer, "Reconstructing Ideal Types of the 'German' in Music," in *Music and German National Identity,* ed. Celia Applegate and Pamela Potter (Chicago: University of Chicago Press, 2002), pp. 36–58.

33. *BAmZ* 1 (5 May 1824): 163, 443. See also Bauer, *Wie Beethoven auf den Sockel kam,* pp. 87–95, and Sanna Pederson, "A. B. Marx, Berlin Concert Life, and German National Identity," *19th-Century Music* 18 (1994): 87–107. Marx did not condemn all Italian opera: during the 1820s, he championed the works of Gaspare Spontini, the musical director at the court of Friedrich Wilhelm III.

34. Fink, "Ueber die Symphonie," pp. 511, 521–22. For other references to the symphony as a distinctively German genre, see Carl Borromäus von Miltitz, "Nachrichten: Dresden," *AmZ* 39 (22 February 1837): 126 ("die so schöne, dem Deutschen allein angehörige Gattung der Sinfonie"); the anonymous review of Gottfried Preyer's Symphony no. 1, *AmZ* 41 (19 June 1839): 484 ("diese grosse Kunstgattung, die Ehre der Teutschen"); and August Kahlert, review of Mendelssohn's "Scottish" Symphony, *AmZ* 45 (10 May 1843): 341.

35. Robert Schumann, "Neue Symphonieen [*sic*] für Orchester," *NZfM* 11 (2 July 1839): 1. A portion of this translation is adapted from Jon Finson, *Robert Schumann and the Study of Orchestral Composition: The Genesis of the First Symphony, op. 38* (Oxford: Clarendon, 1989), p. 19.

36. Richard Wagner, *Über deutsches Musikwesen* (1840), in his *Gesammelte Schriften und Dichtungen,* I, 156; *Ein glücklicher Abend* (1841), in ibid., I, 147–48.

37. See James Parakilas, "Political Representation and the Chorus in Nineteenth-Century Opera," *19th-Century Music* 16 (1992): 181–202.

38. David B. Dennis, *Beethoven in German Politics, 1870–1989* (New Haven: Yale University Press, 1996); Ulrich Schmitt, *Revolution im Konzertsaal: Zur Beethoven-Rezeption im 19. Jahrhundert* (Mainz: Schott, 1990), pp. 255–66. On the ideologies underlying the work of various critics in the twentieth century, see Rumph, *Beethoven after Napoleon,* pp. 222–45. On divergent interpretations and uses of the Ninth Symphony in particular, see Andreas Eichhorn, *Beethovens Neunte Symphonie: Die Geschichte ihrer Aufführung und Rezeption* (Kassel: Bärenreiter, 1993), and Esteban Buch, *Beethoven's Ninth: A Political History,* trans. Richard Miller (Chicago: University of Chicago Press, 2003).

39. Adorno, *Beethoven: Philosophie der Musik,* pp. 175–76; the translation here is from *Beethoven: The Philosophy of Music,* p. 120.

40. "Musikalisches Leben in Braunschweig," *NZfM* 6 (1837): 57. The translation here is a slightly modified version of that given in Gramit, *Cultivating Music,* pp. 159–60. The anonymous essay is attributed in the journal's table of contents to Wolfgang Robert Griepenkerl, author of *Das Musikfest,* discussed later in this chapter.

41. On the role of amateur orchestral musicians (particularly string players) in music festivals in the first half of the nineteenth century, see Ottmar Schreiber, *Orchester und Orchesterpraxis in Deutschland zwischen 1780 und 1850* (Berlin, 1938; reprint, Hildesheim: Georg Olms, 1978), pp. 51–63. On the growth of festival orchestras in general, see Klaus Wolfgang Niemöller, "Die Entwicklung des

Orchesters bei den Musikfesten des 19. Jahrhunderts," in *Festschrift Christoph-Hellmut Mahling zum 65. Geburtstag*, 2 vols., ed. Axel Beer, Kristina Pfarr, and Wolfgang Ruf (Tutzing: Schneider, 1997), II: 1009–22.

42. See Chytry, *The Aesthetic State*.

43. "Grosses Musikfest zu Zerbst, den 15ten und 16ten Juny 1827," *AmZ* 29 (25 July 1827): 522.

44. Dr. Deycks, "Das grosse Niederrheinische Musikfest 1826, in Düsseldorf," *Cäcilia* 5 (1826): 61.

45. Anonymous, "Ueber ein neuerlich aufgefundenes Manuscript des Lasus von Hermione, betitelt: Das Musikfest zu Ephyrae (Korinth), im dritten Jahre der 16. Olympiade," *BAmZ* 1 (1824): 365–69, 373–78.

46. On the tendency of Germans to identify themselves with the ancient Greeks, see Eliza May Butler, *The Tyranny of Greece over Germany* (Cambridge: The University Press, 1935); Edward Craig, *The Mind of God and the Works of Man* (Oxford: Clarendon, 1987), pp. 162–64 (on Hölderlin's *Hyperion*); and Suzanne L. Marchand, *Down from Olympus: Archaeology and Philhellenism in Germany, 1750–1970* (Princeton: Princeton University Press, 1996), pp. 4–6.

47. Friedrich Engels, "Rheinische Feste," *Rheinische Zeitung*, no. 134 (14 May 1842), in Karl Marx and Friedrich Engels, *Gesamtausgabe*, section 1, volume 3 (Berlin: Dietz, 1985), p. 353: "Und wohl mag der Deutsche die Musik, in der er König ist vor allen Völkern, feiern und pflegen, denn wie es nur ihm gelungen ist, das Höchste und Heiligste, das innerste Geheimniß des menschlichen Gemüths aus seiner verborgenen Tiefe an's Licht zu bringen und in Tönen auszusprechen, so ist es auch nur ihm gegeben, die Gewalt der Musik ganz zu empfinden, die Sprache der Instrumente und des Gesanges durch und durch zu verstehen."

48. See William Weber, *The Rise of Musical Classics in Eighteenth-Century England: A Study in Canon, Ritual, and Ideology* (Oxford: Clarendon, 1992), chapter 8, "The 1784 Handel Commemoration as Political Ritual."

49. George L. Mosse, *The Nationalization of the Masses: Political Symbolism and Mass Movements in Germany from the Napoleonic Wars through the Third Reich* (New York: New American Library, 1975), p. 13; Mona Ozouf, *Festivals and the French Revolution*, trans. Alan Sheridan (Cambridge, Mass.: Harvard University Press, 1989); Laura Mason, *Singing the French Revolution: Popular Culture and Politics, 1787–1799* (Ithaca: Cornell University Press, 1996).

50. Carl Maria von Weber, "Musikfest zu Frankenhausen in Thüringen," *AmZ* 17 (27 September 1815): 653–55.

51. "Nachrichten," *AmZ* 17 (15 November 1815): 770.

52. Cecilia Hopkins Porter, "The New Public and the Reordering of the Musical Establishment: The Lower Rhine Music Festivals, 1816–67," *19th-Century Music* 3 (1980): 211–24.

53. Anonymous, "Das Musikfest in Köln am Rhein 1821," *AmZ* 23 (12 September 1821): 633.

54. See appendix 1 in Julius Alf, *Geschichte und Bedeutung der Niederrheinischen Musikfeste in der ersten Hälfte des neunzehnten Jahrhunderts*, 2 vols. (Düsseldorf: Lintz, 1940–41) (Düsseldorfer Jahrbuch, 42–43), II, 241–43.

55. Levinger, *Enlightened Nationalism*, p. 21.

56. Contemporary accounts vary between 362 and 432; see *Letters to Beethoven and Other Correspondence*, 3 vols., ed. Theodore Albrecht (Lincoln: University of Nebraska Press, 1996), III, 101, note 3.

57. "Das Niederrheinische Musikfest, 1825 in Aachen," *Cäcilia* 4 (1826): 67: "Uns scheint, dass der Meister in diesen Instrumental-Sätzen . . . das Verworrene, das Treiben und Drängen grosser Massen—z.B. bei einem Volksfeste—habe darstellen wollen, in welchem sich zuweilen hie und da eine gewaltige Stimme Bahn schafft, aber bald im Gewirre, im Taumel und wilden Jubel untergeht, bis endlich dem Sänger es gelingt, den Tumult zu stillen. Seiner Auffoderung folgen dann Alle, und nun beginnt das Lied der Freude, in welches das ganze Volk einstimmt. Die Melodie dieses Liedes kann nur in möglichst grosser Masse gesungen, Wirkung thun." A similar interpretation of Ferdinand Ries's Symphony in D Major can be found in Deycks's report of the Lower Rhine Music Festival in 1826, where once again the symphony itself is heard to reflect the joyous gathering of a large assembly; see Deycks, "Das grosse Niederrheinische Musikfest 1826, in Düsseldorf," *Cäcilia* 5 (1826): 72.

58. Anonymous, "Felix Mendelssohn-Bartholdy, in Stettin," *BAmZ* 4 (14 March 1827): 86–87: "Auch eine Fuge hat der Komponist aus dem immer länger ausgesponnenen Volksthema gemacht, wahrscheinlich um die Menge der immer mehr theilnehmenden Gesellschaft dadurch zu versinnlichen."

59. For a discussion of the role of the Ninth Symphony in Griepenkerl's novel, see David Levy, "Wolfgang Robert Griepenkerl and Beethoven's Ninth Symphony," in *Essays on Music for Charles Warren Fox*, ed. Jerald C. Graue (Rochester, N.Y.: Eastman School of Music Press, 1979), pp. 103–13.

60. Griepenkerl, *Das Musikfest; oder, Die Beethovener*, 2nd ed. (Braunschweig: Leibrock, 1841), pp. 89–90, 62–63.

61. Griepenkerl, *Das Musikfest*, pp. 152–53. On the association of Pindar and the symphony, see above, p. 46.

62. Griepenkerl, *Das Musikfest*, p. 185; p. 206: "Wer da weiss, welche öffentliche Metze diese verkappte 'Freude' Schillers von Geburt war, der fahe sie!" "Es war die Freiheit."

63. For an overview of the myth of "Freude" as a euphemism for "Freiheit" in Schiller's *An die Freude*, see Christoph Bruckmann, " 'Freude! sangen wir in Thränen, Freude! in dem tiefsten Leid.' Zur Interpretation und Rezeption des Gedichts 'An die Freude' von Friedrich Schiller," *Jahrbuch der Deutschen Schillergesellschaft* 35 (1991): 108–12.

64. Griepenkerl, *Das Musikfest*, pp. 59–60: "Es gab eine Zeit, wo das einsame Träumen am murmelnden Bach, langweiliges Turteltaubengeschwätz und eine im Schweiß des Angesichts herausgequälte Form für wahre Kunst galten. Diese Zeit ist nicht mehr. Jener lächerliche Kunstabsolutismus des Individuums hat seine Endschaft erreicht. Das große öffentliche Leben . . . dieses ist jetzt die eigentliche Werkstatt des Künstlers. Hier soll er die Pulse einer bedeutenden Krise verfolgen. . . . So ist also die Kunst nicht mehr das Armesünderglöckchen eines vereinzelten Individuums, sondern die große Glocke der Nationen, welche durch die Jahrhunderte hallt."

65. Griepenkerl, *Das Musikfest*, pp. 33, 78.

66. Griepenkerl, *Das Musikfest*, p. 79: "Der Haken ist: die Gegensätze, deren Glieder für Manche Welten auseinander liegen, werden nicht schroff genug herausgestellt, man wagt est nicht, dem Meister zu folgen, man hält ängstlich vorgespiegelte Grenzen fest, man will ausgleichen, man will Brücken über Abgründe bauen, wo man eben auf Adlerfittigen hinüberschweben sollte."

67. Thayer, *Thayer's Life of Beethoven*, p. 1057.

EPILOGUE
LISTENING TO FORM: THE REFUGE OF ABSOLUTE MUSIC

1. Robert Schumann, review of two overtures by Kalliwoda, *NZfM* 1 (5 May 1834): 38.

2. Gottschald, "Robert Schumann's zweite Symphonie," 137–38.

3. Franz Brendel, "Fragen der Zeit. III: Die Forderungen der Gegenwart und die Berechtigung der Vorzeit," *NZfM* 29 (2 September 1848): 102.

4. Franz Brendel, "Fragen der Zeit. II: Die Ereignisse der Gegenwart in ihrem Einfluß auf die Gestaltung der Kunst," *NZfM* 28 (22 April 1848): 193–95.

5. Richard Wagner, *Die Kunst und die Revolution*, in his *Gesammelte Schriften und Dichtungen*, III, 32.

6. The term *Zukunftsmusik* was coined by Wagner's opponents but later embraced by him; see Christa Jost and Peter Jost, "*Zukunftsmusik*: Zur Geschichte eines Begriffs," *Musiktheorie* 10 (1995): 119–35. On Wagner's use of the term *absolut*, see Dahlhaus, *The Idea of Absolute Music*, chapter 2; and Thomas Grey, *Wagner's Musical Prose: Texts and Contexts* (Cambridge: Cambridge University Press, 1995), chapter 1.

7. Wagner, *Das Kunstwerk der Zukunft* (1849) in his *Gesammelte Schriften und Dichtungen*, III, 100–101.

8. Ibid., III, 93.

9. Eduard Krüger, "Beziehungen zwischen Kunst und Politik," *AmZ* 50 (21 June 1848): 401, 405.

10. Johann Christian Lobe, *Musikalische Briefe: Wahrheit über Tonkunst und Tonkünstler*, 2 vols. (Leipzig: Baumgärtners Buchhandlung, 1852), I, 132–33; I, 170; II, 164. For further accounts of conservative critics of the 1840s, see Schmitt, *Revolution im Konzertsaal*, pp. 180–90.

11. Hanslick, *Vom Musikalisch-Schönen*, I, 75: "Tönend bewegte Formen sind einzig und allein Inhalt und Gegenstand der Musik." Hanslick emended the final sentence from the third edition (1865) onward to read: "Der Inhalt der Musik sind tönend bewegte Formen."

12. See Lothar Schmidt, "Arabeske: Zu einigen Voraussetzungen und Konsequenzen von Eduard Hanslicks musikalsichem Formbegriff," *AfMw* 46 (1989): 91–120.

13. Hanslick, *Vom Musikalisch-Schönen*, I, 109–10.

14. Ibid., I, 139: "[W]irklich ästhetisches Hören ist eine Kunst." From the fourth edition (1874) onward, the formulation is much more detached: "[E]s gibt eine Kunst des Hörens."

15. Ibid., I, 171: "Dieser geistige Gehalt verbindet nun auch im Gemüth des Hörers das Schöne der Tonkunst mit allen andern großen und schönen Ideen."

16. Ibid., I, 171: "Dieser geistige Gehalt verbindet nun auch im Gemüth des Hörers das Schöne der Tonkunst mit allen andern großen und schönen Ideen. Ihm wirkt die Musik nicht blos und absolut durch ihre eigenste Schönheit, sondern zugleich als tönendes Abbild der großen Bewegungen im Weltall. Durch tiefe und geheime Naturbeziehungen steigert sich die Bedeutung der Töne hoch über sie selbst hinaus und läßt uns in dem Werke menschlichen Talents immer zugleich das Unendliche fühlen. Da die Elemente der Musik: Schall, Ton, Rhythmus, Stärke, Schwäche im ganzen Universum sich finden, so findet der Mensch wieder in der Musik das ganze Universum." From the third edition (1865) onward, Hanslick went even further to suppress any appeal to idealism, deleting the first sentence about "spiritual content" being united within the "disposition of the listener." Because it is based on the eighth German edition (1891), the most frequently cited English translation of Hanslick's treatise, by Geoffrey Payzant (*On the Musically Beautiful* [Indianapolis: Hackett, 1986]), does not include the material quoted here.

17. Hanslick, *Vom Musikalisch-Schönen*, I, 75: "Frägt es sich nun, was mit diesem Tonmaterial ausgedrückt werden soll, so lautet die Antwort: Musicalische Ideen. Eine vollständig zur Erscheinung gebrachte musikalische Idee aber ist bereits selbstständiges Schöne, ist Selbstzweck und keineswegs erst wieder Mittel oder Material zur Darstellung von Gefühlen und Gedanken; wenn sie gleich in hohem Grad jene symbolische, die großen Weltgesetze wiederspiegelnde Bedeutsamkeit besitzen kann, welche wir in jedem Kunstschönen vorfinden. Tönend bewegte Formen sind einzig und allein Inhalt und Gegenstand der Musik." Hanslick emended the final sentence from the third edition (1865) onward to read, "Der Inhalt der Musik sind tönend bewegte Formen."

18. Robert Zimmerman, review of Hanslick's *Vom Musikalisch-Schönen*, originally published in *Oesterreichische Blätter für Literatur und Kunst* (1854) and republished with minor changes in Zimmerman's *Studien und Kritiken zur Philosophie und Aesthetik*, vol. 2: *Zur Aesthetik* (Vienna: Wilhelm Braumüller, 1870), p. 253: "Mich dünkt, hier hat er sich unwillkürlich durch Reminiscenzen derselben Aesthetik überraschen lassen, die er sonst so schlagend und siegreich bekämpft!" Zimmerman (1824–98) would himself write a treatise on formalist aesthetics in all the arts: The second volume of his *Aesthetik* bears the title *Allgemeine Ästhetik als Formwissenschaft* (Vienna: Wilhelm Braumüller, 1865).

19. Marx, *Ludwig van Beethoven*, I, 276–77: "Das Spiel der Töne ist die Urmusik, es war und wird immer der Mutterboden sein, aus dem das Alles, was in Musik lebt, seine Lebenskraft, sein Dasein zieht. Allein der Mensch kann . . . nicht end- und zwecklos fortspielen. Er sucht vor allen Dingen sich selber im Spiel, das Spiel soll Sein Spiel sein, das Gepräge, den Ausdruck Seines Daseins . . . haben. Seine Phantasie sucht auch im Spiel der Töne das Gefühl seines Daseins. . . . Eben darin aber, daß der Mensch die im realen Leben zwingenden Verhältnisse und Stimmungen in der Kunst selbst gestaltet, fühlt er sich Herr dieser selbstgeschaffenen Welt und von der realen Welt in diesem verklärenden Spiegelbild erlöst und frei."

20. Hanslick, *Vom Musikalisch-Schönen*, I, 46. In the second edition, Hanslick qualified this last passage to read: "can perhaps ascend from there to an intimation

of the Absolute." From the third edition (1865) onward, "the Absolute" is replaced with "an eternal, otherworldly peace" ("Ahnung eines ewigen jenseitigen Friedens").

21. See Edward Lippman, *A History of Western Musical Aesthetics* (Lincoln: University of Nebraska Press, 1992), p. 322. These writers include August Wilhelm Ambros, Friedrich Theodor Vischer, Adolf Kullak, and Moritz Carriere.

22. Gotthold Kunkel, "Die Programmmusik und Raff's Lenorensymphonie," *NZfM* 71 (12 February 1875): 65.

23. Eduard Hanslick, "Censur und Kunst-Kritik," *Wiener Zeitung,* 24 March 1848, republished in his *Sämtliche Schriften,* vol. 1, part 1: *Aufsätze und Rezensionen, 1844–1848,* ed. Dietmar Strauß (Vienna and Cologne: Böhlau, 1993), p. 157. The reference to Schubert is presumably to the "Great" C-Major Symphony, D. 944; Hanslick was not alone at the time in hearing "Hungarian" inflections in this and other works by Schubert. Ostrolenka was the site of an unsuccessful Polish uprising in 1831 against the occupying forces of Russia.

24. Ibid., p. 157: "Die Werke der großen Tondichter sind mehr als Musik, sie sind Speigelbilder der *philosophischen, religiösen* und *politischen* Weltanschauungen ihrer Zeit. Webt nicht in Beethovens letzten Werken, und in Berlioz die stolze Hoheit und die schmerzliche Scepsis der Deutschen Philosophie?" Emphasis in the original. The translation here is by Leon Botstein, "The Search for Meaning in Beethoven: Popularity, Intimacy, and Politics in Historical Perspective," in *Beethoven and His World,* ed. Scott Burnham and Michael P. Steinberg (Princeton: Princeton University Press, 2000), p. 349.

25. Eduard Hanslick, *Aus meinem Leben,* 2nd ed., 2 vols. (Berlin: Allgemeiner Verein für Deutsche Litteratur, 1894), I, 135–36.

26. Hanslick, *Vom Musikalisch-Schönen,* I, 88: "Was nicht zur Erscheinung kommt, ist in der Musik gar nicht da, was aber zur Erscheinung gekommen ist, hat aufgehört, bloße Intention zu sein."

27. For a summary of responses to Hanslick's treatise, with references to further literature, see James Deaville, "The Controversy Surrounding Liszt's Conception of Programme Music," in *Nineteenth-Century Music: Selected Proceedings of the Tenth International Conference,* ed. Jim Samson and Bennett Zon (Aldershot: Ashgate, 2002), pp. 98–124.

28. Walter Pater, "The School of Giorgione" (1877), in his *The Renaissance: Studies in Art and Poetry,* ed. Donald L. Hill (Berkeley and Los Angeles: University of California Press, 1980), p. 106.

29. Virgil Thomson, *The Art of Judging Music* (New York: Alfred A. Knopf, 1948), p. 303.

30. Willi Stoph, address to the Konstituierende Sitzung des Komitees für die Beethoven-Ehrung der DDR, *Neues Deutschland,* 28 March 1970, quoted in Eggebrecht, *Zur Geschichte der Beethoven-Rezeption,* p. 84; idem, "Festansprache . . . auf dem Festakt zur Beethoven-Ehrung der Deutschen Demokratischen Republik am 16. Dezember 1970," in *Bericht über den Internationalen Beethoven-Kongress 10.–12. Dezember 1970 in Berlin,* ed. Heinz Alfred Brockhaus and Konrad Niemann (Berlin: Verlag Neue Musik, 1971), pp. 2–3.

31. For an account of these celebrations in both East and West Germany, see Dennis, *Beethoven in German Politics,* pp. 177–97.

32. "Man weicht der Welt nicht sicherer aus als durch die Kunst, und man verknüpft sich nicht sicherer mit ihr als durch die Kunst." This maxim appears in "Ottilie's Diary" in chapter 5 of Goethe's *Die Wahlverwandtschaften* (1809), in his *Sämtliche Werke*, IX, 439.

33. Lydia Goehr, *The Quest for Voice: On Music, Politics, and the Limits of Philosophy* (Berkeley and Los Angeles: University of California Press, 1998), pp. 11–12.

Bibliography

Abrams, M. H. *The Mirror and the Lamp: Romantic Theory and the Critical Tradition.* New York: Oxford University Press, 1953.

Adelung, Johann Christoph. *Grammatisch-kritisches Wörterbuch der hochdeutschen Mundart.* 4 vols. Vienna: Pichler, 1808.

Adorno, Theodor W. *Aesthetic Theory.* Ed. Gretel Adorno and Rolf Tiedemann, trans. Robert Hullot-Kentor. Minneapolis: University of Minnesota Press, 1997.

———. *Beethoven: Philosophie der Musik: Fragmente und Texte.* Ed. Rolf Tiedemann. Frankfurt/Main: Suhrkamp, 1993. Translated by Edmund Jephcott as *Beethoven: The Philosophy of Music.* Stanford, Calif.: Stanford University Press, 1998.

———. *Einleitung in die Musiksoziologie.* Frankfurt/Main: Suhrkamp, 1962.

Albrecht, Theodore, ed. and trans. *Letters to Beethoven and Other Correspondence.* 3 vols. Lincoln: University of Nebraska Press, 1996.

Alf, Julius. *Geschichte und Bedeutung der Niederrheinischen Musikfeste in der ersten Hälfte des neunzehnten Jahrhunderts.* 2 vols. Düsseldorf: Lintz, 1940–41. (Düsseldorfer Jahrbuch, 42–43).

Alperson, Philip. "The Arts of Music." *Journal of Aesthetics and Art Criticism* 50 (1992): 217–30.

Applegate, Celia. "How German Is It? Nationalism and the Idea of Serious Music in the Early Nineteenth Century." *19th-Century Music* 21 (1998): 274–96.

Applegate, Celia, and Pamela Potter, eds. *Music and German National Identity.* Chicago: University of Chicago Press, 2002.

Aris, Reinhold. *History of Political Thought in Germany from 1789 to 1815.* London: George Allen & Unwin, 1936.

Armstrong, Charles I. *Romantic Organicism: From Idealist Origins to Ambivalent Afterlife.* New York: Palgrave Macmillan, 2003.

Arnold, Ignaz Theodor Ferdinand. *Gallerie der berühmtesten Tonkünstler des achtzehnten und neunzehnten Jahrhunderts.* Erfurt, 1810. Reprint, Buren: Knuf, 1984.

Baillie, John. *Essay on the Sublime.* London: R. Dodsley, 1747.

Batteux, Charles. *Les beaux-arts réduits à un même principe.* Paris, 1746. Reprint, New York: Johnson, 1970.

Bauer, Elisabeth Eleonore. *Wie Beethoven auf den Sockel kam: Die Entstehung eines musikalischen Mythos.* Stuttgart: J. B. Metzler, 1992.

Becker, Max. *Narkotikum und Utopie: Musik-Konzepte in Empfindsamkeit und Romantik.* Kassel: Bärenreiter, 1996.

Beethoven, Ludwig van. *Briefwechsel: Gesamtausgabe.* 7 vols. Ed. Sieghard Brandenburg. Munich: G. Henle, 1996–2001.

———. *Letters.* Ed. and trans. Emily Anderson. 3 vols. London: St. Martin's, 1961.

Beiser, Frederick C. "The Enlightenment and Idealism." In *The Cambridge Companion to Idealism*, pp. 18–36. Ed. Karl Ameriks. Cambridge: Cambridge University Press, 2000.

———. *Enlightenment, Revolution, and Romanticism: The Genesis of Modern German Political Thought, 1790–1800*. Cambridge, Mass.: Harvard University Press, 1992.

———, ed. *The Early Political Writings of the German Romantics*. Cambridge: Cambridge University Press, 1996.

Bekker, Paul. *Die Sinfonie von Beethoven bis Mahler*. Berlin: Schuster & Loeffler, 1918.

Bernstein, J. M., ed. *Classic and Romantic German Aesthetics*. Cambridge: Cambridge University Press, 2003.

Besseler, Heinrich. *Das musikalische Hören der Neuzeit*. Berlin: Akademie-Verlag, 1959.

Biba, Otto. "Concert Life in Beethoven's Vienna." In *Beethoven, Performers, and Critics: The International Beethoven Congress, Detroit, 1977*, pp. 77–93. Ed. Robert Winter and Bruce Carr. Detroit, Mich.: Wayne State University Press, 1980.

Blackbourn, David. *The Long Nineteenth Century: A History of Germany, 1780–1918*. Oxford: Oxford University Press, 1998.

Bonds, Mark Evan. *After Beethoven: Imperatives of Originality in the Symphony*. Cambridge, Mass.: Harvard University Press, 1996.

———. "The Symphony as Pindaric Ode." In *Haydn and His World*, pp. 131–53. Ed. Elaine Sisman. Princeton, N.J.: Princeton University Press, 1997.

———. *Wordless Rhetoric: Musical Form and the Metaphor of the Oration*. Cambridge, Mass.: Harvard University Press, 1991.

Botstein, Leon. "The Consequences of Presumed Innocence: The Nineteenth-Century Reception of Joseph Haydn. In *Haydn Studies*, pp. 1–34. Ed. W. Dean Sutcliffe. Cambridge: Cambridge University Press, 1998.

———. "Listening through Reading: Musical Literacy and the Concert Audience." *19th-Century Music* 16 (1992): 129–45.

———. "The Search for Meaning in Beethoven: Popularity, Intimacy, and Politics in Historical Perspective." In *Beethoven and His World*, pp. 332–366. Ed. Scott Burnham and Michael P. Steinberg. Princeton, N.J.: Princeton University Press, 2000.

———. "Toward a History of Listening." *MQ* 82 (1998): 427–31.

Bowie, Andrew. *Aesthetics and Subjectivity: From Kant to Nietzsche*, 2nd ed. Manchester: Manchester University Press, 2003.

———. *From Romanticism to Critical Theory: The Philosophy of German Literary Theory*. London: Routledge, 1997.

———. "German Idealism and the Arts." In *The Cambridge Companion to Idealism*, pp. 239–57. Ed. Karl Ameriks. Cambridge: Cambridge University Press, 2000.

Brendel, Franz. "Fragen der Zeit. II: Die Ereignisse der Gegenwart in ihrem Einfluß auf die Gestaltung der Kunst." *NZfM* 28 (22 April 1848): 193–96.

———. "Fragen der Zeit. III: Die Forderungen der Gegenwart und die Berechtigung der Vorzeit." *NZfM* 29 (2 September 1848): 101–5.

Brinkmann, Reinhold. "In the Time(s) of the *Eroica*." In *Beethoven and His World*, pp. 1–26. Ed. Scott Burnham and Michael P. Steinberg. Princeton, N.J.: Princeton University Press, 2000.

Broyles, Michael. "Organic Form and the Binary Repeat." *MQ* 66 (1980): 339–60.

———. "The Two Instrumental Styles of Classicism." *JAMS* 36 (1983): 210–42.

Bruckmann, Christoph. "'Freude! sangen wir in Thränen, Freude! in dem tiefsten Leid.' Zur Interpretation und Rezeption des Gedichts 'An die Freude' von Friedrich Schiller." *Jahrbuch der Deutschen Schillergesellschaft* 35 (1991): 96–112.

Buch, Esteban. *Beethoven's Ninth: A Political History*. Trans. Richard Miller. Chicago: University of Chicago Press, 2003.

Burke, Edmund. *A Philosophical Enquiry into the Origin of Our Ideas of the Sublime and Beautiful* (1757, rev. 1759). Ed. James Boulton. Notre Dame, Ind.: University of Notre Dame Press, 1968.

Burnham, Scott. *Beethoven Hero*. Princeton, N.J.: Princeton University Press, 1995.

———. "How Music Matters: Poetic Content Revisited." In *Rethinking Music*, pp. 193–216. Ed. Nicholas Cook and Mark Everist. New York: Oxford University Press, 1999.

Butler, Eliza May. *The Tyranny of Greece over Germany*. Cambridge: The University Press, 1935.

Caduff, Corina. *Die Literarisierung von Musik und bildender Kunst um 1800*. Munich: Wilhelm Fink, 2003.

Carpani, Giuseppe. *Le Haydine, ovvero Lettere sulla vita e le opere del celebre maestro Giuseppe Haydn*. Milan: Candido Buccinelli, 1812.

Chastellux, François Jean de. *Essai sur l'union de la poësie et de la musique*. The Hague and Paris, 1765. Reprint, Geneva: Slatkine, 1970.

Christensen, Thomas. "Four-Hand Piano Transcription and Geographies of Nineteenth-Century Musical Reception." *JAMS* 52 (1999): 255–98.

Chua, Daniel K. L. *Absolute Music and the Construction of Meaning*. Cambridge: Cambridge University Press, 1999.

Chytry, Josef. *The Aesthetic State: A Quest in Modern German Thought*. Berkeley and Los Angeles: University of California Press, 1989.

Craig, Edward. *The Mind of God and the Works of Man*. Oxford: Clarendon, 1987.

Dahlhaus, Carl. "E.T.A. Hoffmanns Beethoven-Kritik und die Ästhetik des Erhabenen." *AfMw* 39 (1981): 79–92.

———. *Die Idee der absoluten Musik*. Kassel: Bärenreiter, 1978. Translated by Roger Lustig as *The Idea of Absolute Music*. Chicago: University of Chicago Press, 1989.

———. "Romantische Musikästhetik und Wiener Klassik." *AfMw* 29 (1972): 167–81.

Daverio, John. *Crossing Paths: Schubert, Schumann, and Brahms*. New York: Oxford University Press, 2002.

Deaville, James. "The Controversy Surrounding Liszt's Conception of Programme Music." In *Nineteenth-Century Music: Selected Proceedings of the*

Tenth International Conference, pp. 98–124. Ed. Jim Samson and Bennett Zon. Aldershot: Ashgate, 2002.

Dennis, David B. *Beethoven in German Politics, 1870–1989*. New Haven: Yale University Press, 1996.

Deutsch, Otto Erich, ed. *Schubert: Die Dokumente seines Lebens*. Kassel: Bärenreiter, 1964.

Deycks, Dr. "Das grosse Niederrheinische Musikfest 1826, in Düsseldorf." *Cäcilia* 5 (1826): 61–76.

Düding, Dieter. "The Nineteenth-Century German Nationalist Movement as a Movement of Societies." In *Nation-Building in Central Europe*, pp. 19–49. Ed. Hagen Schulze. Leamington Spa: Berg, 1987.

———. *Organisierter gesellschaftlicher Nationalismus in Deutschland (1808–1847): Bedeutung und Funktion der Turner- und Sängervereine für die deutsche Nationalbewegung*. Munich: R. Oldenbourg, 1984.

Dwight, Henry E. *Travels in the North of Germany in the Years 1825 and 1826*. New York: G. & C. & H. Carvill, 1829.

Eggebrecht, Hans Heinrich. "Das Ausdrucks-Prinzip im musikalischen Sturm und Drang." *Deutsche Vierteljahrsschrift für Literaturwissenschaft und Geistesgeschichte* 29 (1955): 323–49.

———. *Musik im Abendland: Prozesse und Stationen vom Mittelalter bis zur Gegenwart*. Munich: Piper, 1991.

———. *Zur Geschichte der Beethoven-Rezeption*, 2nd ed. Laaber: Laaber-Verlag, 1994.

Eichhorn, Andreas. *Beethovens Neunte Symphonie: Die Geschichte ihrer Aufführung und Rezeption*. Kassel: Bärenreiter, 1993.

Engell, James. *The Creative Imagination: Enlightenment to Romanticism*. Cambridge, Mass.: Harvard University Press, 1981.

Engels, Friedrich. "Rheinische Feste" (1842). In Karl Marx and Friedrich Engels, *Gesamtausgabe*, section 1, volume 3, pp. 352–54. Berlin: Dietz, 1985.

"Etwas über den Werth der Musik überhaupt, und die Mittel, ihn zu erhöhen." *AmZ* 2 (1800): 817–23, 833–41, 849–56.

"Felix Mendelssohn-Bartholdy, in Stettin." *BAmZ* 4 (14 March 1827): 83–87.

Fillion, Michelle. "E. M. Forster's Beethoven." *Beethoven Forum* 9 (2002): 171–203.

Fink, Gottfried Wilhelm. "Symphonie." In *Encyclopädie der gesammten musikalischen Wissenschaften*, vol. 6. Ed. Gustav Schilling. Stuttgart: Köhler, 1838.

———. "Ueber die Symphonie, als Beitrag zur Geschichte und Aesthetik derselben." *AmZ* 37 (1835): 505–11, 521–24, 557–63.

Finson, Jon. *Robert Schumann and the Study of Orchestral Composition: The Genesis of the First Symphony, op. 38*. Oxford: Clarendon, 1989.

———. "'To Our Sincere Regret': New Documents on the Publication of Robert Schumann's D-Minor Symphony." Paper delivered at the annual meeting of the American Musicological Society, Columbus, Ohio, November 2002.

Forkel, Johann Nikolaus. *Über die Theorie der Musik insofern sie Liebhabern und Kennern nothwendig und nützlich ist*. Göttingen: Wittwe Vandenhöck, 1777.

———. *Ueber Johann Sebastian Bachs Leben, Kunst und Kunstwerke* (1802). Ed. Walther Vetter. Berlin: Henschelverlag, 1966.

Frank, Manfred. *Einführung in die frühromantische Ästhetik*. Frankfurt/Main: Suhrkamp, 1989.

———. *Der kommende Gott: Vorlesungen über die neue Mythologie*. Frankfurt/ Main: Suhrkamp, 1982.

Fröhlich, Joseph. *Joseph Haydn* (1828). Ed. Adolf Sandberger. Regensburg: Gustav Bosse, 1936.

Furst, Lillian. *Romanticism in Perspective*, 2nd ed. London: Macmillan, 1979.

Gay, Peter. *The Naked Heart*. New York: Norton, 1995.

Geck, Martin. *Von Beethoven bis Mahler: Die Musik des deutschen Idealismus*. Stuttgart: J. B. Metzler, 1993.

"Gedanken über die Symphonie." In *Großes Instrumental- und Vocal-Concert*, XVI, 57–63. Ed. Ernst Ortlepp. Stuttgart: Köhler, 1841.

Gerber, Ernst Ludwig. "Eine freundliche Vorstellung über gearbeitete Instrumentalmusik, besonders über Symphonien." *AmZ* 15 (14 July 1813): 457–62.

———. *Historisch-biographisches Lexikon der Tonkünstler*. 2 vols. Leipzig: J.G.I. Breitkopf, 1790–92.

Goehr, Lydia. *The Quest for Voice: On Music, Politics, and the Limits of Philosophy*. Berkeley and Los Angeles: University of California Press, 1998.

Goethe, Johann Wolfgang. *Sämtliche Werke*. 34 vols. Ed. Karl Richter. Munich: Hanser, 1985–98.

———. *Wilhelm Meister's Apprenticeship*. Ed. and trans. Eric A. Blackall. New York: Suhrkamp, 1989.

Goldschmidt, Hugo. *Die Musikästhetik des 18. Jahrhunderts*. Zurich and Leipzig: Rascher, 1915.

Gottschald, Ernst. "Robert Schumann's zweite Symphonie. Zugleich mit Rücksicht auf andere, insbesondere Beethoven's Symphonien. Vertraute Briefe an A. Dörffel." *NZfM* 32 (1850): 137–39, 141–42, 145–48, 157–59.

Gramit, David. *Cultivating Music: The Aspirations, Interests, and Limits of German Musical Culture, 1770–1848*. Berkeley and Los Angeles: University of California Press, 2002.

Greenfeld, Liah. *Nationalism: Five Roads to Modernity*. Cambridge, Mass.: Harvard University Press, 1992.

Grey, Thomas S. "Metaphorical Modes in Nineteenth-Century Music Criticism: Image, Narrative, and Idea." In *Music and Text: Critical Inquiries*, pp. 93–117. Ed. Steven Paul Scher. Cambridge: Cambridge University Press, 1992.

———. *Wagner's Musical Prose: Texts and Contexts*. Cambridge: Cambridge University Press, 1995.

Griepenkerl, Wolfgang Robert. "Musikalisches Leben in Braunschweig." *NZfM* 6 (1837): 57–58, 60–61, 65–66, 69–70, 74.

———. *Das Musikfest; oder, Die Beethovener*, 2nd ed. Braunschweig: Leibrock, 1841.

"Grosses Musikfest zu Zerbst, den 15ten und 16ten Juny 1827." *AmZ* 29 (25 July 1827): 522–25.

Hanslick, Eduard. *Aus meinem Leben*, 2nd ed. 2 vols. Berlin: Allgemeiner Verein für Deutsche Litteratur, 1894.

Hanslick, Eduard. *On the Musically Beautiful: A Contribution towards the Revision of the Aesthetics of Music.* Trans. Geoffrey Payzant. Indianapolis, Ind.: Hackett, 1986.

———. *Sämtliche Schriften.* Ed. Dietmar Strauß. Vienna and Cologne: Böhlau, 1993–.

———. *Vom Musikalisch-Schönen: Ein Beitrag zur Revision der Ästhetik der Tonkunst* (1854). 2 vols. Ed. Dietmar Strauß. Mainz: Schott, 1990.

Hanson, Alice M. *Musical Life in Biedermeier Vienna.* Cambridge: Cambridge University Press, 1985.

Haydn, Joseph. *Gesammelte Briefe und Aufzeichnungen.* Ed. Dénes Bartha. Kassel: Bärenreiter, 1965.

Hegel, Georg Wilhelm Friedrich. *Aesthetics: Lectures on Fine Art.* Trans. T. M. Knox. 2 vols. Oxford: Clarendon, 1975.

———. *Phänomenologie des Geistes* (1807). Ed. Eva Moldenhauer and Karl Markus Michel. Frankfurt/Main: Suhrkamp, 1970. Translated by A. V. Miller as *Phenomenology of Spirit.* Oxford: Clarendon, 1977.

Herder, Johann Gottfried. *Erstes Kritisches Wäldchen* (1769). In his *Schriften zur Ästhetik und Literatur, 1767–1781.* Ed. Gunter E. Grimm. Frankfurt/Main: Deutscher Klassiker Verlag, 1993.

———. *Sämmtliche Werke.* 33 vols. Ed. Bernhard Suphan. Berlin: Weidmann, 1877–1913.

Hoeckner, Berthold. *Programming the Absolute: Nineteenth-Century German Music and the Hermeneutics of the Moment.* Princeton, N.J.: Princeton University Press, 2002.

Hoffmann, E.T.A. *E.T.A. Hoffmann's Musical Writings:* Kreisleriana, The Poet and the Composer, *Music Criticism.* Ed. David Charlton, trans. Martyn Clarke. Cambridge: Cambridge University Press, 1989.

———. Review of Beethoven's Fifth Symphony. *AmZ* 12 (4 and 11 July 1810): 630–42, 652–59.

———. *Sämtliche Werke.* 6 vols. Ed. Hartmut Steinecke and Wulf Segebrecht. Frankfurt/Main: Deutscher Klassiker Verlag, 1993.

———. *Schriften zur Musik: Aufsätze und Rezensionen.* Ed. Friedrich Schnapp. Darmstadt: Wissenschaftliche Buchgesellschaft, 1979.

Hohnbaum, D. "Gedanken über den Geist der heutigen deutschen Setzkunst." *AmZ* 7 (20 March 1805): 397–402.

Horn, Franz. "Musikalische Fragmente." *AmZ* 4 (1802): 401–8, 416–26, 433–37, 449–57, 785–91, 801–11, 817–31, 841–48.

Hosler, Bellamy. *Changing Aesthetic Views of Instrumental Music in 18th-Century Germany.* Ann Arbor, Mich.: UMI Research Press, 1981.

Jarvis, Simon. *Adorno: A Critical Introduction.* New York: Routledge, 1998.

Jean Paul [Jean Paul Friedrich Richter]. *Werke.* 10 vols. Ed. Norbert Miller. Munich: Hanser, 1959–1985.

Johnson, James H. *Listening in Paris: A Cultural History.* Berkeley and Los Angeles: University of California Press, 1995.

Johnson, Mark. *The Body in the Mind: The Bodily Basis of Meaning, Imagination, and Reason.* Chicago: University of Chicago Press, 1987.

Jost, Christa, and Peter Jost. "*Zukunftsmusik*: Zur Geschichte eines Begriffs." *Musiktheorie* 10 (1995): 119–35.

Kahlert, August. *Blätter aus der Brieftasche eines Musikers*. Breslau: C. G. Förster, 1832.

Kaiser, David Aram. *Romanticism, Aesthetics, and Nationalism*. Cambridge: Cambridge University Press, 1999.

Kalbeck, Max. *Johannes Brahms*. 4 vols. Vienna and Leipzig: Wiener Verlag; Berlin: Deutsche Brahms-Gesellschaft, 1904–14.

Kant, Immanuel. *Kritik der Urteilskraft* (1790, rev. 1793). Ed. Heiner F. Klemme. Hamburg: Felix Meiner, 2001. Translated by James Creed Meredith as *The Critique of Judgement*. Oxford: Clarendon, 1952.

Kelly, George Armstrong. *Idealism, Politics and History: Sources of Hegelian Thought*. Cambridge: Cambridge University Press, 1969.

Kerman, Joseph. *The Beethoven Quartets*. New York: Knopf, 1967.

Kirby, F. E. "The Germanic Symphony of the Nineteenth Century: Genre, Form, Instrumentation, Expression." *Journal of Musicological Research* 14 (1995): 193–221.

Kivy, Peter. *Music Alone: Philosophical Reflections on the Purely Musical Experience*. Ithaca, N.Y.: Cornell University Press, 1990.

Kluckhohn, Paul. *Persönlichkeit und Gemeinschaft: Studien zur Staatsauffassung der deutschen Romantik*. Halle: Max Niemeyer, 1925.

Koch, Heinrich Christoph. *Kurzgefasstes Handwörterbuch der Musik*. Leipzig, 1807. Reprint, Hildesheim: Olms, 1981.

———. *Musikalisches Lexikon*. Frankfurt/Main, 1802. Reprint, Kassel: Bärenreiter, 2001.

———. "Über den Charakter der Solo- und Ripienstimmen." *Journal der Tonkunst* 2 (1795): 143–55.

———. *Versuch einer Anleitung zur Composition*. 3 vols. Leipzig, 1782–1793. Reprint, Hildesheim: Olms, 1969.

Kohn, Hans. "Romanticism and the Rise of German Nationalism." *Review of Politics* 12 (1950): 443–72.

Kollmann, August F. C. *An Essay on Practical Musical Composition*. London, 1799. Reprint, New York: Da Capo, 1973.

Köpke, Rudolf. *Ludwig Tieck: Erinnerungen aus dem Leben des Dichters*. Leipzig, 1855. Reprint, Darmstadt: Wissenschaftliche Buchgesellschaft, 1970.

Körner, Christian Gottfried. "Ueber Charakterdarstellung in der Musik" (1795). In Wolfgang Seifert, *Christian Gottfried Körner: Ein Musikästhetiker der deutschen Klassik*, pp. 147–58. Regensburg: Gustav Bosse, 1960.

Kramer, Richard. "Between Cavatina and Overture: Opus 130 and the Voices of Narrative." *Beethoven Forum* 1 (1992): 165–89.

Kramer, Ursula. "Auf den Spuren des Häßlichen: Zur ästhetischen und musikalischen Bedeutung von J. F. Reichardts *Hexenszenen zu Shakespeares Macbeth*." In *Aspekte historischer und systematischer Musikforschung: Zur Symphonie im 19. Jahrhundert*, pp. 349–66. Ed. Christoph-Hellmut Mahling and Kristina Pfarr. Mainz: Are Edition, 2002.

Kropfinger, Klaus. "Klassik-Rezeption in Berlin (1800–1830)." In *Studien zur Musikgeschichte Berlins im frühen 19. Jahrhundert*, pp. 301–79. Ed. Carl Dahlhaus. Regensburg: Bosse, 1980.

Krüger, Eduard. "Beziehungen zwischen Kunst und Politik." *AmZ* 50 (21 June 1848): 401–5.

Kunkel, Gotthold. "Die Programmmusik und Raff's Lenorensymphonie." *NZfM* 71 (12 February 1871): 65–66.

La Cépède, Comte de (Bernard Germain Etienne de La Ville sur Illon). *La poëtique de la musique*. 2 vols. Paris: Author, 1785.

Lafont, Cristina. *The Linguistic Turn in Hermeneutic Philosophy*. Trans. José Medina. Cambridge, Mass.: MIT Press, 1999.

Landon, H. C. Robbins. *Haydn: Chronicle and Works*. 5 vols. Bloomington: Indiana University Press, 1976–80.

———. "Haydniana (II)." *Haydn Yearbook* 7 (1970): 307–19.

LaRue, Jan. *A Catalogue of 18th-Century Symphonies*, vol. 1: *Thematic Identifier*. Bloomington: Indiana University Press, 1988.

le Huray, Peter, and James Day, eds. *Music and Aesthetics in the Eighteenth and Early-Nineteenth Centuries*. Cambridge: Cambridge University Press, 1981.

Leitl-Zametzer, Ursula. "Der Unendlichkeitsbegriff in der Kunstauffassung der Frühromantik bei Friedrich Schlegel und W. H. Wackenroder." Ph.D. diss., Munich, 1955.

Levinger, Matthew. *Enlightened Nationalism: The Transformation of Prussian Political Culture, 1806–1848*. Oxford: Oxford University Press, 2000.

Levinson, Jerrold. *Music, Art, and Metaphysics: Essays in Philosophical Aesthetics*. Ithaca, N.Y.: Cornell University Press, 1990.

Levy, David. "Wolfgang Robert Griepenkerl and Beethoven's Ninth Symphony." In *Essays on Music for Charles Warren Fox*, pp. 103–13. Ed. Jerald C. Graue. Rochester, N.Y.: Eastman School of Music Press, 1979.

Lippman, Edward. *A History of Western Musical Aesthetics*. Lincoln: University of Nebraska Press, 1992.

———, ed. *Musical Aesthetics: A Historical Reader*. 3 vols. New York: Pendragon, 1986–90.

[Lobe, Johann Christian]. *Musikalische Briefe: Wahrheit über Tonkunst und Tonkünstler*. 2 vols. Leipzig: Baumgärtners Buchhandlung, 1852.

Lockwood, Lewis. "Beethoven, Florestan, and the Varieties of Heroism." In *Beethoven and His World*, pp. 27–47. Ed. Scott Burnham and Michael P. Steinberg. Princeton, N.J.: Princeton University Press, 2000.

———. *Beethoven: The Music and the Life*. New York: Norton, 2003.

Maniates, Maria Rika. "'Sonate, que me veux-tu?' The Enigma of French Musical Aesthetics in the 18th Century." *Current Musicology*, no. 9 (1969): 117–40.

Marchand, Suzanne L. *Down from Olympus: Archaeology and Philhellenism in Germany, 1750–1970*. Princeton, N.J.: Princeton University Press, 1996.

Marx, Adolf Bernhard. "Etwas über die Symphonie und Beethovens Leistungen in diesem Fache." *BAmZ* 1 (1824): 165–68, 173–76, 181–84.

———. *Ludwig van Beethoven: Leben und Schaffen*. Berlin, 1859. Reprint, Hildesheim: Olms, 1979.

———. *Die Musik des neunzehnten Jahrhunderts und ihre Pflege*. Leipzig: Breitkopf & Härtel, 1855.

Marx, Karl, and Friedrich Engels. *Gesamtausgabe*. Berlin: Dietz, 1972–.

Mason, Laura. *Singing the French Revolution: Popular Culture and Politics, 1787–1799*. Ithaca, N.Y.: Cornell University Press, 1996.

Mattheson, Johann. *Der vollkommene Capellmeister*. Hamburg, 1739. Reprint, Kassel: Bärenreiter, 1954.

Mathy, Dietrich. "Zur frühromantischen Selbstaufhebung des Erhabenen im Schönen." In *Das Erhabene: Zwischen Grenzerfahrung und Größenwahn*, pp. 143–60. Ed. Christine Pries. Weinheim: VCH, 1989.

Meinecke, Friedrich. *Cosmopolitanism and the National State*. Trans. Robert B. Kimber. Princeton, N.J.: Princeton University Press, 1970.

Meyer, Ahlrich. "Mechanische und organische Metaphorik politischer Philosophie." *Archiv für Begriffsgeschichte* 13 (1969): 128–99.

Michaelis, Christian Friedrich. "Ein Versuch, das innere Wesen der Tonkunst zu entwickeln." *AmZ* 8 (23 July 1806): 673–83, 691–96.

———. "Noch einige Bemerkungen über den Rang der Tonkunst unter den schönen Künsten." *AmZ* 6 (15 August 1804): 765–73.

———. "Ueber das Idealische in der Tonkunst." *AmZ* 10 (13 April 1808): 449–52.

———. *Über den Geist der Tonkunst*. 2 vols. Leipzig, 1795–1800. Reprint, Brussels: Culture et Civilisation, 1970.

Miltitz, Carl Borromäus von. "Nachrichten: Dresden." *AmZ* 39 (22 February 1837): 125–26.

Momigny, Jérôme-Joseph de. *Cours complet d'harmonie et de composition*. 3 vols. Paris: Author, 1806.

Moritz, Karl Philipp. *Schriften zur Ästhetik und Poetik*. Ed. Hans Joachim Schrimpf. Tübingen: Max Niemeyer, 1962.

———. *Werke*. 3 vols. Ed. Horst Günther. Frankfurt/Main: Insel, 1981.

Morrow, Mary Sue. "Building a National Identity with Music: A Story from the Eighteenth Century." In *Searching for Common Ground: Diskurse zur deutschen Identität, 1750–1871*, pp. 255–68. Ed. Nicholas Vazsonyi. Cologne: Böhlau, 2000.

———. *German Music Criticism in the Late Eighteenth Century: Aesthetic Issues in Instrumental Music*. Cambridge: Cambridge University Press, 1997.

Mosse, George L. *The Nationalization of the Masses: Political Symbolism and Mass Movements in Germany from the Napoleonic Wars through the Third Reich*. New York: New American Library, 1975.

Mueller-Vollmer, Kurt. "Romantic Language Theory and the Art of Understanding." In *The Cambridge History of Literary Criticism*, vol. 5: *Romanticism*, pp. 162–84. Ed. Marshall Brown. Cambridge: Cambridge University Press, 2000.

"Das Musikfest in Köln am Rhein 1821." *AmZ* 23 (12 September 1821): 631–34.

"Musikzustand und musikalisches Leben in Wien." *Cäcilia* 1 (1824): 193–200.

Nägeli, Hans Georg. *Vorlesungen über Musik, mit Berücksichtigung der Dilettanten*. Stuttgart and Tübingen, 1826. Reprint, Darmstadt: Wissenschaftliche Buchgesellschaft, 1983.

Neubauer, John. *The Emancipation of Music from Language: Departure from Mimesis in Eighteenth-Century Aesthetics*. New Haven: Yale University Press, 1986.

"Das Niederrheinische Musikfest, 1825 in Aachen." *Cäcilia* 4 (1826): 63–70.

Niemöller, Klaus Wolfgang. "Die Entwicklung des Orchesters bei den Musikfesten des 19. Jahrhunderts." In *Festschrift Christoph-Hellmut Mahling zum 65. Geburtstag*, II, 1009–22. 2 vols. Ed. Axel Beer, Kristina Pfarr, and Wolfgang Ruf. Tutzing: Schneider, 1997.

Novalis [Friedrich von Hardenberg]. *Schriften*, 3rd ed. Ed. Paul Kluckhohn and Richard Samuel. Stuttgart: Kohlhammer, 1977–.

———. *Schriften*. Ed. J. Minor. 4 vols. Jena: Eugen Diederichs, 1923.

Ozouf, Mona. *Festivals and the French Revolution*. Trans. Alan Sheridan. Cambridge, Mass.: Harvard University Press, 1988.

Panofksy, Erwin. *Idea: A Concept in Art Theory*. Trans. Joseph J. S. Peake. Columbia: University of South Carolina Press, 1968.

Parakilas, James. "Political Representation and the Chorus in Nineteenth-Century Opera." *19th-Century Music* 16 (1992): 181–202.

Parry, C. Hubert H. "Symphony." In *A Dictionary of Music and Musicians*. 4 vols. Ed. George Grove. London: Macmillan, 1880–89.

Parsons, James. "*Deine Zauber binden wieder*: Beethoven, Schiller, and the Joyous Reconciliation of Opposites." *Beethoven Forum* 9 (2002): 1–53.

Pater, Walter. "The School of Giorgione" (1877). In his *The Renaissance: Studies in Art and Poetry*. Ed. Donald L. Hill. Berkeley and Los Angeles: University of California Press, 1980.

Pederson, Sanna. "A. B. Marx, Berlin Concert Life, and German National Identity." *19th-Century Music* 18 (1994): 87–107.

Pinkard, Terry. *German Philosophy, 1760–1860: The Legacy of Idealism*. Cambridge: Cambridge University Press, 2002.

———. *Hegel: A Biography*. Cambridge: Cambridge University Press, 2000.

Porter, Cecilia Hopkins. "The New Public and the Reordering of the Musical Establishment: The Lower Rhine Music Festivals, 1816–67." *19th-Century Music* 3 (1980): 211–24.

Pregizer, Richard. *Die politischen Ideen des Karl Follen: Ein Beitrag zur Geschichte des Radikalismus in Deutschland*. Tübingen: J.C.B. Mohr, 1912.

Raynor, Henry. *Music and Society since 1815*. New York: Schocken, 1976.

Reimer, Erich. "Nationalbewußtsein und Musikgeschichtsschreibung in Deutschland, 1800–1850." *Die Musikforschung* 46 (1993): 17–31.

Reiss, H. S., ed. *The Political Thought of the German Romantics, 1793–1815*. Oxford: Basil Blackwell, 1955.

Reissmann, August. "Symphonie." In *Musikalisches Conversations-Lexikon*. Ed. Hermann Mendel and August Reissmann. 11 vols. Berlin: L. Heiman & Robert Oppenheimer, 1870–79.

Reynolds, Christopher. *Motives for Allusion: Context and Content in Nineteenth-Century Music*. Cambridge, Mass.: Harvard University Press, 2003.

Riley, Matthew. *Musical Listening in the German Enlightenment: Attention, Wonder and Astonishment*. Aldershot: Ashgate, 2004.

Rochlitz, Friedrich. "Vorschläge zu Betrachtungen über die neueste Geschichte der Musik." *AmZ* 1 (3 July 1799): 625–29.

Rosen, Charles. *The Frontiers of Meaning: Three Informal Lectures on Music*. New York: Hill and Wang, 1994.

Rousseau, Jean Jacques. *Dictionnaire de musique.* Paris, 1768. Reprint, Hildesheim: Olms, 1969.

———. *Écrits sur la musique.* Ed. Catherine Kintzler. Paris: Stock, 1979.

Ruiter, Jacob de. *Der Charakterbegriff in der Musik: Studien zur deutschen Ästhetik der Instrumentalmusik, 1740–1850.* Stuttgart: Franz Steiner, 1989.

Rumph, Stephen. *Beethoven after Napoleon: Political Romanticism in the Late Works.* Berkeley and Los Angeles: University of California Press, 2004.

Salmen, Walter. *Johann Friedrich Reichardt.* Zurich: Atlantis, 1963.

Saul, Nicholas. "The Pursuit of the Subject: Literature as Critic and Perfecter of Philosophy, 1790–1830." In *Philosophy and German Literature, 1700–1990,* pp. 57–101. Ed. Nicholas Saul. Cambridge: Cambridge University Press, 2002.

Schelling, Friedrich Wilhelm Joseph. *Sämmtliche Werke.* Ed. K.F.A. Schelling. 14 vols. Stuttgart and Augsburg: Cotta, 1856–61.

———. *System des transzendentalen Idealismus* (1800). Ed. Horst D. Brandt and Peter Müller. Hamburg: Felix Meiner, 1992.

———. *Vorlesungen über die Methode des akademischen Studiums* (1803). In *Die Idee der deutschen Universität: Die fünf Grundschriften aus der Zeit ihrer Neubegründung durch klassischen Idealismus und romantischen Realismus,* pp. 1–123. Ed. Ernst Anrich. Darmstadt: Wissenschaftliche Buchgesellschaft, 1964.

Scheuner, Ulrich. *Der Beitrag der deutschen Romantik zur politischen Theorie.* Opladen: Westdeutscher Verlag, 1980.

Schiller, Friedrich. *On the Aesthetic Education of Man in a Series of Letters.* Ed. and trans. E. M. Wilkinson and L. A. Willoughby. Oxford: Clarendon, 1967.

———. *Über die ästhetische Erziehung des Menschen.* Ed. Käte Hamburger. Stuttgart: Reclam, 1965.

———. *Werke und Briefe.* Ed. Klaus Harro Hilzinger et al. 12 vols. Frankfurt/Main: Deutscher Klassiker Verlag, 1988–2004.

Schlegel, August Wilhelm. *Vorlesungen über schöne Literatur und Kunst* (1801–2). Erster Teil: *Die Kunstlehre.* In his *Kritische Ausgabe der Vorlesungen,* vol. 1: *Vorlesungen über Ästhetik I (1798–1803),* pp. 181–463. Ed. Ernst Behler. Paderborn: Schöningh, 1989.

Schlegel, Friedrich. *Kritische Friedrich-Schlegel-Ausgabe.* Ed. Ernst Behler. Paderborn, Munich, and Vienna: Ferdinand Schöningh, 1958–.

Schleiermacher, Friedrich. *Über die Religion: Reden an die Gebildeten unter ihren Verächtern* (1799). Hamburg: Felix Meiner, 1958.

Schmidt, Lothar. "Arabeske: Zu einigen Voraussetzungen und Konsequenzen von Eduard Hanslicks musikalsichem Formbegriff." *AfMw* 46 (1989): 91–120.

Schmitt, Ulrich. *Revolution im Konzertsaal: Zur Beethoven-Rezeption im 19. Jahrhundert.* Mainz: Schott, 1990.

Schnabel, Franz. *Deutsche Geschichte im neunzehnten Jahrhundert,* vol. 1: *Die Grundlagen.* Freiburg im Breisgau: Herder, 1929.

Schönfeld, Johann Ferdinand Ritter von. *Jahrbuch der Tonkunst Wien und Prag 1796.* Translated by Kathrine Talbot as "A Yearbook of the Music of Vienna and Prague, 1796," in *Haydn and His World,* pp. 289–320. Ed. Elaine Sisman. Princeton, N.J.: Princeton University Press, 1997.

Schreiber, Ottmar. *Orchester und Orchesterpraxis in Deutschland zwischen 1780 und 1850.* Berlin, 1938. Reprint, Hildesheim: Olms, 1978.

Schröder, Cornelia, ed. *Carl Friedrich Zelter und die Akademie: Dokumente und Briefe zur Entstehung der Musik-Sektion in der Preußischen Akademie der Künste.* Berlin: Akademie der Künste, 1959.

Schumann, Robert. "Neue Symphonieen [*sic*] für Orchester." *NZfM* 11 (2 July 1839): 1–3, 17–18.

———. Review of Hector Berlioz's *Symphonie fantastique.* *NZfM* 3 (1835): 1–2, 33–35, 37–38, 41–44, 45–48, 49–51.

———. "Schwärmerbriefe: Eusebius an Chiara." *NZfM* 3 (20 October 1835): 126–27.

———. "Die 7te Symphonie von Franz Schubert." *NZfM* 12 (1840): 81–83.

Seifert, Wolfgang. *Christian Gottfried Körner: Ein Musikästhetiker der deutschen Klassik.* Regensburg: Gustav Bosse, 1960.

Sheehan, James J. *German History, 1770–1866.* Oxford: Clarendon, 1989.

Sisman, Elaine. "Haydn's Theater Symphonies." *JAMS* 43 (1990): 292–352.

———. *Mozart: The "Jupiter" Symphony.* Cambridge: Cambridge University Press, 1993.

———. "'The Spirit of Mozart from Haydn's Hands': Beethoven's Musical Inheritance." In *The Cambridge Companion to Beethoven,* pp. 45–63. Ed. Glenn Stanley. Cambridge: Cambridge University Press, 2000.

Solomon, Maynard. *Beethoven,* 2nd ed. New York: Schirmer Books, 1998.

———. *Beethoven Essays.* Cambridge, Mass.: Harvard University Press, 1988.

———. *Late Beethoven: Music, Thought, Imagination.* Berkeley and Los Angeles: University of California Press, 2003.

Sparshott, F. E. "Aesthetics of Music." In *The New Grove Dictionary of Music and Musicians,* 20 vols. London: Macmillan, 1980.

Spitzer, John. "Metaphors of the Orchestra—The Orchestra as Metaphor." *MQ* 80 (1996): 234–64.

Sponheuer, Bernd. "Reconstructing Ideal Types of the 'German' in Music." In *Music and German National Identity,* pp. 36–58. Ed. Celia Applegate and Pamela Potter. Chicago: University of Chicago Press, 2002.

Stark, Gary D. "The Ideology of the German *Burschenschaft* Generation." *European Studies Review* 8 (1978): 323–48.

Steinberg, Michael P. *Listening to Reason: Culture, Subjectivity, and Nineteenth-Century Music.* Princeton, N.J.: Princeton University Press, 2004.

Steinkrüger, August. *Die Aesthetik der Musik bei Schelling und Hegel: Ein Beitrag zur Musikästhetik der Romantik.* Bonn: Verein Studentenwohl, 1927.

Stendhal [Henri Beyle]. *Lives of Haydn, Mozart and Metastasio* (1814). Ed. and trans. Richard N. Coe. New York: Calder & Boyars, 1972.

Stoph, Willi. "Festansprache . . . auf dem Festakt zur Beethoven-Ehrung der Deutschen Demokratischen Republik am 16. Dezember 1970." In *Bericht über den Internationalen Beethoven-Kongress 10.–12. Dezember 1970 in Berlin,* pp. 1–8. Ed. Heinz Alfred Brockhaus and Konrad Niemann. Berlin: Verlag Neue Musik, 1971.

Stützel-Prüsener, Marlies. "Die deutsche Lesegesellschaften im Zeitalter der Aufklärung." In *Lesegesellschaften und bürgerliche Emanzipation: Ein europäischer Vergleich*, pp. 71–86. Ed. Otto Dann. Munich: C. H. Beck, 1981.

Sulzer, Johann Georg. *Allgemeine Theorie der schönen Künste*. 2 vols. Leipzig, 1771–74. Reprint, 2nd ed., 1792–99. Hildesheim: Olms, 1994.

Taylor, Ronald. *Hoffmann*. New York: Hillary House, 1963.

"Teutschland im ersten Viertel des neuen Jahrhunderts." *Cäcilia* 4 (1825): 89–112.

Thayer, Alexander Wheelock. *Thayer's Life of Beethoven*, rev. ed. Ed. Elliot Forbes. Princeton, N.J.: Princeton University Press, 1969.

Thomson, Virgil. *The Art of Judging Music*. New York: Alfred A. Knopf, 1948.

Tonelli, Giorgio. "Ideal in Philosophy from the Renaissance to 1780." In *Dictionary of History of Ideas,* vol. 2. Ed. Philip P. Wiener. New York: Charles Scribner's Sons, 1973.

Triest, Johann. "Bemerkungen über die Ausbildung der Tonkunst in Deutschland im achtzehnten Jahrhundert." *AmZ* 3 (1801). Translated by Susan Gillespie as "Remarks on the Development of the Art of Music in Germany in the Eighteenth Century." In *Haydn and His World*, pp. 321–94. Ed. Elaine Sisman. Princeton, N.J.: Princeton University Press, 1997.

"Ueber ein neuerlich aufgefundenes Manuscript des Lasus von Hermione, betitelt: Das Musikfest zu Ephyrae (Korinth), im dritten Jahre der 16. Olympiade." *BAmZ* 1 (1824): 365–69, 373–78.

Vanden Heuvel, Jon. *A German Life in the Age of Revolution: Joseph Görres, 1776–1848*. Washington, D.C.: Catholic University of America Press, 2001.

Vendrix, Philippe. "La reine, le roi et sa maîtresse: Essai sur la représentation de la différence pendant la Querelle des Bouffons." *Il Saggiatore musicale 5* (1998): 219–44.

Wackenroder, Wilhelm Heinrich. *Sämtliche Werke und Briefe: Historisch-kritische Ausgabe*. Ed. Silvio Vietta and Richard Littlejohns. 2 vols. Heidelberg: Carl Winter Universitätsverlag, 1991.

Wagner, Cosima. *Die Tagebücher*. 2 vols. Ed. Martin Gregor-Dellin and Dietrich Mack. Munich: R. Piper, 1976–77.

Wagner, Richard. *Gesammelte Schriften und Dichtungen*. 10 vols. Ed. Wolfgang Golther. Berlin: Deutsches Verlagshaus Bong & Co., n.d.

Waldvogel, Nicolas. "The Eighteenth-Century Esthetics of the Sublime and the Valuation of the Symphony." Ph.D. diss., Yale University, 1992.

Wallace, Robin. *Beethoven's Critics: Aesthetic Dilemmas and Resolutions during the Composer's Lifetime*. Cambridge: Cambridge University Press, 1986.

Weber, Carl Maria von. "Musikfest zu Frankenhausen in Thüringen." *AmZ* 17 (27 September 1815): 653–55.

Weber, Ernst. *Lyrik der Befreiungskriege (1812–1815): Gesellschaftspolitische Meinungs- und Willensbildung durch Literatur*. Stuttgart: J. B. Metzler, 1991.

Weber, William. "Did People Listen in the 18th Century?" *Early Music 25* (1997): 678–91.

———. *The Rise of Musical Classics in Eighteenth-Century England: A Study in Canon, Ritual, and Ideology*. Oxford: Clarendon, 1992.

Webster, James. *Haydn's "Farewell" Symphony and the Idea of Classical Style: Through-Composition and Cyclic Integration in His Instrumental Music.* Cambridge: Cambridge University Press, 1991.

von Weiler. "Ueber den Begriff der Schönheit, als Grundlage einer Ästhetik der Tonkunst." *AmZ* 13 (13 February 1811): 117–24.

Weinzierl, Stefan. *Beethovens Konzerträume: Raumakustik und symphonische Aufführungspraxis an der Schwelle zum modernen Konzertwesen.* Frankfurt/Main: E. Bochinsky, 2002.

Wellmer, Albrecht. *The Persistence of Modernity: Essays on Aesthetics, Ethics and Postmodernism.* Trans. David Midgley. Cambridge, Mass.: MIT Press, 1991.

Wendt, Amadeus. "Von dem Einfluss der Musik auf den Character." *AmZ* 11 (1808): 81–89, 97–103.

Will, Frederic. *Intelligible Beauty in Aesthetic Thought from Winckelmann to Victor Cousin.* Tübingen: Max Niemeyer, 1958.

Winckelmann, Johann Joachim. *Sämtliche Werke.* 12 vols. Ed. Joseph Eiselein. Donaueschingen: Verlag deutscher Classiker, 1825–35.

Zaminer, Frieder. "Über die Herkunft des Ausdrucks 'Musik verstehen.' " In *Musik und Verstehen: Aufsätze zur semiotischen Theorie, Ästhetik und Soziologie der musikalischen Rezeption*, pp. 314–19. Ed. Peter Faltin and Hans-Peter Reinecke. Cologne: Arno Volk/Hans Gerig, 1973.

Zaslaw, Neal. *Mozart's Symphonies: Context, Performance Practice, Reception.* Oxford: Clarendon, 1989.

Zeller, Hans. *Winckelmanns Beschreibung des Apollo im Belvedere.* Zurich: Atlantis, 1955.

Zimmerman, Robert. Review of Eduard Hanslick's *Vom Musikalisch-Schönen* (1854). In his *Kritiken zur Philophie und Aesthetik*, vol. 2: *Zur Aesthetik*, pp. 239–53. Vienna: Wilhelm Braumüller, 1870.

Zuidervaart, Lambert. *Adorno's Aesthetic Theory: The Redemption of Illusion.* Cambridge, Mass.: MIT Press, 1991.

———. *Artistic Truth: Aesthetics, Discourse, and Imaginative Disclosure.* Cambridge: Cambridge University Press, 2004.

Index